READING
TESTIMONY,
WITNESSING
TRAUMA

READING TESTIMONY, WITNESSING TRAUMA

CONFRONTING RACE, GENDER, AND VIOLENCE IN AMERICAN LITERATURE

Eden Wales Freedman

University Press of Mississippi / Jackson

The University Press of Mississippi is the scholarly publishing agency of the Mississippi Institutions of Higher Learning: Alcorn State University, Delta State University, Jackson State University, Mississippi State University, Mississippi University for Women, Mississippi Valley State University, University of Mississippi, and University of Southern Mississippi.

www.upress.state.ms.us

The University Press of Mississippi is a member of the Association of University Presses.

First printing 2020
∞

Library of Congress Cataloging-in-Publication Data

Names: Wales Freedman, Eden, author.
Title: Reading testimony, witnessing trauma : confronting race, gender, and violence in American literature / Eden Wales Freedman.
Description: Jackson : University Press of Mississippi, 2020. | Includes bibliographical references and index.
Identifiers: LCCN 2019034392 (print) | LCCN 2019034393 (ebook) | ISBN 9781496827333 (hardback) | ISBN 9781496827340 (trade paperback) | ISBN 9781496827357 (epub) | ISBN 9781496827364 (epub) | ISBN 9781496827371 (pdf) | ISBN 9781496827388 (pdf)
Subjects: LCSH: Race in literature. | Psychic trauma in literature. | American literature—20th century. | BISAC: LITERARY CRITICISM / American / African American | LCGFT: Literary criticism.
Classification: LCC PS169.R28 W35 2020 (print) | LCC PS169.R28 (ebook) | DDC 810.9/3552—dc23
LC record available at https://lccn.loc.gov/2019034392
LC ebook record available at https://lccn.loc.gov/2019034393

British Library Cataloging-in-Publication Data available

To Matthew, "a friend of my mind,"
and to all who bear witness

Contents

Acknowledgments. ix

Introduction
Reading Trauma in (African) American Literature. 3

1 "To Be Free to Say So"
Witnessing Trauma in the Narratives of Harriet Jacobs,
Sojourner Truth, and Elizabeth Keckley. 41

2 "You Cant Understand It"
William Faulkner's Anti-Witnessing of Race and Gender. 77

3 "You Got Tuh Go There Tuh Know There"
Dual- and Communal Witnessing in Zora Neale Hurston's
Their Eyes Were Watching God and Margaret Walker's *Jubilee*. 115

4 "This Thing We Have Done Together"
Haunted Witnessing in the Novels of Toni Morrison and Jesmyn Ward. 145

Conclusion
Dual-Witnessing as Revolution. 181

Glossary of Terms. 187

Notes 191

Bibliography 205

Index 221

Acknowledgments

This book would not have been possible without the generous assistance of my editor, Katie Keene, who solicited the project and guided me through its writing process; the University Press of Mississippi, which invested in, edited, and published my monograph; the University of New Hampshire Graduate School and English Department, which funded research that served as this book's foundation; and Adams State and Mount Mercy Universities, which awarded me grants to draft and complete this project.

I am grateful to Cathy Caruth, Diane Freedman, Robin Hackett, Delia Konzett, Courtney Marshall, and Reginald Wilburn, my friends and colleagues, whose feedback helped me transform early theories into a completed monograph, and to Aaron Abeyta, Audrey Brunetaux, Ren Denton, and Mount Mercy English faculty, who supported me through the writing process. I am thankful for my students, who continue to help me articulate and refine my literary theories and who work zealously to develop their own critical thinking and engaged scholarship. Teaching and learning from them is a joy.

I am indebted to those who paved the way for my scholarly explorations and without whose foundational efforts I would not have written this book. Thank you to Maya Angelou, Gloria Anzaldúa, Cathy Caruth, Kimberlé Crenshaw, Shoshanna Felman, Judith Herman, bell hooks, Audre Lorde, Cherríe Moraga, Toni Morrison, Elaine Scarry, Patrocinio Schweickart, and Valerie Smith. I am honored to stand on your shoulders and beside you. I hope to carry your important work forward.

To my parents, Luke and Anna Wales, thank you for your loving dedication to my teaching, scholarship, and person and for asking questions that helped clarify my theoretical framework. Thank you for seeking always to grow and for compelling me to do the same. Thank you to the Freedmans for welcoming me into your family and making me feel loved. Thank you to Anne Williamson for adopting me as goddaughter and reminding me that "all shall be well." I am grateful for you all.

To my husband, Matthew Freedman, thank you for accepting without complaint the significant time and energy my academic pursuits have taken from our life together. Thank you for reading and revising this book in its early stages, for following me from state to state each time I accepted a position at a different university, and for cheering me on through every professional milestone. Your insight, sensitivity, and sense of balance (and often humor) have long sustained me. You are my first reader and secondary witness, my partner and best friend. I could not have written this book without you.

READING TESTIMONY, WITNESSING TRAUMA

Introduction
Reading Trauma in (African) American Literature

I n 1985, Elaine Scarry published *The Body in Pain,* detailing the ways physical pain shapes and shatters language and the concurrent difficulty this (de)construction presents authors who write accounts of torture and warfare. Scarry's investigation opened for critics the connection between trauma and literature, giving birth to "trauma theory" in the 1990s. In 1996, Cathy Caruth impelled this field forward, proposing in *Unclaimed Experience: Trauma, Narrative and History* that, in America, the experience of trauma no longer rests "outside the range of usual human experience" (as established by the American Psychiatric Association in 1980) but infuses our culture as a whole. Following 9/11, trauma theory has become a salient critical lens to those theorists alongside Caruth (e.g., Shoshana Felman, Kirby Farrell, Deborah Horvitz, Kali Tal, and Laurie Vickroy) who perceive American culture and literature as pervaded by technological advances in warfare; a rise in the number of natural disasters; ongoing abuse, addiction, and oppression; and a growing exposure to violence in the media. A body of theoretical literature on trauma has proliferated. Critics analyze the (in)capacity of language to articulate traumatic experience, the avowal and disavowal of meaning in trauma narratives, and how trauma theory clarifies and complicates representations of suffering. In addressing these topics, theorists investigate literary depictions of war, genocide, rape, torture, and natural disaster to examine how trauma narratives "witness"—or work through—psychosocial injury.

3

Defining Trauma

What critics classify as "trauma" shifts from theorist to theorist. Caruth defines trauma as an experience so "overwhelming," "sudden," and "catastrophic" as to penetrate the "membrane" of the psyche (qtd. in Hartman 12).[1] Caruth clarifies that one's response to trauma is often "belated" (in Freudian terms), manifesting in the "delayed, uncontrolled, repetitive appearance" of hallucinations and other intrusive phenomena (*Unclaimed* 11). Judith Herman defines trauma as "an affliction of the powerless," an experience in which "the victim is rendered helpless by overwhelming force" (2). Herman explains that, after a traumatic event, the survivor may experience intense emotion but without clear memory of the actual incident (what she calls "hyperarousal") or may remember everything in detail but without emotion (what she calls "constriction"). She adds that traumatic symptoms are often disconnected from their source and take on a life of their own (a state she labels "intrusion"). Anne Whitehead builds on Caruth and Herman's work to define trauma as both a seismic event (e.g., a railway accident) and the symptomatic responses to that event (a shattered psyche) (162). Dominick LaCapra defines trauma simply as a condition of "incomprehensible pain" (23), and Roger Luckhurst conceives of the psychic state as a "knot" that "tangle[s] up questions of science, law, technology, capitalism, politics, medicine, and risk" (14–15) and, I would add, literature and culture. Given these overlapping definitions, Nancy Miller rightly recognizes that, in literary theory at least, "trauma" becomes a "portmanteau that covers a multitude of disparate injuries," states, and experiences (1). I also define trauma openly, as an event or series of events that an author-narrator frames as psychically shattering—from the ravages of war to rape to that ineffable "something" that haunts William Faulkner's protagonist, Temple, in the novel *Sanctuary* (1931) and Lauren Slater's speaker in the memoir *Lying* (2000).[2]

Because this book analyzes the national trauma of slavery alongside literary depictions of the oppressions[3] African Americans and women can face due to their marginalized status as black and/or female, my treatment of trauma includes in its scope not only psychic but also sociocultural positioning, fragmentation, and suffering.[4] With Laurie Vickroy, I consider trauma to be a psychological, cultural, and sociopolitical phenomenon (*Contemporary* xiv). While trauma theory derives from psychoanalysis, trauma is not limited to one's individual psyche but can encompass what Michael Rothberg calls "other disruptive social forces" (xiii), such as collective, national, and cultural catastrophes and individuals' and groups' responses to them. Examples include the national traumas of institutionalized slavery, the September 11 terrorist attacks, and the catastrophic destruction and aftermath of Hurricane Katrina, which carry individual and communal effects and which can endure for generations, shattering survivors both psychically and culturally.

The Call to Witness

While individual definitions of trauma differ, critics all underscore the necessity of traumatic witnessing—the speaking, writing, or otherwise conscious acknowledgment of a traumatic event—in order to overcome it (Caruth, Felman, Herman, Laub, LaCapra, Vickroy). To endure and prevail, Shoshana Felman and Dori Laub claim, the wounded subject must face one's "buried truths," "piece together" an individual history, and voice a "fully realized narrative" (qtd. in Farrell 1). "The survivor," Laub maintains, must "tell his story in order to survive" (63). Suzette Henke substantiates that the effort to witness offers the speaker the "potential for mental healing," alleviating the "persistent symptoms" of Herman's constriction, hyperarousal, and intrusion (xii). Herman writes that "the only way" a survivor can take "control of her recovery" is to witness (97). "Healing takes place," bell hooks asserts, when survivors "speak the truth" about their traumatic histories (*Yam* 11). The same, Ron Eyerman suggests, is true of national and cultural traumas, which also must be "understood, explained, and made coherent"—or witnessed— "through public reflection and discourse" (*Cultural* 2).

In American literature, the call to witness is also emphasized.[5] In William Faulkner's *Requiem for a Nun* (1950), Temple Drake Stevens, the novel's protagonist (and a rape survivor from Faulkner's earlier novel, *Sanctuary*), asserts her need to testify to sexual violence in order to prevail over it. She confesses that, years after the assault, she feels impelled to witness her rape, "just to get it told, breathed aloud, into words, sound" (79). This desire prompts Temple to say to the governor, "[S]o this is the witness stand" (101), even though she is in his office, not in court. She acknowledges: "I've got to say it all, or I wouldn't be here" (112). In James Weldon Johnson's *Autobiography of an Ex-Colored Man* (1912), the narrator, an African American man passing as white, parallels Temple's drive to witness when he professes that, "although he knows that the act is likely . . . to lead to his undoing," he must "divulg[e] the great secret of my life": he must witness his racial passing (3). Temple witnesses individual, psychic trauma (sexual assault). The Ex-Colored Man witnesses both individual (psychic) and collective (cultural) trauma: how systemic racism and white supremacy have psychically shattered him as an individual, leading him to pass as white in order to succeed in antiblack America. Howsoever their traumas and oppressions manifest, both protagonists feel compelled to witness in order to work through their experiences.

Temple and the Ex-Colored Man's determination to witness, however much time has passed and whatever the cost, emphasizes the necessity and challenge of traumatic witnessing. This fictive stance is critically substantiated. While theorists recognize the benefit to witnessing trauma, they also acknowledge its difficulty. Herman explains that the conflict between the "will to deny" and the will "to proclaim" catastrophe "aloud" is the "central dialectic" of psychological trauma (1). Susan Brison, a philosophy professor at Dartmouth and survivor of sexual assault, recalls that when she first sat down to write about her rape, "things stopped making sense" (ix). "I thought it was quite possible that I was brain-damaged," she writes. "I couldn't explain what had happened to me" (ix). In her memoir, *Hunger* (2017), Roxane Gay echoes Brison's experience: Gay attempts to witness childhood rape but struggles to write through her trauma. Even after publishing her story, Gay acknowledges the difficulty of writing to witness. *Hunger* offers details of Gay's rape but still elides elements of the experience that she "will never be able to talk about" (44). Even for professional writers, witnessing can seem insurmountable, as traumatic experience can belay language, skill, and effort.

Despite the obstacles that surface when a victim attempts to witness, theorists underscore the need to do so. When survivors do not narrate their history, Janet Ellerby asserts, traumatic aftermath intensifies (25). An affected person or group may repress traumatic memory for a time, but, until witnessed, the experience haunts. Gay substantiates that witnessing in *Hunger* was "the most difficult thing" she ever attempted (303). Nevertheless, she writes, the effort was "necessary," representing a "freeing" step on the path to recovery (304). In *Option B: Facing Adversity, Building Resilience, and Finding Joy* (2017), Sheryl Sandberg cites psychologist Jamie Pennebaker's research, which found that the day after college students journaled about the "most traumatic experiences of their lives," their blood pressure rose. This result, Sandberg writes, makes "sense, since confronting trauma is painful" (62). Six months after the students began journaling, however, Pennebaker discovered that the negative effects they had initially demonstrated "reversed" and that those who had consistently witnessed trauma were now "significantly better off emotionally and physically" than a control group that had not (62). Following Pennebaker's work, Sandberg writes, countless other experiments have "documented the therapeutic effect[s]" of witnessing (62), such as decreased anxiety, depression, and anger; reduced symptoms of posttraumatic stress disorder; higher grades; and reduced absences from school and work (63). Recorded physical benefits include "higher T-cell counts, better liver function, and stronger antibody responses" (36). Theorists conclude that witnessing empowers shattered subjects not only to survive but also to thrive. Those who do not or cannot witness demonstrate continued hyperarousal, constriction, and intrusion (Herman 162). In his memoir, *Fire Shut Up in My Bones* (2014), Charles Blow corroborates these findings, acknowledging that, as long as he "suppressed" memories of childhood sexual assault, his trauma consumed him (69–70). Only when he witnessed the abuse he suffered as a child was he able to release the fire (or trauma) trapped within.

Critical Intervention: Dual-Witnessing and Venn Liminality

My work builds on the theories above to investigate a readerly engagement of traumatic and testimonial literature. If we accept the premise that survivors must witness trauma in order to prevail, this book explores readers' ensuing responsibility in engaging that testimony. Although theorists devote attention to how, when, and why narrators witness, few delineate the role of the reader-respondent in analyzing testimonial literature. Some critics note the importance of an addressee's response to trauma narratives without clarifying what readerly engagement entails. Caruth, for example, affirms that "one needs to learn to listen" or respond to survivors (*Listening* 73). Laub portrays the reader-respondent as a "midwife," who helps deliver another's testimony (qtd. in Caruth *Listening* 58). Evelyn Jaffe Shreiber asserts that, if the survivor is to recover, one needs an "empathic witness to hear the trauma story" (2). Memoirists also speak to the need for readerly response without explaining what this role requires. In her memoir, *After Silence* (1998), Nancy Raine quotes H. D. Thoreau's adage: "It takes two to speak the truth—one to speak, and another to hear" (118). Brison resolves: "Bearing witness makes more sense . . . once one is able to be heard by those willing to help" (52). Those who witness need to be understood by reader-respondents. The succeeding question is: "How?" In answer, I consider intersections of traumatic witnessing and reception theory to articulate a theory of reading trauma—what I term *Venn liminality* (figure 2)—that affords narrators and readers the opportunity to *dual-witness* (figure 1), that is, to witness trauma collectively.

Critics maintain that reading is not only a passive but an active process. Hans Robert Jauss describes reading as "a dialog between work and audience" (19). James Phelan defines reading not only as "the act of taking in" but also as "the act of responding" (227). When reading, Phelan expounds, one is "both passive and active, as the text acts upon us and we act upon it; the text calls upon—and we respond with—our cognitive, emotive, social, and ethical selves" (228). Patrocinio Schweickart similarly portrays a reader not as a "passive recipient" but as an "active listener or producer of meaning" (qtd. in Goldstein and Machor "Introduction," xiv). According to these theorists (and others, such as Stanley Fish, Stuart Hall, and Patricia Hill Collins), reading is what Phelan calls a "two-sided, multi-dimensional, multileveled activity" (228). The same, I argue, is true of witnessing, which, like reading, is not one-sided or passive but dual and active.

Clearly, I am not the first to suggest that meaning is generated in conversation between text and reader. I am, however, the first to place reception theory in conversation with trauma theory to interrogate how readers work with and against authors, characters, and texts to witness mutually. When testifying through spoken or written language,[6] I argue, a narrator bears witness to an addressee who absorbs the teller's story and testifies to its veracity. This relational mode is conveyed in the definition of the word "witness." The *Oxford English Dictionary* defines a witness as both the speaker who bears witness "from personal observation" (what I term the *primary witness*) and the "spectator or auditor" (or *secondary witness,* a term borrowed from Dominick LaCapra) who bears witness to the speaker's testimony (sense 6a).[7] When a reader enters into a speaker's narrative and an account is mutually witnessed, *dual-witnessing* occurs.[8]

The active, dual nature of witnessing is acknowledged by other writers. In *Lynching and Spectacle* (2009), Amy Louise Wood clarifies that witnessing includes not only the "public testimonials of faith or truth" (or primary witnessing) but also the "act of being a spectator of significant and extraordinary events" (or secondary witnessing) (4). Whitehead describes witnessing as a "highly collaborative relationship" between speaker-survivor and reader-listener (7), and Schweickart insists that a traumatic text "accomplish[es] nothing" if no one is "willing and able to undertake a careful and just understanding of what the writer has written" (13). "Traumatized human beings," Bessel Van der Kolk explains, "witness in the context of relationships" (212): a given author, text, or narrator cannot witness primarily when reader-listeners do not also witness secondarily.

Witnessing's duality is upheld in literature as well. In *Fire Shut Up in My Bones,* Blow details his boyhood need to find a secondary witness to help him work through childhood trauma (28). Unfortunately, Blow's need is not met: "No one seemed to notice this need in me," he writes, "and I was too young and ashamed of it to articulate it" (28). Determined to secure a secondary witness, Blow asks for a ventriloquist's puppet one Christmas "just so I would have someone to talk to" (28). Denied a secondary witness in boyhood, Blow seeks an engaged respondent in a doll, but his attempt falls short, since he witnesses only to a plastic prototype.[9] Similarly, in Alice Walker's novel *The Color Purple* (1982), the protagonist, Celie, writes letters to God because she wants to witness her stepfather's physical and sexual violence, and her abuser has forbidden her to disclose her trauma to "nobody but God" (1). In framing her novel in this way, Walker underscores not only the drive to witness primarily but also the need to witness to an engaged respondent, even if the only one available is the invisible, unknowable God (or the equally invisible, unknowable reader). *The Color Purple* also emphasizes that dual-witnessing is not restricted to those who share identical social constructs (such as race, gender, sexuality, and class) or circumstances (such as sexual and physical abuse) but is open to anyone willing to engage another's life narrative. For this reason, Celie can witness primarily both to God and to her readers—and ask them to witness secondarily—even if she does not know which identity constructs they embody or which circumstances they have endured.

In my framework, two types of secondary witnesses exist. The first engages the primary witness's testimony. Another, the *secondary witness by proxy*, testifies on behalf of a primary witness who is unable to do so. Examples include lawyers, civil rights' activists (e.g., abolitionists during slavery), and those primary witnesses who speak out of their own experiences on behalf of others (e.g., former slave narrators who witness trauma both to work through their own experiences and to speak for those silenced by slavery, society, or death). Cathy Caruth, Dori Laub, and Shoshana Felman contend that one cannot witness in place of another, that the secondary witness by proxy cannot exist. Caruth cites Paul Celan as writing that "no one bears witness for the witness" (*Trauma* 15), but I align with critics such as Elaine Scarry who maintain that, because the traumatized narrator is often "bereft of the resources of speech," witnessing is often "brought into being" by those who are not traumatized but who speak on behalf of those who are (Scarry 6). Although, as Scarry recognizes, "impediments" arise when witnessing trauma secondarily by proxy, "good reasons" exist as to why one may need to do so (e.g., in the cases of emancipatory narratives, edited by amanuenses and abolitionists) (Scarry 6).

Consider, for example, Mamie Till Mobley's insistence in 1955 that the lynched body of her son, Emmett Till, be placed in an open casket at a public funeral, so the community could bear witness to the violence done to Till in particular and to black bodies in general. "Let the people see what I see," Mobley commanded (qtd. in Rankine 148). In refusing to conceal Till's corpse from view, Mobley witnessed primarily her grief at her son's death. She also witnessed secondarily by proxy the violence done to black bodies in America.[10] Mobley's witnessing (and the response it inspired in those who viewed Till's corpse) galvanized the American civil rights movement. A literary example of a secondary witness by proxy is Claudia MacTeer, the narrator of Toni Morrison's *The Bluest Eye* (1970), who witnesses protagonist Pecola Breedlove's history of violence in an attempt to help her work through it.

When dual-witnessing takes place on a larger scale, such as when the primary witness speaks to a group of listeners, who collectively respond to the testimony (as at an Alcoholics Anonymous meeting) or when a group of people mutually witness with and for one another (as in group therapy), I call the exchange *communal witnessing*. The form such witnessing takes shifts from group to group: Mobley invited America to witness collectively the injustice done to her son for being black. Feminist consciousness-raising groups, introduced in the 1960s, and contemporary Black Lives Matter protests also invite participants to witness communally. Communal witnessing can even take place through social media platforms, such as Twitter and Facebook. While some may dismiss internet spaces as not "real" enough to foster witnessing, the venues also open the opportunity to witness with those one may otherwise not encounter. In her introduction to *The Fire This Time* (2016), Jesmyn Ward writes that when George Zimmerman killed an unarmed black teenager, Trayvon Martin, in 2012, she "took to Twitter" (3). "I wanted to hear what others, black writers and activists, were thinking about what happened," she writes (3). Twitter provided the ideal "social forum" to witness as a "community" with other grieving Americans, who could work collectively through their shared "frustration," "anger," and "fear" about Martin's murder (3).[11] In *So You Want to Talk about Race* (2018), Ijeoma Oluo upholds the witnessing potential of social media. "Thanks to the power and freedom of the Internet," she writes, many "people of color have been able to speak their truths" and to witness with one another (4). "We've been able to reach out across cities, even countries," she writes, "to share and reaffirm that yes, what we are experiencing is true" (5). Such is the power of communal witnessing.

Communal witnessing is celebrated in Gloria Naylor's *The Women of Brewster Place* (1983). The novel is narrated through seven distinct chapters, each of which details the storyline of an individual character. Read together, the chapters witness communally the individual and shared traumas and testimonies of a select group of women (the residents of Brewster place). The novel's communal witnessing, however, does not overwhelm the textual attention granted to dual-witnessing. Of the seven chapters, six evince dual-witnessing by centering on the relationship between individual characters. The final chapter, "Block Party," differs from these in witnessing communally the story of the entire neighborhood. In structuring her novel in this manner, Naylor reveals how dual-witnessing between two persons can extend into communal witnessing among a larger group and teaches readers that what they may view as a solitary activity (the act of reading) is in fact an interactive and communal process wherein the individual reader dual-witnesses with a single text and also joins author, work, characters, and other discourse communities in witnessing communally.

How do reader-respondents witness dually and communally? In answer, I turn to the work of psychoanalysts, survivors, and memoirists who elucidate when and how their witnessing has not been well-received. That is, as no one clearly delineates the reader's role in engaging trauma, I formulate my theories out of what experts suggest *not* to do. I call the failure to engage another's testimony *anti-witnessing*.[12] Writers outline three principal ways a reader can anti-witness a speaker's testimony. First, the reader may position herself alongside the victimizer instead of the victim. This mode of reading is *aggressive anti-witnessing* in my schema. In such cases, the anti-witness may add to a speaker's trauma either by (1) blaming her for her own experience (e.g., when a rape victim is censured for what she wore or how she acted before being raped) or by (2) objectifying her experience and treating it sensationally (e.g., when the details of a personal trauma are salaciously consumed by a scandal-hungry public). The former I term *accusatory anti-witnessing* and the latter *voyeuristic anti-witnessing*.

A reader may also anti-witness by disengaging from the primary witness' testimony altogether. Here, the reader aligns with the so-called "impartial bystander," ignoring or denying the narrator's story, pretending it does not exist, and adding to the narrator's trauma by increasing her feelings of worthlessness and isolation. I label this type of anti-witnessing *a-witnessing*. To a-witness, a reader may (1) ignore a speaker and her testimony, silencing the primary witness by refusing to acknowledge her trauma (what I call *ignorant a-witnessing*) or (2) negate a speaker's testimony (*negative a-witnessing*), claiming that the events a survivor witnesses did not happen or could not have happened (as in the case of Holocaust deniers).

Finally, a reader may align too closely with a speaker-survivor. I deem this mode of response *co-optive anti-witnessing*, of which two kinds exist. The first, *empathic anti-witnessing*, occurs when one mistakenly believes that—by virtue of having heard or read a victim's testimony—one understands intimately what an actual victim has endured (as when those who read the 1845 emancipatory narrative of Frederick Douglass believe falsely that they understand fully the trauma of slavery). The second, *appropriative anti-witnessing*, occurs when a reader usurps the speaker's trauma for some other purpose (e.g., when amanuenses utilized slave testimony to forward abolitionism). All three types of anti-witnessing are mutually viable: one may, throughout the course of a narrative, aggressively anti-witness, a-witness, and/or co-optively anti-witness. A reader is not restricted to one form of anti-witnessing or another.

These styles of anti-witnessing are critically substantiated (in Scarry, Herman, LaCapra, and Miller), although they have yet to be discussed together as a whole. Nor do such forms of anti-witnessing appear elsewhere under the terminology I provide. Still, the above approaches represent standard, not aberrant, reactions to encountering trauma secondhand. In fact, I uphold that aggressive anti-witnessing is, to some degree, unavoidable. Howsoever we respond to traumatic narratives, our mere entry into another's testimony necessarily contaminates it. Readers probe texts for meaning and symbolism. We interrogate what happens in a narrative, what is at stake, what is "successful" or not, and why. In doing so, we penetrate text and speaker alike, which, to those who have survived tragedy, can feel like further violation. In attempting to dual-witness, one always risks anti-witnessing. In light of this fact, I maintain that, in order to witness as a reader-respondent, one must first recognize (and take responsibility for) the victimizing position one adopts toward text and speaker. If one denies one's tendency to anti-witness aggressively, one may a-witness (by disengaging from the text entirely), co-optively anti-witness (by pretending one is not a victimizer but a victim), or aggressively anti-witness anyway through victimization and voyeurism.

However, if the reader recognizes one's tendency to anti-witness and learns to situate oneself at the core of a *Venn diagram of secondary witnessing* (figure 2), one may align not only with the victimizer but also with the impartial bystander and victim all at once. This type of reading or *Venn liminality* represents a careful navigating of a liminal space in which the reader realizes one's indivisible roles as (1) potential victimizer of the narrative; (2) empathic bystander outside the narrative; and (3) survivor-in-solidarity, a reader who—though not a victim oneself—witnesses alongside and with the traumatized speaker. In navigating this triune space, the reader can become a secondary witness. In engaging trauma narratives with this *Venn consciousness*, one may engage in dual and communal witnessing, in which speaker and reader(s) witness trauma collaboratively.

Aggressive Anti-Witnessing

The first impulse of most respondents is to align oneself with the victimizer: to blame the survivor for her victimhood, and, in doing so, to contribute to her victimization (i.e., to anti-witness aggressively). In confronting trauma,

Herman explains, "most people" (even trained therapists and literary critics) side with the perpetrator, doubting the speaker's story or minimizing or rationalizing her abuse (145). We feel "revulsion and disgust" at the witness' narrative, Herman clarifies, which we transfer to the witness herself, judging and blaming her when she "fails to live up to" our "idealized notion" of how a victim "ought to behave" (145). Ronnie Janoff-Bulman, a psychology professor at UMass Amherst, explains that respondents anti-witness out of desire to preserve meaning and order. If we can blame survivors for their victimhood, we can maintain our own sanity, assuring ourselves that, while bad things may happen to "deserving" people, the world remains safe for us (Janoff-Bulman 149). Reader-respondents who refuse to engage traumatic narratives may fear that they will discover in their lives the same catastrophes the speaker-survivor has encountered. In his foreword to Toni Morrison's *The Origin of Others* (2017), Ta-Nehisi Coates explains that the "danger of sympathizing"—or witnessing—"with the stranger is the possibility of becoming a stranger" (xiii). If we engage a primary witness's trauma, we risk associating with her and thereby becoming, if only secondarily, "other." Rather than risk the feelings of contamination that can accompany dual-witnessing, we distance ourselves; we blame the victim. We anti-witness the other to protect ourselves from becoming other.

Following the 2012 gang rape of an eleven-year-old girl by eighteen men in Cleveland, Texas, for example, neighbors reported that they held the child responsible for her own rape since she was known to "hang out" with teenage boys and to wear "makeup and fashions more appropriate to a woman in her twenties" (McKinley). "She wanted this to happen," Angie Woods told the *Houston Chronicle.* Community members also blamed the girl's mother for "neglect" for permitting her daughter to partake in such "risky" behavior (Raphael 62). No one interviewed held the rapists accountable but repeatedly blamed an eleven-year-old victim for her own assault (Raphael 62). These destructive responses are unfortunately quite common. In *Tainted Witness* (2017), Leigh Gilmore explains that if the contemporary era is an "age of testimony and witness," it is also one of "judgement"—particularly of those who dare to witness primarily (1). As a result of reader-listeners' tendency to anti-witness aggressively, when survivors disclose trauma, Gilmore argues, their witnessing is repeatedly "discredited by a host of means" meant to "contaminate by doubt," "stigmatize through association," and "dishonor through shame," such that "not only the testimony" but also the primary witness herself is "smeared" (*Limits* 2). In such instances, a survivor struggles to work through her trauma, as those called to witness dually and communally instead anti-witness accusatorily.

Readers also exhibit the propensity to treat trauma narratives voyeuristically. Miller explains that we have become so "accustomed in American culture to stories of pain, from the annihilation of the Holocaust to the devastation of AIDS," that we are culturally "addicted" to trauma narratives (2). When, therefore, a speaker summons the courage to witness her history (or to perform a divergent identity construct), readers follow her testimony with rapt delight (Miller 2). In *The Vulnerable Observer* (1996), Ruth Behar offers Isabel Allende's story of Omaira Sánchez, a thirteen-year-old girl trapped in mud who became the subject of "obsessive media attention" (1). The "news-hungry" media, which could do nothing to save the girl's life, "descended upon her," Behar writes, "fixing their curious and useless eyes on her suffering" (1). To this image of voyeuristic anti-witnessing, Behar contrasts the actions of photographer Rolf Carlé, who found he could "no longer bear to watch from behind the camera" and, "crouching down in the mud, flung his arms around Sánchez, as her heart and lungs collapsed" (1). This story exemplifies the difference between anti-witnessing and secondary witnessing. Carlé recognizes his role as voyeur-victimizer (snapping pictures of a dying child without entering into her experience) and then moves beyond victimization into dual-witnessing (embracing the girl as she dies). Here, the photographer acts as secondary witness to Sánchez's death: Carlé does not deny his propensity as a photojournalist to victimize those whom he photographs. He acknowledges that standing behind the camera is an attempt, as a purveyor of sensationalism, to "document tragedy" (1), but he also transcends his victimizing position by standing in solidarity with the sufferer, by putting his lens aside and embracing her pain.

The distinction between secondary and aggressive anti-witnessing surfaces in fiction as well. Naylor's *Brewster Place* emphasizes dual-and communal witnessing but also underscores the dangers of aggressive anti-witnessing. In the chapter "The Two," a lesbian character, Lorraine, attempts to join the community by attending a tenant-association meeting. Instead of being welcomed (or witnessed secondarily and communally), she is aggressively anti-witnessed by her neighbor, Sophie, who verbally attacks Loraine for performing queer sexuality.[13] Although Lorraine has done nothing to offend either Sophie or her neighbors (other than to exist as a lesbian and to rent an apartment with her partner, Tee), Sophie accuses Lorraine of "causin' a disturbance with [her] nasty ways" (145). When Lorraine asks what she has done to "disturb" anyone, Sophie censures Lorraine for stepping out of the shower naked and asking Tee to bring her a towel (145). To Sophie, this sequence of events is neither innocuous nor routine but something for which she can accusatorily anti-witness Lorraine. "Don't stand there like you a Miss Innocent," Sophie condemns, "I'll tell ya what I seen!" (145).

Note too the voyeurism implicit in Sophie's aggressive anti-witnessing. How has Sophie managed to observe what transpired in Lorraine and Tee's bathroom? Sophie provides the answer. She peered through the women's window to "catch" them doing something "nasty": "You forgot to close your shades last night," Sophie indicts, "I saw . . . you . . . standin' in the bathroom door, drippin' wet and . . . naked . . . Calling to the other one to put down her book and get you a clean towel . . . I saw it—I did!" (145). Although Sophie anti-witnesses Lorraine for stepping out of her shower and calling for a towel, the reader recognizes that fault lies with the accuser, not the accused: Drying off after a shower is not "nasty." What *is* "nasty" is a neighbor stationing herself outside another's bathroom window, hoping to catch sight of sexual behavior. That Sophie recognizes that Lorraine "forgot to close" her shades that night also suggests that Lorraine typically does close her shades and that Sophie has waited outside Lorraine's window consistently enough to know that the night in question is an anomaly, which allows her, finally, to anti-witness Lorraine. Sophie's rant highlights the accusatory and voyeuristic components of aggressive anti-witnessing.

A-Witnessing

In addition to blaming a primary witness for her struggles or identity or voyeuristically consuming her story, a respondent may a-witness another's testimony. "More often than not," Herman explains, "family and authorities" alike "block out" a survivor's story (161). Instead of witnessing trauma, reader-listeners wish victims would "stop harping on their suffering" (115). Raine recalls that after her rapist repeatedly told her to "shut up," so too did those in whom she confided. One woman, after reading an essay Raine had written about her rape, remarked, "No one wants to hear about such terrible things" (119). A-witnessing represents another way reader-respondents disassociate from the reality of traumas they do not want to face. "In the presence of victims," Janoff-Bulman maintains, we feel "uncomfortable, ill at ease" (144). For some, this discomfort results in "outright, even hostile, rejection of victims," that is, in aggressive anti-witnessing (144). For others, it "results in avoidance" or a-witnessing (148). In *Post Traumatic Slave Syndrome* (2005), Joy DeGruy asserts that the response to witnessed trauma is commonly "denial and disbe-lief" (25). The speaker-survivor, having "reopened wounds" in attempting to witness trauma, is "left frustrated and reinjured" (25), a-witnessed ignorantly and negatively. Jessica Stern, an American policy consultant on terrorism and a survivor of childhood rape, corroborates: "Denial [or a-witnessing] helps the bystander. We would rather not be confronted with evil. This is as true about Abu Ghraib as it is about personal assaults and ... private crimes" (144). Involvement can seem too difficult to risk engaging another's narrative. In a-witnessing trauma, however, potential secondary witnesses join victimizers in "unmaking" (to quote Scarry) a survivor's sense of self (23). "Silence" (or a-witnessing) in response to another's trauma, Sandberg writes, "can increase" a primary witness's "suffering" (34).

Consider, for example, many white Americans' a-witnessing of the traumatic aftermath of institutionalized slavery and the persistence of anti-black racism in the United States. In *Tears We Cannot Stop: A Sermon to White America* (2017), Michael Eric Dyson suggests that many white Americans choose "to forget" (74)—or to a-witness—America's legacy of antiblack violence. When white Americans, for instance, respond to the call to action, Black Lives Matter, with the slogan, "All Lives Matter," they a-witness the nation's history of racism and the expressed hope that black people will one day matter in antiblack America. ("If indeed all lives mattered," Angela Davis emphasizes, "we would not need to emphatically proclaim that 'Black Lives Matter'" [qtd. in Dyson 87]). Black Lives Matter, Dyson explains, needs to be witnessed primarily, secondarily, and communally, because American history has long elided black worth (87). When black people proclaim that black lives matter, they are seeking "simple recognition" (Dyson 92). They are asking to be witnessed. When white Americans ignore and negate Black Lives Matter, they a-witness the trauma antiblack racism has wrought and the value of black lives in America. In doing so, they contribute to black dehumanization.

The dangers of a-witnessing are explicit in Ralph Ellison's *Invisible Man* (1947), a novel whose titular character has become "invisible" not by "biochemical accident" but by the refusal of others to acknowledge his existence (4). The narrator explains: "I am invisible, understand, simply because people refuse to see me" (3). Because the protagonist has been raced as "black" in American society, white people a-witness him both ignorantly (by ignoring his presence) and negatively (by denying that he exists at all). He describes those white characters who a-witness his existence as sleepwalkers who move through a dream in which he does not appear (5), and he conveys his anguished, aching need for others (such as his readers) to wake from their collective a-witnessing to witness him secondarily—a development he also recognizes is unlikely (4) and, by the end of the novel, has yet to occur. The negative effects of such widespread a-witnessing are marked. After years of invisibility, the narrator himself begins to question whether or not he exists.

The a-witnessing of others inhibits his ability to witness primarily (either to himself or to others), and the a-witnessed protagonist begins to a-witness himself. The inherent message to readers is to wake from individual and collective a-witnessing and to witness instead those persons and narratives we ignore and negate.

Co-Optive Anti-Witnessing

Finally, a respondent may co-optively anti-witness by aligning too closely with a survivor or by appropriating her narrative. In the first instance, one may convince oneself that one has gained a thorough understanding of victimhood merely by having encountered a survivor's testimony. In the second instance, one may co-opt the speaker's testimony for personal purposes (as in the case of politicians who utilize others' stories of suffering to garner votes and campaign contributions or to buttress political platforms). These co-optive forms of anti-witnessing enable the respondent to believe one is engaging the victim's narrative, while one actually directs attention to oneself (as one does when aggressively anti-witnessing and a-witnessing). In "Narrating Pain" (2007), Richard Kearney cautions that the empathic reader may "veer towards over-identification" with a primary witness unless "checked by a countervailing movement of distance and detachment" (53). Even in attempting to assist a survivor in witnessing trauma, a co-optive anti-witness may manipulate the survivor's story to further one's own purposes, damaging the speaker's ability to work through trauma. For this reason, secondary witnesses should strive to stand in solidarity with the speaker-survivor while also fulfilling the dual roles of acknowledged victimizer and engaged bystander. If one does not maintain a certain distance from the primary witness, one risks co-opting her testimony. Molly Andrews warns that, when we over-identify with primary witnesses, we "appropriate their subject positions as our own" (33). However well-intentioned, this co-optive mode anti-witnesses the speaker's experience for, if one forsakes the survivor's individuality in an attempt at engagement, her opportunity to witness is cut short and her personhood is silenced, just as if she had been victimized or ignored, aggressively anti-witnessed or a-witnessed.

Co-optive anti-witnessing is embodied in the person and performance of Rachel Dolezal, a Caucasian woman who successfully passed as African American until her white parents outed her in 2015. (Since her outing and the subsequent media frenzy concerning her identity, Dolezal continues to maintain she is black.) To appear Afra-American, Dolezal applies bronzer to her skin and wears braids and weaves. She has posed with black men she falsely claimed were her biological father and sons. She has misrepresented herself on job applications as African American (Pérez-Peña). She also served as the Afra-American president of the NAACP chapter in Spokane, Washington, and taught and as an instructor of Africana studies at Eastern Washington University. She gave lectures with artificially blackened skin on the natural hair movement (Thrasher) and reported (falsely) that she had received anti-black hate mail (Blanchfield). Dolezal's father speculates that his daughter posed as black after "assimilat[ing] herself into the African-American community through her various advocacy work" (qtd. in Bouie). While the work Dolezal did for the NAACP is laudable, in passing as black, she co-optively anti-witnesses experiences lived by actual Afra-Americans—people who, due their doubly marginalized status as black and female, have likely suffered (where Dolezal has not) commingled racist and sexist subjugation.

In *This Will Be My Undoing: Living at the Intersections of Black, Female, and Feminist in (White) America* (2018), Moran Jerkins explains that Dolezal's appropriation of black womanhood insults those Afra-Americans who are "not afforded the privilege of malleable identity" (46). While Dolezal darkens her skin and braids her hair, Jerkins writes, she "still inhabits a white female body" and thus possesses the privilege to take on and off again "black female characteristics," that is, to wear black womanhood "as a kind of costume" (46). Black women are not afforded this privilege but continue to be "stigmatized" for the black and female bodies they inhabit (Jerkins 46). Oluo explicates that Afra-Americans can never "escape" the fact that they exist as both black and female in a "white supremacist" and sexist country (1). By co-opting black womanhood, Dolezal does not stand in solidarity with African American women but uses white privilege to anti-witness Afra-American culture (e.g., natural hair), experiences (disenfranchisement), status (leadership), and traumas (hate mail), regardless of whether she empathizes so deeply with African American women that she confuses herself for one of them and/ or has appropriated an Afra-American identity to further her career as a black scholar-advocate. Dolezal's book deal and "massive press junket" about her professed black identity have allowed her to profit from co-optive anti-witnessing (Jerkins 46).

Contrast to Dolezal essayist Leslie Jamison, who works against her propensity to anti-witness co-optively. Before recognizing her appropriative tendencies, Jamison writes, whenever "bad things happened to other people," she imagined them happening to herself (20). When, for example, her brother was diagnosed with Bell's palsy, she quickly became "obsessed with his condition," spending "large portions" of her day imagining how she would feel if her face were also paralyzed. In doing so, Jamison acknowledges, she "projected" onto herself—or co-optively anti-witnessed—her brother's experience, a response she now identifies not as empathy but as "*in*pathy" and "theft" (20). To avoid such anti-witnessing, Jamison endeavors to enter into another's narrative without becoming other. Her example is one all secondary witnesses can follow: to stand in solidarity with the speaker-survivor while also fulfilling the dual roles of acknowledged victimizer and engaged bystander. Only in doing so can one overcome the inclination to anti-witness to dual-witness instead. As Whitehead underscores and Jamison recognizes, secondary witnesses "bear a dual responsibility" to receive another's testimony without appropriating it as one's own (Whitehead 7), to witness secondarily without anti-witnessing co-optively.

In Harper Lee's *To Kill a Mockingbird* (1959), the protagonist, Atticus Finch, tells his daughter, Scout, "you never really understand a person until you . . . climb into his skin and walk around in it" (48). Atticus encourages Scout (and the reader through her) to engage empathically different persons and diverse narratives, that is, to witness secondarily. The way he frames his lesson, however, is problematic in that he incites his daughter not only to enter into another's "skin" but also to walk around in—or away with—it, potentially co-optively anti-witnessing it. In some ways wiser than her father, Scout practices the core of Atticus' message as she also rejects and revises its co-optive implications. Toward the end of the novel, Scout reminds readers that Atticus "said you never really know a man until you stand in his shoes and walk around in them" (463). To her father's lesson, she adds: Sometimes "just standing on [another's] porch [is] enough" (463). In this way, Scout provokes readers to engage another's life and narrative—to stand on the other's porch, so to speak—without falsely imagining that one can also inhabit the other's shoes, skin, and circumstances. Scout thus teaches readers to witness secondarily without co-optively anti-witnessing, modeling what LaCapra calls "empathic unsettlement" or "empathy without over-identification" (40) and what Vickroy describes as the "reader's double position" as "outsider and insider," as "engaged yet separate witness" (*Contemporary* 96). This readerly stance resists co-optive anti-witnessing and facilitates dual-witnessing.

Learning to Dual-Witness

No single approach to dual-witnessing exists. As there is not one, essential definition of "trauma," no chart or code can engage all trauma narratives empathically. Sandberg asserts that "there is no one way to grieve" and "no one way to comfort" (51). There is also no one way to witness primarily or secondarily. Sandberg recognizes, "What helps one person won't help another, and even what helps one day might not help the next" (51). Still, this book distills how a reader may position oneself as a secondary witness in relation to traumatized narrators and testimonial literature.[14] In *Extremities* (2002), Wendy Chun cites Barbara Johnson's query: "Is the witness the one who sees, the one who undergoes, or the one who propagates the [trauma] to which he bears witness?" (149). To Johnson's question, I answer "yes": the secondary witness simultaneously sees trauma as an engaged bystander (combating the tendency to a-witness), undergoes trauma in solidarity with the victim (contravening the propensity to anti-witness co-optively), and propagates trauma as acknowledged victimizer (resisting the inclination to anti-witness aggressively). In embodying this tripart role, the reader becomes a secondary witness, occupying a space that opens for speaker and reader alike (to borrow from Kaja Silverman) a "heteropathic identification": the ability to say, with the bystander, "It could have been me," with the victim, "It was me, also," and, at the same time, with the victimizer, "But it was not me" (40). Here, standing in the core of Venn liminality, the reader-respondent, as coincident bystander, victim, and victimizer, may begin the critical work of dual-witnessing.

In *This Bridge Called My Back* (1981), Cherríe Moraga asserts that everyone can witness secondarily another's life experiences, as each person has experienced in childhood some traumatic event, however seemingly insignificant. If we can access those original encounters, we can empathize with others, independent of the severity of their individual experiences (Moraga 29). In recalling one's own history of pain, one can move from self to other, identifying psychologically with and responding compassionately to another's trauma (Moraga 29). Moraga's contention resonates with theorists' claim that trauma is ubiquitous in American culture. Because of the prevalence of trauma in the contemporary era, critics argue, everyone has likely encountered some shattering experience before engaging another's. One does not have to enter extreme situations to encounter trauma, Van der Kolk asserts. Trauma infuses contemporary life, affecting everyone (1). Research by the Centers for Disease Control and Prevention indicates that one in five Americans has been sexually abused; one in four has been physically abused; one in three couples "engage in physical violence"; one in four have alcoholic relatives; and one in eight have "witnessed their mother being beaten or hit" (qtd. in Van der Kolk 1). While the minority of Americans (e.g., one in four or one in eight) have directly experienced a specific catastrophe, by adulthood, the majority has encountered trauma in some form. A personal understanding of psychic pain, Andrews asserts, helps us respond empathically to others' traumas (37).

Dual- and communal witnessing, however, can be more challenging than Moraga, Van der Kolk, and Andrews acknowledge. In fact, as primary witnessing can seem impossible to traumatized speakers, even well-meaning reader-respondents may find themselves debilitated by engaging trauma narratives. Adrienne Rich upholds that engaging others' trauma can feel "confusing, disorienting and painful" (18), and Caruth recognizes that responding to traumatic narratives presents a problem to therapists and literary critics alike (8), a phenomenon she attributes to the "contagious" nature of trauma, which seeps out "like a plague," distressing all who confront it (16). Despite their best efforts, Judith Butler underscores, both speaker-survivor and reader-listener can be "undone" by the witnessing process ("Violence" 389).

The difficulty that accompanies dual-witnessing is substantiated by neuroscientist Jean Decety who used fMRI scans to measure what happens in a person's brain when responding to another's pain and discovered that imagining pain activates the same areas in the brain (the prefrontal cortex, anterior insula, and anterior cingulate) as experiencing it directly (200). Based on this research, Decety concludes that to engage another's trauma is to risk feeling traumatized oneself (200). In "Learning to Listen," Richard Orton, the first man to volunteer at the Austin Rape Crisis Center (in 1978), corroborates these findings, underscoring the difficulty of secondary witnessing. The first time Orton heard a survivor witness, he acknowledges, he felt "numb" (241). Several hours later, he recounts, "I broke down. One moment I was fine, the next I was sobbing uncontrollably" (241). "I hadn't seen this coming," he confesses, and "I was unable to control it when it did. I was shocked and frightened at what was happening to me. I had never experienced anything like this before. I was falling apart" (242). Orton's portrayal of the effects of secondary witnessing takes on a traumatized tone, and he describes his response to the speaker's rape narrative as many survivors depict the aftermath of rape itself. Orton's experience does not make him a rape victim, but his breakdown emphasizes the dangers and difficulties of dual-witnessing: One cannot engage trauma without experiencing trauma.

Ann Petry exposes the difficulty of both dual-witnessing and refusing to dual-witness in her novel, *The Street* (1946). After the protagonist, Lutie, learns that her son, Bub, has been arrested, her neighbors are "reluctant to meet head on" (or to witness secondarily and communally) Bub's trauma and Lutie's anguish (390). Whenever they encounter Lutie, their "faces [fill] with dread" (390) They regard Bub's detention as "a symbol of doom" (390) and attempt to avoid traumatic contamination by a-witnessing his mother, turning "their faces away from the sight of her" and walking "faster to get away from the sound of her" (390). Just as dual-witnessing can prove difficult to sustain, so too can anti-witnessing. Thus, while Lutie's neighbors hurry "to close the doors of their apartments" to shut out her grief, her sobbing sounds through "the flimsy walls" of their apartments and "tight-shut doors" (390). As trauma intrudes upon the psyche of the survivor, it can also haunt those who would a-witness it. Although Lutie's neighbors turn on their radios "full blast in order to drown out" her "familiar, frightening, unbearable sound," they can still hear it, for they too have begun crying—or suffering and perhaps even witnessing—with her (390). The neighbors are impelled to witness secondarily, whether they wish to or not, as Lutie's "perpetual weeping" flows through them, "carrying pain and a shrinking from pain, so that the music and the voices coming from the radios couldn't possibly shut it out, for it was inside them" (390). Here, Petry depicts the contagion of trauma, suggesting that once one experiences trauma (whether primarily or secondarily), one cannot discount it. One witnesses trauma or succumbs to it.

However traumatic dual-witnessing may feel, the results of refusing to dual-witness can be equally disastrous, particularly to the primary witness. In *Testimony*, Laub relays the narrative of Chaium Guri's film *The 81st Blow* (1975), which "portrays the image of a man who narrates the story of his sufferings in the [concentration] camps only to hear his audience say: 'All this could not have happened. You must have made it up'" (68). This negation of the speaker's testimony wreaks, according to the film, the fateful blow, beyond the eighty the speaker, in Jewish tradition, can endure. Thus, though the man survives the trauma of the Holocaust, he dies witnessing it. He cannot prevail over the a-witnessing of his audience (68). Memoirists affirm Guri's thesis. "After my assault, Brison confesses, "I was afraid of people finding out—afraid of their reactions and of their inability to respond" (19). Of her teenage pregnancy and the forced adoption of her birth-daughter, Ellerby writes that, even now that she has published her narrative, she still "dreads those [readers] that, knowing all [her] secrets"—anti-witness her tale with "rejection" and "condemnation" (71). These writers confirm the necessity of secondary witnessing, for, unless readers can learn to engage trauma productively, primary witnesses may find themselves forever silenced and traumatized, like Pecola, the traumatized protagonist of Morrison's *The Bluest Eye*, who, denied secondary and communal witnesses, is driven insane. In *Frames of War* (2010), Judith Butler emphasizes how difficult it is "to stay responsive" to another's imparted trauma (184). "And yet," she underscores, "the precarity of life"—the pervasiveness of trauma—"imposes an obligation upon us" to do so (2). "The work is hard," Eesha Pandit acknowledges, "but, of course, it's the only way" (164).

Sometimes a narrator may not know how her testimony is received. If, for example, she publishes a memoir about a traumatic experience, she cannot know (other than what is published in book reviews) how individuals treat her testimony. If an author is deceased, she does not know whether her text is posthumously anti- or dual-witnessed. One may wonder how secondary witnessing functions when a primary witness has no knowledge of how her testimony is treated. In such cases, I focus on the readerly reception not only of an author but also of her text. This attention to textual reception should not suggest that a primary witness's experience is less important than her published work. Instead, I argue that a sustained empathic response to both author and text is vital. Reception theory investigates how readers' interpretative practices interact with textual meaning. With theorists such as Stanley Fish, Wolfgang Iser, and Louise Rosenblatt, I maintain that, while a reader cannot always communicate with an author, one can always converse with—or witness secondarily—a text. While a speaker-survivor may gain or suffer the most, depending on how her narrative is read, both dual- and anti-witnessing can take place beyond the purview of an author-narrator. In such cases, the text serves as primary witness, and the reader continues to function as secondary witness.

To consider one's readerly response to physical texts alongside traumatized speakers may seem counterintuitive. While a demonstrated lack of empathy may prove damaging to survivors who struggle to witness their histories only to discover that their traumas remain unrecognized, written narratives do not suffer from a reader's inability to enter into them. Even so, an engaged response to traumatic texts (not just traumatized speakers) is crucial. For one, texts have the power to witness trauma, as they continue to testify (often beyond the lifespan of their authors) to the existence of both individual tragedies and cultural catastrophes, encouraging generations of readers to enter into the reality of their depicted traumas. While trauma narratives are not psychically harmed through readerly anti-witnessing, they neverthe-less stand in for and alongside actual people and situations that readers could maltreat in "real life" by refusing to witness their incidents secondarily. Traumatic testimony thus deserves to be met with the critical empathy that speaker-survivors encounter when witnessed secondarily.

To dual-witness, one must commit to sustained and active reading and listening. While this instruction may seem obvious, in *We Need to Talk: How to Have Conversations That Matter* (2017), Celeste Headlee explains that "very few of us" ever listen to—or dual-witness with—one another (209). We may "hear" what a primary witness says or read what she writes, but few "also understand, respond [to], and remember" her testimony (209). Engaging another's narrative, Headlee writes, asks us to do more than to sit "passively in toleration while someone else speaks; a robot could do that" (219). Dual-witnessing requires rigorous self-reflection and awareness. To start, a secondary witness must first consider the ways one is particularly disposed to anti-witness. The addressee is called to interrogate how one responds both productively and problematically to others so that one may consciously combat the proclivity to anti-witness. Laub explains that respondents help speakers overcome past traumas by listening to their narratives, that is, by witnessing secondarily. He also maintains that one's ability to witness secondarily depends largely on the degree to which one can "listen to oneself" (qtd. in Trezise 8). Rich affirms that until reader-respondents acknowledge the ways they are personally inclined to anti-witness, they can neither "know themselves" nor "read others" (19). In short, dual-witnessing depends not only on how well one engages another's testimony but also on how well one engages oneself. As one strives to dual-witness, one must remain alert not only to the primary witness's testimony but also to one's reactions to it. Headlee maintains that, while few people are "good active listeners" or secondary witnesses, "most of us are blissfully unaware of our incompetence" (214). A reader-respondent can make strides toward dual-witnessing by acknowledging first the ways one tends to anti-witness and then repositioning oneself against (in order to resist) potentially destructive responses.

Dual-witnessing, however, requires more than recognizing that one anti-witnesses. The mere acknowledgment of difficulty or error is not enough. Instead, secondary witnesses must continue to check their problematic responses in order to push back against them. As Mia McKenzie writes, "heightened consciousness" can devolve into the opportunity simply to "pat [oneself] on the back" for being so "aware" (112) without pushing oneself to move beyond anti-witnessing into dual-witnessing. For this reason, this book invites reader-respondents first, to acknowledge their tendency to anti-witness; second, to recognize the specific ways they are inclined to anti-witness (e.g., aggressively, ignorantly, negatively, and/or co-optively); and third, to position themselves against these damaging tendencies by residing at the liminal core of a Venn diagram of secondary witnessing, where they may align not merely aggressively with victimizers, passively with bystanders, or co-optively with victims but with and against all at once (figure 2).

Because dual-witnessing and Venn liminality emerge out of anti-witnessing, the theories could appear more proscriptive than generative. However, my approach to dual-witnessing does not berate readers for the various ways they anti-witness but calls reader-respondents (myself included), first, to acknowledge a collective propensity to anti-witness and, second, to discern (in order to position oneself against) the individual and intersectional ways one is inclined to anti-witness.[15] An aggressive reader, for example, may wish to establish some distance from a witnessed trauma and also to engage its subjects more empathically to avoid blaming a survivor or sensationalizing her experience. In doing so, the reader employs strategies derived from a-witnessing and co-optive anti-witnessing to prevent aggressive anti-witnessing. In contrast, one who typically ignores or negates traumatic testimony may choose instead to enter into a narrative both critically and empathically, thereby combatting a-witnessing with what otherwise could manifest as aggressive and co-optive anti-witnessing. Finally, the appropriative or overly-empathic reader may need to separate oneself from a text and also to interrogate its contexts more aggressively to impede readerly appropriation and emotional debilitation. Here, the reader employs aggressive anti-witnessing and a-witnessing to circumvent co-optive anti-witnessing. In short, each reader exploits contrasting modes of anti-witnessing to transform one's characteristic style of anti-witnessing into dual-witnessing. With this *Venn consciousness,* readers may witness secondarily the traumas they encounter in life and literature.

If a secondary witness is uncertain how to dual-witness, one can ask questions—both of the primary witness and of oneself. Sandberg upholds this claim in her reflection following the death of her husband, David Goldberg, in 2015. When Goldberg died, Sandberg writes, her connections with others disintegrated. Friends "wanted to help" but "weren't sure how." Thus, they approached her with "fear in their eyes." When Sandberg confronted her loved ones about the growing distance between them, they reported feeling "paralyzed" when Sandberg was around, worried they "might say the wrong thing." Because Sandberg's friends were afraid to anti-witness, they a-witnessed instead. This hurtful response could have been avoided if they had asked Sandberg what she needed and how to help. Jamison asserts that empathy (or, in this case, dual-witnessing) "isn't just listening. It's asking . . . questions" (5). Thus, the practice "requires inquiry as much as imagination" (5). In *How to Be a Friend to a Friend Who's Sick* (2014), Letty Cottin Pogrebin encourages potential secondary witnesses to pose such questions as "How can I help?" (36) or "What [not how] are you feeling right now?" (167). These responses, Pogrebin explains, express "empathy" and "availability" without assuming that one already knows how to respond (36). The questions also enable the primary—not secondary—witness to control the pace and tenor of the conversation. If a respondent reads (rather than listens to) a speaker's testimony, one can still pose questions to oneself and the text: "How am I positioned in relation to this narrative?" "How 'successfully' am

I responding?" "What could I do differently?" In making these inquiries, one guards against anti-witnessing and works to dual-witness.

Potential secondary witnesses, like Sandberg's friends, may avoid asking questions if they are afraid of making mistakes. Indeed, in the attempt not to anti-witness, many respondents avoid traumatic engagement altogether, a coping mechanism that can result in a-witnessing. One strategy to combat the fear of not knowing how to respond is to accept that, even as a secondary witness, one can never fully understand another's traumatic experience. Sandberg's friends may have believed that they needed to understand exactly how Sandberg felt in order to respond to her, but they did not. They needed to bear witness to her grief rather than to elide it. In *The Body Is Not an Apology* (2018), Sonya Renee Taylor encourages readers to "make peace with not understanding" (19). Understanding, she writes, is "not a prerequisite" for empathy or dual-witnessing. In fact, recognizing that we do not and cannot understand another's narrative "leaves room for the possibility" of empathic connection (Taylor 19). If a secondary witness begins to dual-witness by recognizing that, even when one shares experiences with a primary witness, one will still never completely understand what she has suffered (as everyone's individual experience differs), one has a better chance of responding to the narrative without a-witnessing (as Sandberg's friends did) or co-optively anti-witnessing (by making the speaker's testimony not about what she suffered but about a situation the reader-listener encountered). Rather than responding to another's testimony: "I do not understand, so I cannot help" (which leads to a-witnessing) or "I know just what you went through; the same thing happened to me" (which engenders co-optive anti-witnessing), a secondary witness can respond: "I know I can never fully understand, but I want to. I hear you and support you." (Reading versus hearing another's testimony allows one to witness secondarily without understanding a narrative.)

To develop as a secondary witness, one should also strive to become more comfortable being uncomfortable. If Sandberg's friends had risked the discomfort of saying the wrong thing, they might have made mistakes in how they responded, but they would not have a-witnessed their friend. They might have even witnessed her secondarily. Dual-witnessing is difficult and can be draining. Identifying and unlearning one's tendencies to anti-witness is challenging, requiring practice and persistence. The process can be uncomfortable for everyone involved, but, as Oluo suggests, the secondary witness must "build a tolerance for discomfort" if one wishes "to help and not hinder" healing (209). Empathic engagement, Oluo acknowledges, can be distressing, but engaging another's pain is ultimately "worth a little discomfort" (Oluo

211). If a secondary witness commits to working through discomfort with a primary witness, one has a better chance of dual-witnessing.

However, when dual-witnessing becomes too uncomfortable or difficult, when a secondary witness recognizes that one is anti-witnessing more than dual-witnessing, one can and should take a break. The reader can put down a text and return to it when ready to engage. The listener can ask a primary witness to resume the conversation at a later time. Interrupting someone's testimony risks a-witnessing by silencing or shutting down her story. In such instances, the secondary witness should assure the primary witness that one wants to continue witnessing but cannot do so at the moment. One needs to rest and process before returning to the narrative. (At other times, a primary witness may need to take a break, so she may understand the secondary witness's wish to do so as well.) Before leaving the conversation, both parties should set a time and date when witnessing will recommence, so the primary witness knows she will have the opportunity to testify further. Before reconvening, the secondary witness should review what went wrong in the previous conversation and then reposition for the next to better engage the traumatic narrative. Oluo explains that taking a break from difficult conversations is sometimes necessary—both for the health of the participants and the conversation itself. "It is very hard," she writes, "to leave an emotional conversation unfinished," but a "resolution" is more likely to happen when one has not "already burned all the conversational bridges" (49). In taking time to reassess, the secondary witness is better prepared to dual-witness moving forward.

If one temporarily suspends witnessing, one must be willing to return to the conversation at a later time. One should not let fear of anti-witnessing or guilt at having previously anti-witnessed prohibit one from dual-witnessing in the future. Pandit suggests, "[K]eep doing the work as best as you can. Learn from it, and don't make the same mistake again" (165). Part of witnessing is accepting not only discomfort but the inevitability that one will err in the process. McKenzie suggests that allyship requires "constant vigilance" and "practice" (26). The same can be written of dual-witnessing. To witness secondarily, one must be willing to make mistakes, to reposition oneself as one learns, and to try again. If, in the course of dual-witnessing, Pandit advises, "you realize you've made a mistake"—or veered toward anti-witnessing—"acknowledge your mistake," apologize, and ask what amends can be made (165). If one is reading, one can ask oneself: "Where did I stumble as secondary witness? How can I position myself in the future to witness more successfully?" If the primary witness no longer wishes to continue with the secondary witness, or one has finished a book and still feels unable to witness its contents secondarily, one can still use what one has learned in an earlier session to improve in the future.

Dual-witnessing is neither simple nor easy. The practice asks the respondent to engage situations that feel difficult (and sometimes impossible) to understand, to empathize with a speaker who differs from oneself, and to step back rather than speak over others. Dual-witnessing requires that one open oneself to a high level of vulnerability and accountability—that one risk secondary traumatization and practice Venn liminality. However, Jarune Uwarjaren and Jamie Utt write about the power of allyship: "It's better to [try] . . . and fail than to avoid making an effort entirely" (2015). In *Thinking in Bets: Making Smarter Decisions When You Don't Have All the Facts* (2018), Annie Duke acknowledges that learning to think probabilistically is "hard, especially initially" (114). The same is true of dual-witnessing. Like "thinking in bets," the practice "has to start as a deliberative process" and will initially feel "clunky, weird, and slow" (Duke 114). One way to improve is to ask for help. One can ask the primary witness to be informed when one responds problematically, so one can apologize and reposition. Secondary witnesses can also seek out larger communities (e.g., book clubs, classrooms, group therapy sessions, etc.) to practice witnessing secondarily and communally. In group sessions, primary and secondary witnesses can discuss not only the imparted narrative but also how well they have engaged it. Duke explains that "it is easier to make . . . changes" to how we behave "if we aren't alone in the process" (117). "Recruiting help" or broadening dual-witnessing to communal witnessing can foster "robust change" (Duke 117). As Oluo recognizes, witnessing "will never become easy," but it will "become easier" (52). Conversations about trauma and oppression will "never be painless, but they can lessen . . . pain. They will never be risk-free, but they will always be worth it" (Oluo 52). Witnessing is not a miracle cure for the traumas and oppressions that pervade our lives, but the practice can help us heal, transforming primary and secondary witnesses alike.

Fictive Witnessing

The examples I offer above derive from nonfiction and fiction. The decision to include fictive instances of dual-and anti-witnessing was purposeful, as, to explicate my theories of reading trauma, this book engages (African) American novels. Although chapter 1 analyzes nineteenth-century emancipatory narratives, the bulk of the book tackles fiction. When one considers a readerly response to traumatized speakers, the decision to analyze fiction alongside nonfiction may seem counterintuitive. While a lack of empathic response may prove damaging to memoirists who struggle to witness their histories only to discover that their testimonies remain unheard and their traumas unrecognized, fictional subjects do not suffer from a reader's inability to enter into their narratives. Additionally, while writing nonfiction may facilitate traumatic witnessing by granting its author the opportunity to work through catastrophe, penning fiction does not require an author to witness her own trauma; a fiction-writer may not have anything to work through. Even when fiction does appear to witness (e.g., in portraying the depths of characters' lives), one could argue that nonfiction witnesses more successfully, as historical truth is more compelling than literary conjecture. Finally, a danger exists that trauma fiction could anti-witness actual trauma, prompting readers to a-witness the reality of trauma; to anti-witness voyeuristically fictional events; and/or to anti-witness co-optively real catastrophe, passing fiction off as truth and undermining the reality of someone's definite experience.

Even so, an engaged response to trauma fiction is critical. Although fiction occupies the realm of the imaginary, the genre nevertheless has the power to witness trauma, as it testifies to the actual existence of both individual tragedies and cultural catastrophes, encouraging readers to enter into the reality of trauma as depicted in fiction.[16] Trauma fiction, Vickroy asserts, helps readers "access" lived "traumatic experience" (*Contemporary* 1). Trauma fiction can also introduce readers to experiences they have yet to encounter but with which they—as empathic and socially responsible human beings—still need to grapple. Arnold Weinstein contends that a primary goal of trauma fiction is to "present readers verbally with a reality they cannot afford to experience literally," that is, to offer them the opportunity to witness secondarily what they have not witnessed (or cannot witness) primarily. "Literature," Weinstein writes, "pulls us out of our torpor" and provokes us to dual-witness "life's ultimacies"—or its manifold traumas and modes of oppression—"while remaining, preciously" literature (439).

The writer of trauma fiction also has the advantage of being able to step outside of her own, individual experience (the central "I" of memoir) into a more communal form of witnessing. In her work, she can not only convey the primary encounters of a single protagonist but can also witness within a single text the divergent, sometimes conflicting viewpoints of multiple characters and perspectives, which may benefit readers by suggesting the diverse identities and possibilities contained in each individual and community. In this way, fiction writers can serve as secondary witnesses by proxy for those who have suffered trauma but may not have the language or social support to testify to their experiences. Toni Morrison acknowledges

that her "single gravest responsibility" as a writer of trauma fiction is to
"expose"—or to witness secondarily by proxy—"truth[s] about the inte-
rior life of people who didn't write" or couldn't witness primarily ("Site of
Memory" 72). Correspondingly, trauma fiction can witness to contemporary
readers the traumas of speaker-survivors who have died (e.g., the experiences
of nineteenth-century slaves, depicted fictively in novels such as Colson
Whitehead's *The Underground Railroad* [2016]).

   Although fictitious characters may not be harmed through readerly anti-
witnessing, these fictive witnesses stand in for and alongside actual people
and situations that readers could maltreat in "real life" by refusing to witness their testimonies secondarily. Learning to engage trauma fiction can
help teach readers empathy in general, modeling to those willing to enter
into such narratives how to dual-witness in literature and life. Although
this stance could be dismissed as naïve or sentimental, Wayne Booth and
Schweickart suggest that the characters in the books we read, like the actual
people in the "company we keep," affect and inform us "for good or ill, so that
we have not only the right but the responsibility to understand and evalu-
ate"—or to witness secondarily—"how these characters live their fictional
lives" (Schweickart 11). Moreover, Schweickart writes, the intersubjectivity of
fictional characters and real people and fictional traumas and actual catastrophes is also substantiated by the concepts of "live entering," "acknowledging,"
and "facing" that Adam Zachary Newton derives from Bakhtin, Cavell, and
Levinas, respectively (Schweickart 11). Perhaps for this reason, theorists have
long placed trauma theory and literature in conversation. Cathy Caruth,
Shoshana Felman, and Geoffrey Hartman developed trauma studies out of
literary criticism, and each demonstrates in their work an appreciation for
the literary. (Caruth in particular uses literature to explain trauma theory
and trauma theory to analyze literature, for example, through the myth of
Tancred in *Unclaimed Experience*.) Upon this critical foundation, this book
analyzes dual-witnessing in nonfiction and fiction.

Witnessing in Postbellum American Literature

The postbellum American era is a rich period in which to explore dual-
witnessing in traumatic and testimonial literature. As Vickroy suggests,
postbellum American fiction marks a "growing awareness"—or witnessing—of the "effects of catastrophe and oppression on the individual psyche,"
a perspective that has "emerged with contemporary examinations" of the
psychological consequences of wars, the Holocaust, poverty, colonization,

and domestic abuse (*Reading* 1). American literature also embodies an inherent multiculturalism that parallels and prompts the Venn liminality dual-witnessing demands. A Venn space, Toni Morrison argues, is already encoded in American language and, by extension, its literature. American English, Morrison asserts, is "one of the best languages in the world to write in, because it is so polyglot—so many languages are already there, so many synonyms, so many antonyms" (qtd. in Borstein 153). Her declaration extends out into my geocultural focus: American testimonial literature lends itself to this book because, like its language and its ancestors, its texts are heterogenic, offering a fertile field in which to cultivate the theories of dual-witnessing and Venn liminality.

Likewise, the postbellum era marks an ideal period in which to investigate traumatic witnessing. Trauma theorists establish that witnessing can feel overwhelming. The struggle to testify is compounded when a writer is limited by the sociopolitical confines of her era. Sexual abuse, for instance, can be a particularly difficult trauma to witness (as it unfortunately carries with it a perceived social stigma or shame), and survivors of sexual assault may find their witnessing further inhibited by the strictures of the time period in which they write and by their own social position or standing (or lack thereof). We know, for instance, that African American slave women were frequently raped by their masters. In emancipatory narratives, however, few female speakers recount the details of their assaults, perhaps fearing a readerly backlash of outraged antebellum sensibilities. As a result, at their narratives' close, the totality of the speakers' experience can remain unwritten and unwitnessed. Twentieth- and twenty-first-century American fiction writers, conversely, benefit from writing out of the modern and postmodern eras, literary periods that grant authors more freedom to write what—and how— they want, without being (as) socially censured. Postbellum authors also have the literary latitude to write into their narratives a variety of combined and contradictory styles and voices that—through intersections of form and content—open for readers Venn liminality and incite dual-witnessing.

Last, postbellum literature may be able to witness more fully than the work of previous eras the lasting effects of American slavery, a central theme of this book. This claim does not imply that antebellum authors did not grapple with institutionalized racism (they did) or that racism and various forms of slavery do not persist today (they do). Instead, I emphasize the belatedness narrators require to testify. Caruth argues that trauma as it first occurs is incomprehensible. Only after a period of latency can a witness integrate catastrophe into narrative (*Unclaimed Experience* 8). Caruth's contention functions on an individual and a communal level. If a survivor takes time to process trauma, the same can be argued for society at large. Thus, rather than distance themselves from the catastrophe of American slavery, postbellum American authors may use the passage of time since Emancipation—a kind of sociocultural belatedness—to witness the trauma of American slavery.

Witnessing American Slavery and Its Aftermath

Within the larger field of postbellum American literature, this book analyzes Venn liminality and dual-witnessing in relation to African American literature and the genre's treatment of American slavery. In fact, it may be impossible to write about personal and sociopolitical American trauma without considering the substance and specter of institutional slavery. DeGruy explains that American slavery represents a national and cultural trauma "incomparable in scope, duration, and consequence to any other incidence of human enslavement" (112). The African American "slave experience," DeGruy writes, was marked by perpetual physical, psychic, and spiritual trauma (13): African American slaves were tortured and murdered. Their families were dismembered. Black women, men, and children were forced into subjugation, illiteracy, and poverty (Anderson 11). Critical race theorists refer to American institutional slavery as the "Maafa," Swahili for "disaster," "calamity," "catastrophe" or trauma (DeGruy 117). The aftermath of the Maafa persists today, as slavery's wounds fester in American society.

Miller explains that tragedies unfold intergenerationally. Traumatic aftermath lives on in survivors' families and culture at large. Trauma, she writes, can "deeply affect" even those who do not "share bloodlines with its victims," who have not "stood directly" in the trauma's path (9). If we apply this reasoning to (African) American culture and the history of racism in the United States, we can presume that, however many years have passed since Emancipation, Americans continue to be affected by slavery's aftermath.[17] In his introduction to *I Was Born a Slave: An Anthology of Classic Slave Narratives* (1999), Charles Johnson upholds that all Americans are "stained" by the history of institutional slavery, including those immigrants who arrived from Europe after Abraham Lincoln's 1863 Emancipation Proclamation (x): No American can claim exemption from the trauma of slavery. To do so would be to a-witness the history of racial trauma imbedded in our nation's culture and literature. In an interview with Michael Dyson, Kamala Harris, the junior United States Senator from California, asserts that one cannot "talk about this history of race in America without talking about slavery. It's the sin, the blemish, the shameful part of our history" (qtd. in Dyson *Truth*

75). Accordingly, this book speaks to the individual and communal histories, cultures, and traumas of African Americans, as witnessed in postbellum American literature, granting particular emphasis to the traumatic aftermath of American slavery.[18]

Regrettably, both American slavery in particular and African American trauma in general are habitually elided from trauma studies' discourse and purview. While trauma theorists address national and cultural catastrophes, such as the Holocaust or the September 11 terrorist attacks, few consider institutionalized slavery and its aftermath. Michael Awkward acknowledges that, despite the "growing scope and influence" of trauma studies over the past twenty years, American slavery is continually ignored and undermined, relegated to "parenthetical asides and afterthoughts" in the field's "most significant texts" (qtd. in Levy-Hussen 23). Caruth's influential edited collection, *Trauma: Explorations in Memory* (1995), for example, includes essays on the Holocaust; sexual assault and rape culture; the AIDS crisis; Hiroshima; and a community's response to an underground gas leak. No mention is made—even in passing—to African American psychosocial life or to the enduring trauma of American slavery. In a-witnessing American slavery and its aftermath, trauma theorists limit the scholarly potential of their field. They also exclude from conversation (and thereby further marginalize) what Levy-Hussen calls a "significant contingent" of (African) American writers, critics, literature, and concerns (23). To address this critical gap (and to advance both trauma and [African] American studies by placing them in conversation with one another), I join scholars, such as Awkard, Levy-Hussen, Keith Byerman, Lisa Woolfork, and Sadia Sahar Ahad, who explore the connections between trauma theory and African American literature and culture—and specifically those who consider literature's treatment of American slavery. This book contributes further to the intersecting fields of (African) American studies and trauma theory by considering how readers can respond to literary representations of (African) American trauma in ways that combat—versus contribute to—depicted catastrophes.

Defining African American Literature

To consider one's readerly response to representations of trauma in (African) American literature requires a clearer understanding of what constitutes "African American literature." At present, no single definition exists. Like that of "trauma," the definition remains open and malleable. Some classify the genre as any writing by and about black people living in the United States

(*Oxford Companion* 67). Others, such as Kenneth Warren, make narrower claims, asserting that the "collective enterprise" of African American literature represents a strict "Jim Crow phenomenon," dating from the US Supreme Court's decision in *Plessy v. Ferguson* (1896) through the end of segregation in the 1960s (8). Scholars such as Dickson Bruce take a more expansive view, tracing the development of African American literature from the seventeenth century into the twenty-first (xi). The genre's definitive parameters are further obscured when considering the overlapping differences between "African-American literature" (literature penned by native-born Africans, now living in America, e.g., Chiminanda Adichie's *Americanah* [2013]), texts with white protagonists written by self-identified black authors (e.g., Zora Neale Hurston's *Seraph on the Suwanee* [1948]), and novels with black protagonists written by self-identified white authors (e.g., Kathryn Stockett's *The Help* [2008]). Divergent classifications of African American literature prompt Morrison to query: "Other than melanin and subject matter," what creates a "black writer" or "African American" text? ("Unspeakable" 146).

The question is further complicated by the illusory quality of race. If, for example, I argue that African American literature witnesses black personhood and culture, how I define "black"—or race in general—affects my analysis of African American literature as a whole. Like African American literature, race is difficult to define without resorting to essentialism. While those who are raced, for example, as "white" or "black," often share common visual characteristics (such as skin color and hair texture) and geographical lineage (such as African or Anglo-European ancestry), Johnson qualifies that race is a socially constructed "*maya*," an illusion (xi). "Race," writes historian Nell Painter, "is an idea, not a fact" (qtd. in Coates "Foreword" xv). Still, simply because race is difficult to define does not mean that I can ignore it in a book about reading (among other constructs) race in African American literature. While speaking of race can lead to forms of aggressive anti-witnessing, in which "race" as a construct is used to denigrate those allocated to racial minority status, a-witnessing race can also augment racial prejudice, allowing those in power who profit from the tyranny of racial ignorance (e.g., whites) to exert racially based control over others (e.g., blacks) and simultaneously deny that they are doing so, as race "does not exist." For this reason, this book upholds that race represents not a biological certainty[19] but a cultural construct denoting how subjects are positioned by society. Race may not be essential, but our conceptions of race affect how we relate to one another. Thus, this book uses "race" to signify cultural positioning (in this case, relating to the culture of those Americans with African heritage) and, alongside Morrison and others, treats race—and, specifically, "blackness"—as "both an empty category" and "one of the most destructive and powerful forms of social categorization" in our race-conscious society (qtd. in Denard ix).

Ultimately, this book considers literature, written by and about African Americans, which is fundamentally testimonial, witnessing black personhood and culture by speaking to (and against) the pervasiveness of racism in the United States.[20] This collection of "African American literature" realizes this historical, cultural, and traumatic witnessing in two principal ways. First, the literature testifies to the individual experiences of an African American speaker, (e.g., Linda Brent/Harriet Jacobs recounts her tribulations in *Incidents in the Life of a Slave Girl* [1861] and Morrison depicts Sethe's anguish in *Beloved* [1987]). Second, alongside and out of her primary witnessing, the speaker typically becomes a secondary witness by proxy, using her individual experiences to testify as a representative member of her larger community. For example, in *Incidents,* Jacobs publishes her narrative both to witness her own life story and to speak for those other Afra-Americans, silenced by slavery, who cannot witness for themselves. *Beloved* also uses the title character's voice to testify to her own experience as well as on behalf of those whom she encompasses and witnesses, namely, the "Sixty Million and more" of the novel's dedication page, who died as a result of slavery and for whom Beloved serves as both surface and symbol. Following examples such as these, this book analyzes those works that witness, through the depth of an individual's strivings, the breadth of her (African) American experience. One could argue that all literature is testimonial, in that it all witnesses something, but the literature this book analyzes stands apart not only in how it witnesses (primarily and secondarily by proxy) but in what it testifies to, namely, the competing foundational precepts of our nation: freedom, equality, and institutionalized racism embodied in the institution of American slavery—all witnessed through the perspective of an African American protagonist or speaker. The "African American literature" this book examines, therefore, is a literature of individual and communal witnessing that testifies to the cultural positioning of African Americans in America, beginning with—and extending out of—the trauma of American slavery.

The assertion that African American literature is distinctly testimonial is critically substantiated. Mae Gwendolyn Henderson emphasizes that African American literature is "primarily testimonial," resulting from a "commonality of history, culture, and language" that "constitutes the basis for a tradition of a black [narrator's] expressive culture" (qtd. in Miles 48). Margaret Walker upholds that African American literature witnesses "the ultimate of Black experience, or the life of Black people, in America," offering readers a record of "what life has been for Black people in America for [over] 350 years"

("Humanistic Tradition" 122–23). Moreover, African American literature testifies not only to black personhood and culture but also to the manifold traumas arising out of slavery, which continue to affect the life narratives of contemporary (African) Americans. In *Women, Violence, and Testimony* (2003), Diana Miles underscores that African American literature "gives voice to an American literary tradition propelled by an ethical imperative" to witness the "psychological and physical trauma of slavery" (48). To link African American literature to witnessing, testimony, trauma, and slavery is not to suggest that the genre lacks other literary characteristics, such as aesthetic or entertainment value. Instead, this book argues, with critics such as Levy-Hussen, that—in addition to its other qualities—the genre belongs fundamentally to the "province of political speech," as, "above all," its "representational aims" are "activist, pedagogical, and documentary" (169). African American literature, Levy-Hussen asserts, is not just beautiful writing or a diversion from real life. The genre "inspirit[s] social change" through "the act of reading" (169). In *What Truth Sounds Like*, Dyson asserts that a "special burden fell on the shoulders" of those black artists, "blessed with great talent: they must use their station to tell the truth; to, in [James] Baldwin's words, be 'a witness'" (231–32). Alongside these writers, this book treats African American literature as a genre that witnesses black personhood, culture, and trauma and provokes readers to do the same.

African American literature also promotes dual-witnessing, underscoring the necessity of primary witnessing, while impelling the reader to enter directly into the narrative experience (to witness secondarily). While most literature encourages readerly engagement, what this book classifies as "African American literature" is noteworthy for its ability to provoke those readers who would rather a-witness the realities of America's racial history than dual-witness the specter of American slavery. In *Quiet as It's Kept: Shame, Trauma, and Race in the Novels of Toni Morrison* (2000), J. Brooks Bouson argues that African American literature invites readers "to understand and to respond viscerally to"—or dual-witness—the "painful race matters" to which they testify (x).

The call to readers to confront racial trauma through fiction underlies the African American literary tradition. Dual-witnessing is built into both African American literature and culture. In "Unspeakable Things Unspoken," Morrison describes the process of reading African American literature as "choos[ing] to examine centers of the self" one may previously have ignored. Here, Morrison seems to uphold this book's claim that, as "subjects" of their own narratives, primarily concerned with the project of telling their personal and communal stories, the narrators in African American literature witness primarily and secondarily by proxy and, in doing so, challenge readers to "choose to examine" or witness secondarily the history of American racism and endurance of African Americans.

While critics do not yet delineate the dual-witnessing inherent in African American literature, they do note the genre's attention to readerly response. Keith Byerman contends that African American literature provokes readers "to face the truth" regarding the "fullness" of American history "in all its ambiguity and ugliness and complicity" (9). Morrison asserts that African American literature inspires readerly participation "in the same way that a Black preacher requires his congregation to . . . join him in the sermon that is being delivered" ("Rootedness" 59), and Henry Louis Gates Jr. upholds that, in African American literature, the story "fires up" its readership, so that even when the text concludes, "the story" does not (*Talk That Talk* 10). Instead, readers "take the story home with them, and the next day they spread the word to the ones who were not there to witness the event" (Gates 10). African American literature impels dual-witnessing, and when readers put down their books and "spread the word" to those who have not encountered the text in question, dual-witnessing transforms into secondary witnessing by proxy and inspires communal witnessing. Thus, the witnessing potential of African American literature does not cease when a book concludes but continues to witness to and through those who engage it.

Ultimately, this book places trauma and reception theory in conversation with cultural criticism to read "African American literature" as a collection of testimonial works, ranging from the nineteenth through the twenty-first centuries, that witnesses primarily and secondarily by proxy and incites readers to witness secondarily and communally black personhood, culture, history, and trauma. In treating texts written and published during the antebellum era and its immediate aftermath (e.g., nineteenth-century emancipatory narratives) through the contemporary era (e.g., Jesmyn Ward's 2017 novel, *Sing, Unburied, Sing*), I join critics who take an expansive historical view of African American literature. "The literature of Black people in America," Walker explains, "is not a recent phenomenon" ("Humanistic Tradition" 121) but has been printed and distributed in the United States "since the colonial days" ("Reflections" 41). Accordingly, Walker continues, contemporary African American writers have neither created nor discovered a new genre (even if the collection is newly recognized by non-African American readers) but instead "continue a tradition" begun by other African American authors "over two-hundred years ago" ("Phillis Wheatley" 37). Critics such as Johnson, Lovalerie King, and Shirley Moody-Turner agree: African American literature "began its prose with the slave [emancipatory] narrative, transitioned in the nineteenth century to the protest novel" (Johnson *Contemporary* xi), and persists today in a "dynamic relationship of continuity and change, rewriting, . . . signifying" and/or witnessing (King and Moody-Turner 5).[21]

Witnessing Race and Gender

Finally, *Reading Testimony* examines the interplay of race and gender in (African) American testimonial literature. As dual-witnessing is the desired consequence of the African American writing this book explores, *Reading Testimony* considers the intersectionality of race and gender in the witnessing process and the crossing of these social identities by speakers and readers to witness together. Black feminist critics such as Joanne Braxton, Barbara Christian, bell hooks, Valerie Smith, and Deborah White underscore the need for African American literature to witness not only a seemingly unified "genderless" black history but to testify to difference, particularly between black men and black women and black women and white women. In American society, black women are doubly marginalized, silenced by black men because of their gender and a-witnessed by white women because of their race, enduring what I term an *embodied triple witnessing* (the para-Du Boisian consciousness of one's "threeness" as an American, a black, and a female). African Americans and women, White writes, are consigned to subservient roles, as both groups share a "relationship of powerlessness vis-à-vis white males" and are thus automatically treated "as outsiders and inferiors" (27). Black men can be "rescued" from what White calls the "myth of the Negro," by aligning themselves with what society considers "masculine" and "dominant" (28). White women, "as part of the dominant racial group" can also overcome the "myth of women," but an "impossible task confronts the black woman. If she is rescued from the myth of the Negro, the myth of woman traps her; if she escapes the myth of woman, the myth of the Negro still ensnares her" (White 27–28). "The black woman," Toni Morrison writes, "has nothing to fall back on: not maleness, not whiteness, not ladyhood, not anything" (qtd. in Jerkins 49). Accordingly, the embodied triple witnessing of Afra-Americans, as black, American, and female,[22] must be witnessed, particularly in a genre as testimonial as African American literature, which already testifies to underrepresented American personhood and should not exclude from its purview black womanhood.

In light of this history, though not every chapter of this book responds to literary representations of both race and gender, most examine one construct or the other and often the interplay of both.[23] The book builds upon the work of black feminists to utilize intersectionality as a mode of traumatic, cultural, and textual analysis and to interrogate what it means to read—or dual-witness—at intersecting constructions of race and gender. In doing so, *Reading Testimony* interrogates how black and white women dual-witness across gender. Of distinct significance is the interracial female dual-witnessing that occurs between black and female witnesses since their shared occupation of the female sphere may enable them to pass over the racial barriers between them. This interracial female dual-witnessing models the type of analysis, a scholarly dual-witnessing, that underlies and informs my book, as I speak back to those textual moments that highlight how testimonial African American literature can be, at once embodying and promoting textual and intertextual, multicultural, and readerly speakerly dual-witnessing out of and through the fraught (literary) histories of race and gender relations in America.

To elucidate how theories of dual-witnessing intersect with (African) American literature, race theory, and gender criticism, *Reading Testimony*'s first chapter examines Afra-American emancipatory narratives as foundational to ensuing Venn readings of trauma, testimony, race, and gender. Explicitly, chapter 1 investigates (1) how well—and to what effect—nineteenth-century Afra-American emancipatory narratives witness and (2) the nature of our readerly response to the texts in question. Chapter 2 analyzes how William Faulkner's fiction (in order to testify to the southern white male "problems" of race and gender) co-optively anti-witnesses black and female characters' traumas, even as his work pushes readers, independent of social positioning, to engage trauma, testimony, and racial and gendered difference, that is, to dual-witness. Chapter 3 analyzes Zora Neale Hurston's *Their Eyes Were Watching God* (1937), in which the protagonist is witnessed secondarily through conversation with her friend, alongside Margaret Walker's *Jubilee* (1966), which moves the conversation from two similar speakers to many diverse participants, in order to explore how African American literature promotes multiethnic and multigendered dual- and communal witnessing. Chapter 4 analyzes how Toni Morrison and Jesmyn Ward's novels witness the traumatic aftermath of slavery and impact of systemic racism and sexism to impel readers to engage the individual and collective histories of marginalized Americans. The conclusion to *Reading Testimony* considers how theories of dual-witnessing may extend beyond reading and listening to incite a revolutionary response.

CHAPTER 1

"To Be Free to Say So"

Witnessing Trauma in the Narratives of
Harriet Jacobs, Sojourner Truth, and Elizabeth Keckley

The capacity for narrative nonfiction to witness trauma is upheld by auto-biographical critics and memoirists alike. Life writing, theorists maintain, permits the author to witness in three principal ways. First, writing out and through one's trauma (what Suzette Henke calls "scriptotherapy") empowers the writer to process and prevail over her tragedies (xxi). Second, life writing allows the speaker to testify to a newly particularized self that emanates directly out of her encounter with catastrophe (Ellerby xxi). Third, writing through trauma permits the survivor to "speak truth to power," to testify publicly not only to the suffering she has endured but also against the systemic oppression and violence that helped facilitate her individual experience (Hill 6). In these ways, autobiography offers primary witnesses the opportunity to (re)assert control over their life narratives, to reform shattered selves, and to combat respective and collective injustice.

Evidence of autobiography's witnessing potential is found in nineteenth-century American emancipatory narratives, which testify to the formerly enslaved speaker's individual trauma and personhood (McBride 16), to the catastrophes borne mutually by all American slaves (Gates xxvi), and to the insidiousness of slavery itself (Foster *Written* 86). Emancipatory narratives also encourage dual-witnessing, exhorting readers to witness their accounts secondarily by reaffirming their speakers' individual and representative personhood and racially induced suffering. On this premise, this chapter analyzes three emancipatory narratives: *Incidents in the Life of a Slave Girl*, by Harriet Jacobs as "Linda Brent" (1861); *Narrative of Sojourner Truth*, by Sojourner Truth and her amanuensis Olive Gilbert (1850); and *Behind the Scenes Or, Thirty Years a Slave and Four Years in the White House* by Elizabeth Keckley (1868) to examine how and to what effect the narratives witness as well as how readers respond to the texts in question. To explore the multiple jeopardies of marginalized race and gender (and intersections of racism and sexism) in traumatic autobiographical witnessing, this chapter considers emancipatory narratives written by or on behalf of African American women.

The distinction drawn between male-and female-voiced narratives is significant. While theorists such as William Andrews, Sterling Bland, and Robert Stepto have written extensively about the testimonial value of androcentric emancipatory narratives, few critics originally considered the witnessing potential of female bondswomen. Joanne Braxton explains that the 1845 *Narrative of the Life of Frederick Douglass* has traditionally been read as the "central text" of the emancipatory narrative genre (19). Based on Douglass' narrative, theorists such as Stepto have identified the principal "Afro-American archetype" as that of the "articulate hero" (or male primary witness), who, through self-acquired literacy, writes to witness his traumatic history (Stepto 17). In exclusively analyzing male slave heroics, however, theorists have ignored the testimonial power of the equally "articulate and rationally enlightened" female slave narrator, eliding Afra-American experiences from their critical purview (Braxton 19). To address this critical gap and build upon the foundation laid by Braxton (and critics such as Houston Baker, Hazel Carby, and Frances Smith Foster), this chapter investigates the interplay of blackness, womanhood, and traumatic witnessing in American emancipatory narratives to discern how such identity constructs work together and against one another to help and hinder witnessing.

Ultimately, the chapter concludes that, despite the narratives' testimonial potential, each narrator is restricted in her ability to witness trauma, particularly as it relates to her compounded marginalization as an enslaved Afra-American. Constricted perhaps by traumatic memory and by those social constraints dictating what a black female speaker may and may not disclose about her life (i.e., her knowledge of the prevalence of sexual abuse in American slavery and the racist misogyny it reflects),[1] Jacobs, Truth, and Keckley witness inconsistently, each testifying more explicitly through what she does not write than through what she does. The bondswomen's struggle to witness, however, need not undermine the traumatic, literary, or historical import of their autobiographies. Instead, the omissions that pervade their recorded histories offer readers the opportunity to engage actively their testimony and witness with them, facilitating the speakers' ability to testify across centuries to the multifarious traumas that arise out of institutional slavery and continue to shape American literary culture.

"Far More Terrible for Women": Witnessing (Sexual) Trauma in Harriet Jacobs's *Incidents*

I begin a-chronologically with an analysis of Harriet Jacobs's *Incidents in the Life of a Slave Girl,* published in 1861 under the pseudonym Linda Brent. Although Sojourner Truth's 1850 narrative precedes Jacobs's and presents similar subjects and themes to those addressed in *Incidents in the Life of a Slave Girl* (such as the struggle for freedom by—and sexual oppression of—female slaves), Jacobs's account remains the most critically cited female-penned emancipatory narrative and thus offers a rich foundation for continued analysis of the genre's (in)ability to witness trauma experienced by American bondswomen. Throughout her narrative, Jacobs (as Brent) testifies out of her "own experience and observation" (81) to what Maya Angelou calls the "tripartite crossfire of masculine prejudice, white illogical hate, and black lack of power" (265) inherent in American slavery. "Slavery," Brent attests, "is terrible for men; but it is far more terrible for women. Superadded to the burden common to all, they have wrongs, and sufferings, and mortifications peculiarly their own" (119). In presenting this charge, Jacobs witnesses both primarily (as "Linda"),[2] highlighting her own traumas and experiences, and also secondarily by proxy (as the titular "Slave Girl"), testifying as a representative of all bondswomen to the violence and oppression of slavery's instilled racism and sexism.

Throughout *Incidents,* Jacobs upholds her commitment to witness primarily and secondarily by proxy. She concludes her narrative with the exclamation "What a comfort it is to be free to say so!" (263), indicating that freedom is not limited to one's physical location or social station but includes the ability to witness as speaker of one's own narrative and spokesperson for African American women in bondage. "Reader," Brent pledges, "it is not to awaken sympathy for myself that I am telling you truthfully what I suffered in slavery. I do it to kindle a flame of compassion in your hearts for my sisters who are still in bondage, suffering as I once suffered" (47). In offering this assurance, Jacobs guards against those who would charge her with arrogance or indecency for daring to disclose the traumas she suffered as a slave. She also emphasizes that her dedication to testify is motivated not by self-interest but by a desire to speak for those other women who are unable to witness slavery's catastrophes. A drawback to Jacobs's effort to witness primarily and secondarily by proxy is that her particular experiences can be eclipsed by those of the collective, rendering her encounters, in Dwight McBride's language, "less meaningful" (11). Accordingly, readers may struggle to witness Jacobs's traumas secondarily, as her experiences belong not exclusively to her (or even to "Linda") but to all bondswomen.

For this reason, readers must strive to dual-witness Jacobs's unique psychic traumas as well as her collectively representative sociopolitical catastrophes. Jacobs invites such secondary witnessing when she addresses her readership above (i.e., "Reader, it is not to awaken sympathy . . ." [47]), and she elicits readerly engagement throughout her narrative. In *Incidents'* preface, Brent speaks directly to her reader. "Reader," she asserts, "be assured this narrative is no fiction. I am aware that some of my adventures may seem incredible; but they are, nevertheless, strictly true. I have not exaggerated the wrongs inflicted by Slavery; on the contrary, my descriptions fall far short of the facts" (5). Here, Brent asks to be witnessed secondarily. Even as she recognizes the difficulty dual-witnessing presents, she prompts readers to engage the veracity of her "adventures" or traumatic encounters. Brent intuits that readers may resist her history but asks them nonetheless to believe, as slavery represents too great a "wrong" to be a-witnessed. And yet, in admitting that her "descriptions fall short of the facts," Jacobs-as-Brent also recognizes that the truths of her narrative remain unwitnessable, defying both language and belief. Accordingly, the author offers readers the opportunity to enter into her history, so they may witness secondarily what her speaker struggles to witness primarily.

Inciting readers to dual-witness is not without challenge. In *To Tell a Free Story*, William Andrews suggests that "black self-writers" who wished to witness slavery's iniquities were "burdened" with the "task" of engaging a "skeptical, if not hostile white audience" (4). Frances Smith Foster acknowledges that in order to incite readers to witness the slave narrator's history, the writer had first to "overcome the incredulity" of those readers whose "surprise" that a black slave could write "overshadowed any attempt" to engage the narrator's testimony (*Witnessing* 9). Cognizant of such obstacles, Jacobs narrows the scope of her intended audience to Northern white women, encouraging white female readers to view her speaker not only as an oppressed African American but also (and principally) as an exploited woman. In doing so, Jacobs helps those white women who may resist her testimony connect instead to her suffering, through a shared sense of sisterhood and outrage at the subjugation women face. Brent rebukes, "Why are ye silent, ye free . . . women of the [N]orth? Why do your tongues falter in maintenance of the right?" (48). She appeals, in the words of the prophet Isaiah, "Rise up, ye women that are at ease! Hear my voice, ye careless daughters! Give ear unto my speech" (Isaiah 32.9; Jacobs 2). In such passages, Jacobs signifies on the biblical language of the Jewish and Christian prophets to call white and free women to cross over race and station and witness secondarily the suffering, personhood, and rights of Brent and, through her, all enslaved black women.

Jacobs models such interracial dual-witnessing throughout *Incidents*. Valerie Smith observes that every time Brent escapes an obstacle on her way to freedom, she does so "only with the aid of someone else"—most often a white woman (32), who, as Jean Yellin notes, "defect[s] from the slaveholders' ranks to help" the African American runaway ("Texts and Contexts" 275). Brent could not have escaped slavery, Yellin contends, but for the assistance of the white woman who attempts to stop Brent's master from molesting her, the female slaveholder who conceals Brent in her home for a month, or the Northern female employer who loans her own child to Brent, so she can evade slave catchers by traveling as a nursemaid instead of a fugitive. In each illustration, Yellin explains, readers observe women who forsake "allegiances of race and class" and "assert their stronger allegiance to the sisterhood of all women" ("Texts and Contexts" 275–76). Readers can follow suit by renouncing those social dictates separating women by race and class; by witnessing Brent's oppression as a woman; and by rallying for Brent's freedom as well as for the emancipation of all (black) women.

Jacobs also models interracial female dual-witnessing by including in her narrative conversations between white and black women that underscore multicultural engagement and cooperation. In one such scene, a white woman, moved by witnessing Brent's trials, agrees to help her. "Among the [white] ladies . . . acquainted with my grandmother," Jacobs writes, "was one who had . . . always been very friendly to her" (151). Jacobs reminds readers that, even when slavery works to divide women by race, interracial friendships can exist. Jacobs relates that, following Brent's escape from slavery, the white woman asked her grandmother to "tell me all about it. Perhaps I can do something to help you" (151). In this scene, the white woman invites the black woman to witness to her and then offers not only to listen but also to act. Jacobs describes: "She listened attentively to the details of my story, and sat thinking for a while. At last she said, . . . 'If you think there is any chance of Linda's getting to the Free States, I will conceal her for a time'" (152). Through this passage, Jacobs demonstrates that interracial female dual-witnessing requires active listening, careful consideration (as when the woman sits "thinking"), and courageous action (when she promises to "do something" to help). Readers are called to follow this example: to read intently, to consider carefully what one has learned, and to cross over race and to unite in sisterhood and "do something" about slavery, presumably by advocating for those, like Brent, who remain enslaved.

Further interracial female dual-witnessing is displayed through the positive interactions exhibited between *Incidents'* white editor, Amy Post, and its black author, Harriet Jacobs. Although Jacobs wields control over her narrative by writing her preface, Post pens its appendix—a coda that models dual-witnessing between women. Post begins by describing Jacobs as her "highly-esteemed friend" (304), placing Jacobs and herself on the same social level without claiming superiority due to race or class. She continues: "If readers knew her as I know her, they could not fail to be deeply interested in her story" (304), suggesting that, if readers engage Jacobs's account and personhood (as Post has), they will engage her life narrative. Post next reveals that Jacobs initially resisted divulging her "bitter experiences": "A woman can whisper her cruel wrongs in the ear of a dear friend much easier than she can record them for the world to read" (305). Post, however, encourages Jacobs to witness anyway, in order to work through her ordeals and to "arouse" readers to "work for the disinthralment" of other bondswomen (305). Jacobs's reticence underscores the difficulty of primary witnessing, and Post's insistence that she witness emphasizes how imperative the editor believes the process to be. The women's conversation also instructs readers to remain mindful of the "mental agony" implicit in witnessing trauma (305) and to treat Jacobs's testimony considerately, as Post has, by reading as an invested friend instead of a distant stranger. In framing her appendix, Post underlines the significance of Jacobs's narrative and the importance of interracial dual-witnessing between women.

As Deborah Gray White demonstrates, Jacobs also celebrates interracial female dual-witnessing by testifying to the difficulties white women face as co-victims (with black women) of white patriarchal power (43). For example, when Brent's master, Dr. Flint, sexually harasses her, she fears for her life, but she also empathizes with her mistress, Mrs. Flint, whose marriage vows have been "desecrated" and "dignity insulted" (White 43). Jacobs is able to read Mrs. Flint not only as a victimizer of Brent, whom the mistress repeatedly abuses, but also as a victim of her husband's infidelity and a larger patriarchal system. *Incidents* does not imply, simply because free white women (such as Flint) and enslaved black women (such as Brent) are both subjugated, that their oppression is commensurate. Instead, as Foster maintains, while

Jacobs "asserts a common sisterhood" between women, she also warns white female readers against empathic anti-witnessing or "conflating the situations of enslaved black women and free white ones" (*Written* 96). In her preface, Jacobs pronounces:

> O, you happy free women, contrast your New Year's day with that of the poor bond-woman! With you it is a pleasant season . . . Friendly wishes meet you everywhere, and gifts are showered upon you. . . . [Your children] are your own, and no [one] . . . can take them from you. But to the slave mother New Year's day comes laden with . . . sorrows. She sits on her cold cabin floor, watching the children who may all be torn from her the next morning. (26)

Here, Jacobs reminds white female readers that, while they are free to celebrate life, family, and the passage of time, for black bondswomen, holidays such as New Year's (when slaves are sold at auction) are not jubilant but traumatic. In illustrating such inequities, Jacobs does not elide racial differences between women but utilizes their disparities in status to embolden free white women to use their privilege to advocate for those without.

As Jacobs does not discount racial inequalities between women, she also does not pretend that interracial female dual-witnessing is effortless. Instead, she provides counterexamples of white women who are unwilling to dialogue with black women, demonstrating the effort required to cross over race to dual-witness as well as the damage that ensues when women refuse to do so. Consider the depicted relationship between Linda Brent and Mrs. Flint. Despite the abuse Brent receives from Mrs. Flint, the bondswoman remains surprisingly willing to dual-witness with her mistress, even as Mrs. Flint refuses to witness her secondarily. When Mrs. Flint demands that Brent tell her "all that has happened between you and your master," she reports: "I did as she ordered. As I went on with my account, . . . she wept, and sometimes groaned. . . . I was touched by her grief" (53). Brent engages Mrs. Flint's emotional response and exhibits empathy for her mistress. "Tears came to my eyes," Jacobs writes, moved by Mrs. Flint's sorrow. "But," she recognizes, "I was soon convinced that her emotions arose" not from sympathy but "from . . . wounded pride. . . . Her dignity [was] insulted, but she had no compassion for the poor victim of her husband's perfidy" (53). Whereas Brent is willing, Mrs. Flint is loath to dual-witness. The passage warns against the patriarchy's ability to divide women who are otherwise united in their shared oppression and encourages readers not to align with Mrs. Flint but with those, such as Brent, who risk everything to witness their suffering and personhood.

However, even as Jacobs elicits dual-witnessing, she struggles to witness her own traumas primarily, particularly those relating to sexual assault. In fact, the author confides to her editor her reluctance to publish *Incidents*, as doing so will require her to print the "whole truth" of her sexual history (Nudelman 942). Such reticence is not unique to Jacobs. Judith Herman explains that, when a life writer is traumatized, formal difficulties specific to her trauma can interfere with her ability to convey her experience. The constricted author, for instance, may lack the language to witness trauma. When she attempts to detail the particulars of her experience, she may circle around the event instead of witnessing it. She may repeat herself without communicating or truncate her sentences before providing crucial information (Herman 7). Dori Laub expounds that, for the traumatized subject, "there are never enough words or the right words, there is never enough time or the right time to articulate the story that cannot be fully captured" (63). Emancipated narrators are no exception, leading Andrews to describe the attempt to witness slavery's traumas as an "anguishing mental and emotional struggle" (9). "Rare [is] the autobiographer," Andrews observes, who does not "lament" his or her inability to testify comprehensively to the pervasive "horrors of slavery" (9).

The struggle to witness trauma is evident in emancipatory narratives written by and for female survivors of sexual assault. Of all traumas, sexual abuse can be exceptionally challenging to witness, as it carries with it a perceived social stigma (Ahrens 3). The difficulty of witnessing sexual trauma pertains in particular to Afra-American slave narrators, whose ability to testify to sexual violation is limited not only by traumatic consciousnesses but also by the societal conventions of the time. Because the antebellum period emphasized even more stridently than the present the ignominy of sexual assault, the pressure placed on survivors not to witness such abuse was tremendous. Braxton notes that according to the Victorian "cult of true womanhood," sexuality of any form was "not to be discussed" (27). The injunction against disclosing the sexual (and sexually traumatic) details of one's life applied especially to triply marginalized black bondswomen, who were socially and legally restricted from testifying to anything, let alone to the (sexual) abuse enacted by their white male masters. Moreover, because white slaveholding society stereotyped African American women as lascivious "Jezebels" who "invited sexual overtures from white men"—thereby aggressively anti-witnessing enslaved black women for being raped by such white men as their masters and plantation overseers—black female slaves were held responsible for their own victimization (White 29–30). Perhaps for these reasons, few female slave narrators published the details of their sexual violation, and, when bondswomen did address sexual trauma, their narratives testify more explicitly to the difficulty of witnessing sexual violence than to its incidence. Accordingly, a former bondswoman's sexual trauma may remain unwritten and unwitnessed. For this reason, Andrews instructs readers to "pay special attention" to the structured blanks that surface in an otherwise "objective reportage of the facts of slavery" (8), as narrative gaps may reveal that an author has written around (instead of through) experiences she cannot witness. When engaging *Incidents,* therefore, readers should attend as closely to what Jacobs elides as to what she describes. Consider the testimony that surfaces through the following passage's structured blanks. To introduce the sexual abuse Brent suffers, Jacobs writes: "I now entered my fifteenth year—a sad epoch in the life of a slave girl" (43). Here, Brent testifies to her personal knowledge of the prevalence of sexual assault in slavery by suggesting that, upon reaching physical maturation, she entered that "sad epoch" during which all bondswomen are victimized. Jacobs does not delineate the specifics of Brent's violation but reports, "My master began to whisper foul words in my ear" (43), while omitting what Dr. Flint said or what made his message foul. Despite this elusiveness, Brent assures her readership that "young as I was, I could not remain ignorant" of her master's meaning (43). In writing thus, Jacobs may hope that—without her having to disclose the particulars of her harassment—readers will not "remain ignorant" of the assault she suffered and will instead engage unspeakable traumas. Jacobs's insistence that Brent could not "remain ignorant" carries a sexual connotation, signifying that, against her will, Brent was forced—through rape—to acquire carnal knowledge. Jacobs, however, does not testify to the veracity of this interpretation but continues to veil the nature of the abuse perpetrated against her.

Throughout *Incidents,* Jacobs utilizes narrative gaps to (a-)witness sexual assault. Of Brent's abuser, Jacobs writes: "He was a crafty man and resorted to many [unspecified] means to accomplish his [unspecified] purposes" (43). Here, Jacobs transfers to her readership the authority to explicate Flint's behavior. Readers are left to decipher for themselves what reprehensible means Flint employed to achieve his purposes. Jacobs discloses only that Flint's actions "violat[ed] the most sacred commandments of nature" (43), most likely by desecrating both his wedding vows and Jacobs's sense of natural law by raping Linda Brent. Although Jacobs does not illustrate the details of Flint's sexual exploitation, she does assert that, when Flint pursued her, Brent "turned from him with disgust and hatred" (43). Jacobs emphasizes the "degradations," "wrongs," and "vices" inherent in Flint's assault of Brent and also—in underscoring the slave's rejection of her master's advances—guards against those who would blame Brent for her own victimization. Concluding unhappily, the narrator states, "But he was my master" (43), emphasizing her legal powerlessness (defending herself once more against anticipated accusatory anti-witnessing) and also witnessing secondarily by proxy for those bondswomen who likewise have no recourse against cruel masters. By suggesting but not stating the degrees of her violation, her master's perfidy, and her own inability to prevent him from achieving "his purposes," Jacobs argues against slavery itself, an institution that sanctions the white male ownership of black female bodies (to abuse as the master pleases) and thus legalizes and facilitates the rape of black women by white men.

In this passage (and throughout *Incidents*), Jacobs simultaneously a-witnesses and witnesses sexual assault by affirming the existence of her abuse while proscribing its particulars. In doing so, she incites readers to enter into her structured blanks, to engage with her narrative gaps, and to witness secondarily their hidden traumas. The danger with this approach is that it leaves interpretation up to Jacobs's audience. When a reader encounters textual aporias in *Incidents*, even the most well-meaning will attempt (as I have above) to determine what happened to Brent, what traumas Jacobs elides, and why. In doing so, readers necessarily penetrate the text, a violent act of interpretation that seems more like anti-witnessing than dual-witnessing. Foster corroborates that "under the label of education" scenes depicting masters' "violence and cruelty" toward their slaves awakened not only "moral outrage against slavery" but also "the public's appetite for sensationalism," leading critics such as Robin Winks to describe emancipatory narratives as the "pious pornography of their day" (qtd. in *Witnessing* 20). A positive outcome of such readerly anti-witnessing is that narrators can exploit the voyeuristic tendencies of their audience to provoke readers to witness secondarily what they may otherwise have anti-witnessed. In fact, Bland reports, fugitive slave narrators were encouraged by abolitionists to "highlight the most lurid and sensational accounts of their lives"—if only through elision, as Jacobs does above—in order to induce indisposed readers to buy and read socially challenging texts (Bland 8). The problem with such a strategy is that readers may approach a text voyeuristically without troubling to witness its contents secondarily. Moreover, authors may feel obligated to present traumatic experiences in a prurient light in order to entice readers to join the abolitionist cause, thereby subverting their own need to witness primarily to meet the appropriative anti-witnessing of abolitionists. Thus, even as emancipatory narratives provoke readers to contest the probity of slavery, their speakers' histories may remain anti-witnessed.

Incidents' reception history is fraught with anti-witnessing. Jacobs's autobiography was first published in serial form by the *New-York Tribune,* a newspaper owned and edited by the abolitionist Horace Greeley. Jacobs's depicted sexual abuse, however, was considered "too shocking for readerly consumption," and the paper stopped printing her work, thereby erasing her history (Yellin "Harriet Jacobs" 394). Jacobs was not able to secure a publisher until Lydia Maria Child, moved by what the bondswoman had suffered, offered to serve as her editor (Yellin "Harriet Jacobs" 394). While Child helped abate the elision of *Incidents,* her assistance underlines another vulnerability slave narrators faced when seeking publication: the threat of appropriative anti-witnessing. Ideally, as editor, Child would serve as secondary witness to (and secondary witness by proxy for) Jacobs, but a blurred boundary exists between dual- and anti-witnessing, and, in editing *Incidents,* Child also risked appropriating it. In her introduction, Child asserts that any "changes" she made to *Incidents* were "for purposes of condensation and orderly arrangement" (7). "With trifling exceptions," she contends, "the ideas and the language are [Jacobs's] own (7). Here, Child preempts the charge of co-optive anti-witnessing but, in doing so, highlights the danger of editorial appropriation, raising the questions: What makes a revision more or less "orderly," and how do such "changes" adhere to the era's social order? (Does Child "condense" Jacobs's mention of rape, for instance, or does she simply reorder paragraphs?) What constitutes a "trifling exception," and which "ideas" and "language" are not Jacobs's own? In offering her validation, Child forestalls those who would reject *Incidents* because it is written by an Afra-American or who would disbelieve that a bondswoman could pen a narrative, but Child also, in submitting this explanation and in editing *Incidents,* risks usurping the power of Jacobs's narrative voice. Indeed, when *Incidents* was first published, Child's name—not Jacobs's or Brent's—appeared on its title page (Yellin "Harriet Jacobs" 394), permitting the editor, consciously or not, to appropriate the narrative's contents.

Whatever was Child's intent, Jacobs's narrative was anti-witnessed by many of her readers. Despite the editor's white envelope attesting to the reliability and character of *Incidents*' black author and authenticating the veracity of her narrative, for over a hundred years after *Incidents*' publication, Jacobs's critics negatively a-witnessed the narrative, asserting that it was false. Some, with the editor and readers of the *New-York Tribune,* censured the narrative's sexual details and denounced both author and publisher for printing them. Others, underscoring the danger of white appropriation of black narratives, expressed confusion as to whether the book was written by Child or Jacobs. Well into the twentieth-century, critical estimation was that *Incidents* was a false memoir, written by Child to further abolitionism (Yellin *Harriet Jacobs* xi-xii). Not until the 1980s did Jean Yellin use historical documents to prove that Harriet Jacobs did exist, that she was sexually assaulted by her master, that she escaped from slavery, and that she wrote her own narrative (Christian 41). *Incidents*'s reception history, fraught with anti-witnessing, emphasizes the difficulty female slave narrators encountered in testifying to their personal experiences with sexual abuse in American slavery, and the importance of contemporary readers who choose not to ignore or negate its contents but to strive instead, with Yellin and Christian, to witness secondarily what Jacobs labored to witness primarily.

"Oh, God, Make the People Hear Me!": (Anti-)Witnessing the *Narrative* of Sojourner Truth

Sojourner Truth is an eminent figure, celebrated as a spokesperson for and icon of black feminism, lauded for her work in the abolitionist and women's rights movements, and acclaimed for her oratorical prowess, exemplified in her speech on racial and gendered inequities, "Ar'n't I a Woman?," at the 1851 Ohio Women's Rights Convention. In praising Truth's ability to testify to personal and sociopolitical oppression, few consider her autobiography, *The Narrative of Sojourner Truth* (1850), which is often eclipsed with analyses of Jacobs's *Incidents*. Yellin, for instance, overlooks Truth's *Narrative* (as well as other female-penned accounts, such as Elizabeth Keckley's *Behind the Scenes*) when she lauds Jacobs's text as the "only known full-length work" by an Afra-American "writing about her experience as a slave woman" (qtd. in Braxton 23). Hazel Carby opts not to mention Truth's *Narrative* in her chapter on slave women's autobiography in *Reconstructing Womanhood*, and Frances Smith Foster omits Truth's text from her analysis in *Witnessing Slavery*. The reason for this critical elision may be that Truth's *Narrative* is not typical of its genre. Yellin may discount Truth's (auto)biography because it was dictated to the white amanuensis Olive Gilbert and is thus not technically written by an Afra-American. Although other slave narrators employed amanuenses, Truth's text is singular in its third-person depiction of the trials of a black woman enslaved in the North (Ulster County, New York), as most emancipatory narratives are first-person accounts, written by enslaved bondswomen in the South. Perhaps for these reasons, theorists exclude Truth's *Narrative* from their critical purview. In doing so, they a-witness the text's historical and literary value and witnessing potential.

Although unique, Truth's *Narrative* is also emblematic of other nineteenth-century emancipatory narratives in its adherence to generic conventions, such as the speaker's witnessing out of her own experiences on behalf of other enslaved black women; the detailing of (physical) traumas; and the direct plea to her reader to enter into the narrative and witness it secondarily. With other emancipatory narratives of the era, Truth witnesses those times when white masters—through the use of physical violence—attempted to strip her of personhood. Gilbert recounts:

> One Sunday morning . . . [Truth] was told to go to the barn . . . [where] she found her master with a bundle of rods, prepared in the embers, and bound together with cords. When he had tied her hands together before her, he . . . whipped her till the flesh was deeply lacerated, and the blood steamed from her wounds—and the scars remain to the present day to testify to the fact. "And now," [Truth] says, "when I hear 'em tell of whipping women on the bare flesh, it makes my flesh crawl, and my very hair rise on my head." (18)

This passage highlights the hypocrisy of Truth's supposedly Christian masters, who do not go to church on Sunday morning but instead whipped a woman in a barn like an animal.[3] Truth also provides a detailed account of the tools and methods of her torture, so that addressees can enter into her experience. She concludes the passage with a subtle plea to her readers to witness her trauma secondarily, to allow—alongside the speaker—our flesh to crawl and hair to rise on end, when we learn how enslaved women like Truth were treated.

Like Jacobs, Truth does not testify exclusively to her own physical suffering. She also witnesses secondarily by proxy for those similarly oppressed. She tells the story, for instance, of the bondswoman Tabby, whose white mistress "beat in" her skull and then, "not content with that, had her tied up and whipped, after her skull was broken" (58). Tabby, Gilbert soberly reports, "died hanging to the bedstead to which she had been fastened" (58). In such passages, Truth witnesses with and for those women who suffer slavery's traumas.

Unlike Jacobs, Truth shows that slavery's malevolence is not restricted to the American South but pervades the North as well. Wherever slavery exists, Truth testifies, calamity follows. Truth's inclusion of Northern slaveowners in her indictment of slavery may account in part for why her *Narrative* is understudied. Most slave narrators address their autobiographies to a Northern audience. In doing so, they exploit Northern regional prejudice against the South in order to rouse their readership to abolitionism. This option is unavailable to Truth, who must portray the ills of slavery even in such states as New York. Accordingly, Northern readers may reject her *Narrative* because, in engaging its contents, they cannot condemn the South exclusively for slavery's villainy but must confront the corruption their own communities perpetuate.

To help readers witness secondarily the affliction of American slavery in the North and South, Truth relies on the power of her voice. Despite Gilbert's decision to publish Truth's narrative in third- rather than first-person, distancing the reader somewhat from Truth's lived experience, the strength of Truth's voice and temperament resound throughout her *Narrative*. When proslavers threaten to "burn down the building" in which Truth stands if she dares to testify against slavery, Truth responds: "Then I will speak upon the ashes" (96). She will allow no person or circumstance, not even the threat of death, to prohibit her from witnessing. In fact, the bondswoman's ability to witness primarily is established long before her work on the abolitionist circuit. Her strength of self is made explicit when she decides, early in her narrative, to leave her master John Dumont's plantation to work (for pay) for Isaac and Maria Van Wagener. When Dumont follows Truth, then known as Isabella Baumfree,[4] to the Van Wageners to collect her, Gilbert demonstrates Truth's agency: "When her master saw her, he said, 'Well, Bell, so you've run away from me,'" to which Truth retorts: "'No, I did not *run* away; I walked away by day-light, and all because you had promised me a year of my time'" (29).[5] Here, Truth grants the reader the opportunity to witness secondarily the speaker's strength as primary witness. Truth is not afraid to assert herself to her former master, demonstrating a subtle command of language and argument by repeating Dumont's words back to him in order to strengthen her own position. When she remarks, "I did not run away; I walked away by day-light," Truth exhibits self-actualization.

Truth is not remorseful that she left Dumont. She did so in daylight for everyone to see, and now—once again in the truth of daylight for everyone to witness secondarily—she testifies to the rectitude of her escape. By maintaining that she walked (not ran) away from Dumont, Truth implies—in and through her tone and attitude—that she left enslavement with a free and proud saunter: She did not secretly flee him then, and she does not secretly denounce him now. She publicly repudiates him for breaking his promise to her. Truth testifies to both Dumont and the reader that the master—not the slave—is the villain in this scenario. In doing so, she subverts the legal and social hierarchies of the time, asserting that a triply marginalized black female slave is not accountable to her white male owner. The representative of the patriarchy is answerable to her. Truth's testimony all but silences Dumont. Her master cannot contravene the argument of his female slave, so he attempts to reassert his authority over her: "You must go back with me" (29). To this order, Gilbert reports, Truth's "decisive answer" is: "No I won't go back with you" (29). Rather than submit to Dumont's demands, the speaker asserts the *Truth* of her personhood. As a result, Dumont leaves Truth's chosen home. The strength of a slave's testimony overpowers the entitlement of her white male oppressor.

Given such textual moments, one may consider Truth's ability to witness unimpeachable. Throughout her life, Truth proved willing to expose herself in order to witness primarily her individual personhood as an Afra-American ex-slave and to witness secondarily by proxy the evils of institutional slavery. Gilbert reports that, on the abolitionist circuit, Truth "thought nothing" of "exposing her back and revealing the scars on her flesh made by whiplashes," in order to testify bodily to the enduring wounds of slavery. Nor did she hesitate, when challenged, to expose her breasts to an audience of proslavery men in order to prove her womanhood (95). Truth's fearless witnessing in public, however, is not consistently exhibited throughout her narrative. Instead, silence overrides the precision and daring of Truth's testimony, particularly when Gilbert prods her to witness traumas she is unwilling or unable to articulate. Though Truth's testimony appears unhindered when she describes the treatment she received from her master, she circles around the handling she received from her mistress, Sally Dumont. These textual gaps disrupt the clarity of Truth's *Narrative*, emphasizing the magnitude and unspeakability of the trauma she suffered at the hands of her mistress as well as the difficulty of witnessing trauma through antebellum autobiography.

Truth's reticence to witness the nature of the "unaccountable," "unreasonable," and "unnatural" abuse she received from her mistress Sally Dumont—while she testifies in detail to her physical abuse at the hands of her master—suggests that Mrs. Dumont may have sexually molested her slave. The *Narrative*'s use of the word "unnatural" and its refusal to name the "unnatural act" sustains the premise that Truth was sexually abused by her mistress. In literary and cultural history, the word "unnatural" has been linked to homosexuality, homosexual acts, and silence. In *Epistemology of the Closet*, Eve Sedgwick traces the textual-historical tradition of connecting sodomy to silence. Gay male sex, Sedgwick explains, has been euphemized (or stigmatized) in literature as silence: for example, "that sin which should not be named nor committed," "things fearful to name," and "the obscene sound of the unbeseeming words" (203). Truth's description of "unaccountable," "unreasonable," and "unnatural" traumas mirrors Sedgwick's list of historically and literarily silenced queer sex. Though the encounter Truth (dis)avows involves female/female (not male/male) sexual contact, the language linking sodomy to silence is applicable to sexual contact between women.[6]

When Truth begins to witness her "standing with . . . her mistress," the speaker skirts around the depth of Truth's trauma. Gilbert writes:

> From this source [i.e., Truth's relationship with Sally Dumont] arose a long series of trials in the life of our heroine, which we must pass over in silence; . . . from motives of delicacy . . . therefore, the reader will not be surprised if our narrative appears somewhat tame at this point, and may rest assured that it is not for want of facts, as the most thrilling incidents of this portion of her life are from various motives suppressed. (20)

The vagueness of Gilbert's language in this passage (e.g., the allusion to a "long series of trials" that the narrator encourages the reader to "pass over in silence" and thus a-witness) points to Gilbert's and Truth's inability or unwillingness to witness those traumatic encounters that remain psychically overwhelming. That Gilbert characterizes this trauma as "indelicate" also betrays Gilbert's or Truth's perceived shame in the face of this particular catastrophe, implying that the event was so appalling, particularly to antebellum sensibilities of female modesty, that speaking to it openly would risk scandalizing the speaker, amanuensis, publisher, and reader. Truth's "trials" therefore remain unwritten—however much they are hinted at—as evidence of trauma that is un-witnessable, either by Truth primarily or Gilbert secondarily as a hearer of Truth's narrative and as a proxy—and perhaps by the reader of Truth's text via Gilbert—and maybe all at once.[7] Accordingly, as Nell Irvin Painter notes, "Despite the familiarity of Truth the symbol," what Truth actually did during her lifetime remains "surprisingly obscure" (vii).

Engaging a historical Truth becomes even more challenging when Truth—or Gilbert through her—structurally shifts her autobiography away from her "trials" and tribulations of enslavement to focus on her Christian conversion and time spent evangelizing for the prophet Matthias. While the turn from personal trauma to a depersonalized, collective Christian testimony may appeal to those readers who would rather engage an ex-slave's call to follow Jesus than consider the possibilities of queer assault, the move also gestures to Truth's potential powerlessness to speak the unspeakable, a powerlessness that subverts both the strength of her individual voice and her capacity to testify.

For this reason, readers must work diligently to witness with Truth and her *Narrative*, which Truth's amanuensis and editors suggest is what Truth seeks most of all. In "The Book of Life," Harriet Beecher Stowe reports that "an audience was what [Truth] wanted . . . She had things to say, and was ready to say them at all times, and to any one" (104). Stowe does not explicate what "things" Truth has to witness, but her appeal (with Truth) for audience participation prompts readers to dual-witness, despite the difficulty of doing so. One reason Truth may have sought secondary witnesses among her readership is that, as Isabella Baumfree, she lived a life of isolation. Painter explains that Baumfree was the household's only slave and worked alone, without "access to a community beyond her masters' tight control" (xiii). Gilbert relates that, at age nine, Baumfree "could only talk Dutch," and her masters spoke only English. Accordingly, "neither of them could understand the language of the other, a formidable obstacle in the way of a good understanding" between them (18).[8] This inability to communicate precipitates accusatory anti-witnessing, as when Baumfree is blamed and beaten for her failure to follow commands given in a foreign language (18). Of this period, Truth recalls: "If they sent me for a frying-pan, not knowing what they meant, perhaps I carried them the pot-hooks and the trammels. Then, oh! how angry mistress would be with me!" (18). Through such counterexamples, Truth and Gilbert encourage readers not to emulate the model of Baumfree's masters but to strive instead to dual-witness Truth's *Narrative,* even when its protagonist wrestles to communicate clearly what readers are asked to witness secondarily.

Truth's desire for dual- and communal witnessing may account for why she shifts in her *Narrative* from witnessing slavery to witnessing through organized religion. Preaching to assemblies about her faith offers Truth the occasion to witness something hopeful (such as her belief in God) instead of traumatic (such as the tribulations she endured as a slave). Witnessing Christianity at revival meetings also affords Truth the opportunity to be well-received (or communally witnessed) by a group of receptive listeners—something Truth, as Isabella Baumfree, was denied. Truth's religious testimony also offers readers a respite from traumatic depictions of slavery and enables them to dialogue with *The Narrative* without becoming distressed by reading about the abuse Truth suffered. Finally, as a devout Christian, Truth may have found religious language to be an effective form through which to witness.

In her *Narrative,* Truth uses the language of faith to witness spiritual conviction more successfully than she employs secular language to testify to sexual trauma. For Truth, faith itself takes the form of dual-witnessing. When she prays, she presents her supplications not as a list of requests made to God but as a series of "talks with God" (41). When Truth converses with (instead of prays to) God, she models dual-witnessing as a mutual, nonhierarchical process and also suggests that God is on her side (and, through her, all enslaved African Americans). Those who resist Truth's *Narrative,* therefore, not only fail to witness secondarily but also implicitly side against God and those with whom God witnesses. Thus, Truth teaches readers not only how to witness but with whom (i.e., with God, with herself, and with all oppressed persons).

Truth also provides examples of ideal secondary witnesses alongside whom readers may position themselves, reconnecting the practice of dual-witnessing to human engagement. Truth prays that God will help her readers witness secondarily: "Oh, God, make the people hear me" (47): that is, "let my readership witness (me) secondarily, as You do." Truth's prayers are answered at such moments as when God directs her to the house of the Van Wagners, who prove excellent secondary witnesses by receiving her "kindly" and "hospitably" and by "listen[ing] to her story," as she "ma[kes] her case known to them" (28). When Truth has finished testifying, the Van Wagners offer her employment and "assur[e]" her that they will "never turn [her] away" (29), demonstrating that dual-witnessing requires not only sustained engagement but prompt action. In passages such as these, Truth uses her relationship with God—and exemplary persons—to exhibit dual-witnessing.

Truth's desire to dual-witness with God and other people may account for why, in 1832, she joined (and preached for) the "Kingdom" of the prophet Matthias. Robert Matthias was a religious leader who foretold the imminent return of Jesus and heralded the need for collective purification in preparation for the Second Coming. He gathered a following in New York, but the Kingdom disbanded when its prophet was charged with adultery, bankruptcy, and the murder of one of his disciples (Painter xix). Truth's active participation in Matthias's Kingdom may represent another reason critics ignore her *Narrative*. Truth serves today as an emblem of black feminism, an image difficult to reconcile with *The Narrative*'s Isabella Baumfree, who worked tirelessly to promote the doctrine of a man now recognized as a cult leader.

Given Truth's history, however, her attraction to the Kingdom and its prophet is understandable. Matthias, Gilbert reports, "pronounced vengeance on the land," preached that the "law of God was the only rule of government," and promised to repossess the world "in the name of the King of kings" (61). Though such promises evoke slave rhetoric (as when a master declares his divinely ordained rule over his slaves), one can appreciate how Matthias' message would have also appealed to Truth, who placed her faith in God above humanity; rightly believed that slave society was wicked; and may thus have wished to see God's justice done—and soon. Moreover, Matthias appears to have witnessed with Truth. Gilbert reports that, at their first meeting, the prophet was "drawn into conversation" with Baumfree, recognizing her as his "equal" (62). Matthias may have also appealed to Truth by championing communal witnessing in organizing his Kingdom around "but one table, and all things in common" (62), differentiating himself from the slave master (who rules singly above his slaves) and heralding a Christian communalism antithetical to hierarchal slavery.

Eventually, however, Matthias revealed a deep-seated misogyny, which may have been what led Truth to abandon his discipleship in favor of feminist abolitionism. When preaching about women, Matthias used slave rhetoric, proclaiming that any man who dared to educate a woman was "wicked," that females who were "not obedient" to male masters were "damned," and that womankind in general was "full of all deviltry" (63–64). After hearing such statements, Gilbert reports, Baumfree decided "she must leave the city," as the Kingdom no longer held a place for her, and she was called to "travel east and lecture"—or to witness with and for her "friends" (such as feminist abolitionists)—rather than to serve a false prophet who performed communal witnessing while preaching bigotry. Only after Baumfree determined to leave Matthias to witness as her own prophet did she rename herself Sojourner Truth (68), a moment in which she no longer sought "truth" elsewhere but elected instead to embody witnessing itself by becoming (in both name and deed) one who sojourns the earth to testify to Truth. Unlike Matthias, Truth did not set herself above others but sought instead a community of "friends" with whom to witness communally.

When the ex-bondswoman committed herself to this life of witnessing, she secured a receptive community in which to do so: the Garrisonian abolitionists and feminists of Northampton, Massachusetts. During this same period, Truth met and began to work with her principal secondary witness (and secondary witness by proxy), the amanuensis, Olive Gilbert (Painter x). In engaging Truth's *Narrative*, however, one may question the degree to which Gilbert witnesses her subject secondarily. Certainly, the amanuensis facilitated the slave woman's witnessing by recording her narrative for all to read. (Since Truth was illiterate, she could not write her story herself. She relied directly on Gilbert to help her witness through their jointly authored *Narrative*). Gilbert's presence may also have helped Truth testify, in that, like the reader, the amanuensis could serve as a secondary witness, empowering the speaker to work through the details of her trauma. Finally, Gilbert and Truth's shared gender may have facilitated mutual witnessing, as a female amanuensis and a female speaker can unite through their common experience of gender-based oppression in order to witness more easily the subjugation Truth faced as an Afra-American slave.

Despite, however, the potential for interracial female dual-witnessing, the danger of amanuensal anti-witnessing remains. Just as the reader contaminates a text by reading it, Gilbert alters Truth's testimony by recording it. To start, Gilbert writes *The Narrative* in third-person (thereby distancing the reader from the protagonist's opinions and experiences) and also inserts throughout the text her own commentary, which appears to disregard and contravene Truth's story. Accordingly, readers struggle to ascertain which language and viewpoints are Truth's, which are Gilbert's, and which are collaborative. Perhaps with good intentions, Gilbert wrote *The Narrative* in third-person and asserted her own sentiments to acknowledge outright the presence of a transcriber, in juxtaposition to those emancipatory narratives penned in first-person and "written by oneself." By conflating two independent voices, however, Gilbert both a-witnesses (in ignoring and negating) and co-optively anti-witnesses (in appropriating) Truth's narrated history. In her analysis of *The Narrative*, Jean Humez suggests that the text produced by Gilbert "implies a process of strenuous contest and negotiation" between amanuensis and protagonist, during which both Gilbert and Truth "won some important points" (35). One may wonder if, as amanuensis, secondary witness, and secondary witness by proxy, Gilbert is entitled to "win points" through Truth's narrative. Should not the truth of the bondswoman's life be hers to witness as she sees fit? Humez explains that both Truth and Gilbert "wished to teach the reader about the meaning" of Baumfree's personal history and endured suffering but that their "vastly different perspectives on slavery" led to "contradiction and even incoherence in crucial sections of the text" (36). That is, in writing *The Narrative*, Gilbert appropriates Truth's life to witness not only the protagonist's views and experiences but also (and principally) her own views. The text thus witnesses Truth's history inconsistently, and the power of the bondswoman's testimony is undercut.

Gilbert most clearly co-opts Truth's life narrative when she injects into it her own abolitionist views. When Truth recalls that her first master, Charles, "was the best of the family," Gilbert adjoins: "—being, comparatively speaking, a kind master to his slaves" (9). Here, Gilbert deconstructs the myth of the good master, an admirable goal that nevertheless seems inconsistent with Truth's characterization of her experience. Gilbert revises Truth's narrative to support abolitionism. In his introduction to Truth's *Narrative*, Jeffrey Stewart explains that female activists such as Gilbert had "few opportunities" to write "publicly about their opinions" of slavery. When given the chance, therefore, they "seized upon" a story such as Truth's, "as a vehicle for [their] own indictment" of slavery (xxix). Appropriating Truth's story to combat slavery as Gilbert does may seem innocuous or even noble and in keeping with Truth's own goals for her *Narrative*. The fact, however, that a speaker supports her amanuensis' political outlook—or the fact that such an outlook is both timely and just—does not negate the co-opting of another's personal experience for political gain. The desire to denounce slavery publicly and in print is commendable—as is the abolitionist's wish to use her voice to champion civil rights—but one should not attempt to witness secondarily by proxy by appropriatively anti-witnessing the traumas of those for whom one advocates. Albeit well-intentioned, such anti-witnessing undermines the primary witness's recovery and the secondary witness's cause.

In her most appropriative moments, Gilbert derides Truth in a misguided attempt to make slavery look worse than the ex-slave already has. "Isabella found herself the mother of five children," Gilbert censures, "and she rejoiced in being permitted to be the instrument of increasing the property of oppressors! Think, dear reader, . . . if you can, . . . of a *mother* thus willingly, and with *pride*, laying her own children, 'the flesh of her flesh,' on the altar of slavery!" (25). Gilbert's tone is pejorative, suggesting that Baumfree is to blame both for birthing children destined to be slaves (and thereby enriching her masters) and also for loving these children. We do not know whether Baumfree wanted or consented to bear children. We do know that her master forcibly "married" her to another slave (who was not the partner of her choosing) and that children resulted from this prescribed union (24). Whatever the circumstances, Truth can hardly be blamed for having children. Nor is it reasonable to expect a mother not to care for her offspring, simply because they—like she—are considered property. Such narrative moments reveal the danger of co-optive anti-witnessing, even for a good cause. Gilbert not only anti-witnesses an already-oppressed bondswoman, potentially exacerbating her trauma, but encourages readers to follow suit. In doing so, she reveals herself to be less of a secondary witness or secondary witness by proxy and more of an accusatory and co-optive anti-witness who would misappropriate Truth's traumas to further her own agenda.

This anti-witnessing does not end with Gilbert. Following *The Narrative's* initial publication, white and female abolitionists, such as Frances Titus, joined Gilbert in co-opting Truth's history and personhood by appending additional materials to her (auto)biography (1875). Consequently, the affixed "History of [Truth's] Labors and Correspondences" (excerpted from a personal collection of Truth's called the "Book of Life") reveals more about Titus' principles than Truth's. As Zachary Hutchins notes, Titus seems "less interested in accuracy than in bolstering Truth's legend" and in using that legend to promote her own causes. The first edition of *The Narrative,* for example, clearly reports that Truth, after refusing to remain John Dumont's slave, was emancipated by her master in 1828. Titus maintains, conversely, that "Sojourner became free in 1817" when "the State of New York emancipated all slaves at the age of forty years" (308). In revising the date of Truth's liberation, Titus can argue against slavery without alienating those readers who do not wish to recall that Northerners continued to own slaves into the late 1820s and sometimes enslaved persons, such as Truth, who were legally free. Titus's approach may appease her Northern readership, but it undermines Truth's history.

Titus continues in this co-optive vein, adding to Truth's "Book of Life" a description of Truth's funeral, assorted poems and obituaries, an article from the *Chicago Inter-Ocean*, and the words of what was supposedly "Truth's favorite song," so that, as Painter notes, Truth appears "now as radical, now as naïve, now as potent, pitiful, popular, well-connected, cunning, patronizing, visionary, questionable, and faltering, depend[ing] on which clipping one heeds" (xix). Following Gilbert and Titus' appropriation, Truth becomes, in the eyes of her readership, less of a human being and more of a symbol of whatever her writers wish her to be. Her witnessing potential is appropriated by those who claim to celebrate her life and work, even as they anti-witness it. At the end of her *Narrative*, Truth remains largely unknown, anti-witnessed even by those who worked alongside her. When critics follow suit by a-witnessing her text, the history of the woman-turned-symbol is all but lost. This fraught reception exposes how psychic constriction, social constraints, and co-optive anti-witnessing collude to make the act of witnessing Truth's (auto)biography difficult, even as *The Narrative* itself prompts readers to enter into and engage Truth's history.

"A Subject Fraught with Pain": Reading Elizabeth Keckley's *Behind the Scenes*

In *Behind the Scenes, Or, Thirty Years a Slave and Four Years in the White House* (1868), Elizabeth Keckley narrates her experiences as a former slave who became a successful seamstress, most notably as personal modiste to Mary Todd Lincoln. As with Jacobs's and Truth's narratives, the testimonial power of Keckley's text is undercut by the author's traumatic consciousness, the era's restrictive social mores, and the readerly resistance to witness secondarily the incidents of an African American bondswoman-turned-businesswoman. Despite these obstacles, Keckley's witnessing attempts are not entirely unsuccessful. With Jacobs's and Truth's narratives, *Behind the Scenes* effectively depicts the physical abuse wrought by slave masters against their slaves. Keckley reports that, when she was a slave, her school teacher, Mr. Bingham, flogged her repeatedly (32). When Keckley inquired what she had done to "deserve punishment," Bingham replied "in his blunt way": "No matter" (33). Bingham beats Keckley for "no matter" (as she has done nothing wrong), and the reason he chooses to do so does "no[t] matter"—at least not to him—since he, the oppressor, has the power to act as he pleases.[9] Keckley describes the "fearful force" of Bingham's inflicted torture: His rawhide whip "cut the skin, raised great welts," and caused "warm blood" to cover her "quivering flesh" (34). From this lesson, Keckley learns (and readers through her) that, in slaveholding society, one's identity, not behavior, determines how one is treated. Because Keckley is an enslaved black woman, she is deemed "deserv[ing of] punishment." Because her persecutor is a free white man, he may dispense that punishment for "no matter" at all. In recording the abuse she has suffered, Keckley witnesses her traumatic history, inciting readers not to align with victimizers, such as Bingham, but with victims, such as herself, who withstand not only individual accounts of violence but also intersecting forms of oppression (e.g., racism and sexism) that help produce the systemic violence and oppression inherent in institutional slavery.

Keckley witnesses the physical catastrophes she confronted and the scope of her resulting trauma. Like Jacobs and Truth, she struggles to depict the sexual abuse she suffered, thereby eliding a significant component of her trauma as a black bondswoman.[10] "I must pass rapidly over the stirring events of my early life," Keckley writes when alluding to her assault (31). She then records not the details of her rape but the fact that she has long been "regarded as fair-looking for one of my race" (31). By linking her physical attraction to her fair skin—as her "fairness" (or beauty) is located in her "fair" (or pale) skin color—Keckley emphasizes the sociopolitical instead of the sexually traumatic, reminding readers that, in America, whiteness (or light skin) is speciously valued above nonwhiteness (or dark skin). At the same time, she testifies to the incidence of sexual assault in her genealogy, as her light skin physically bears witness to the rape of darker-skinned female forebears by white male oppressors. The implication also exists that, because Keckley is considered "fair-looking" (both beautiful and pale), she is a target for white male predators who prefer light skin. In denoting her fairness, Keckley thus connotes the fear of white rapists that plagues her and other (light-skinned) Afra-Americans. As Jacobs pronounces in *Incidents*: "If God has bestowed beauty"—in this case, "fairness"—"upon [a bondswoman], it will prove her greatest curse. That which commands admiration in the white woman only hastens the degradation of the female slave" (43).[11] Keckley's mention of skin color distances her narrative from the details of her own assault even as it exposes yet another way white men abuse black women: by causing them to curse their own skin color instead of the white men who rape them. Accordingly, Keckley is able to testify secondarily by proxy to the prevalence of sexual assault in American slavery, even if she chooses not to witness primarily her personal experience of it.

When it becomes necessary for Keckley to mention rape outright (in order to explain the birth of her son), she does so through veiled language: "For four years a white man—I spare the world his name—had base designs upon me" (39). By refusing to name her assailant, Keckley potentially exposes traumatic consciousness, suggesting that she is too constricted to write the name of her rapist and that her narrative omission "spare[s]" her as much as it does "the world." The possibility also exists that Keckley refuses to name her rapist in order to avoid granting him undue power over her. In identifying her rapist only as "a white man," Keckley allows her assailant to serve as a representative for all white male oppressors who similarly assault black bondswomen—from Keckley's female ancestors to contemporary Afra-Americans. Thus, while traumatic memory and nineteenth-century social constraints intrude upon Keckley's narrative, the author manages to testify through structured blanks to sociopolitical catastrophes, even as she avoids disclosing her own familiarity with the trauma in question. Thus, as in her treatment of skin color, while Keckley remains reticent to witness her sexual trauma primarily, she does not hesitate to witness secondarily by proxy the proliferation of sexual assault in American slavery.

And yet, Keckley's gestures to common rape seem to be all she is prepared to offer. She confesses: "I do not care to dwell upon this subject, for it is one that is fraught with pain. Suffice it to say that he [the white man mentioned above] persecuted me for four years, and I—I became a mother" (39). Keckley's use of the asexual verb, "persecute"—instead of the sexually explicit verb, "rape"—suggests that she cannot bear to narrate the sexual element of her abuse. The fact that her rape-induced pregnancy takes place in the structured blank between the repetition of "I" ("I—I became a mother") indicates that the abuse Keckley suffered caused the shattering of a unitive identity (or "I") into multiple selves (or "I's") from which she struggles to witness now. Trauma theorists may argue that Keckley cannot repair her fragmented psyche without first having witnessed her sexual trauma. The irony (and danger) of such a claim is that a narrator's shattered identity can itself obstruct her ability to witness, as—haunted by the aftermath of sexual assault—the traumatized speaker may not be able to reassemble the shards of a divided consciousness in order to testify to the very trauma that ruptured her psyche in the first place.

Perhaps as a result of such challenges, Keckley's sexual trauma remains largely unwritten and unwitnessed. Evidence of rape, however, does surface in depictions of other forms of violence. One can read into Keckley's descriptions of physical abuse a coinciding history of sexual assault, revealing that the extent of her trauma is not written onto the pages of her text but is, as her title suggests, staged behind the scenes. Keckley's graphic representations of flagellation, for example, evoke rape. When Bingham beats her, Keckley writes that, though young, she was "fully developed," and yet he still "bade me take down my dress" (33). Bingham presumably asks Keckley to disrobe to facilitate the whipping, but the command carries a sexual connotation, suggesting that the school teacher, aroused by Keckley's "fully developed" body, wishes to dominate his victim both physically and sexually.[12] Keckley responds to Bingham's advances like a sentimental heroine facing rape: She "resist[s]" her attacker "with all [her] . . . strength," but Bingham proves "the stronger," and, "after a hard struggle," he succeeds "in binding [her] . . . hands and tearing [her] . . . dress from [her] . . . back" (37). This passage reads less like a traumatic narrative and more like the sensationalized rape narratives of Victorian novels and Harlequin romances. Though one could argue that Keckley voyeuristically anti-witnesses assault by sensationalizing it[13]—another indication that she has trouble witnessing sexual abuse—the salient point is that Keckley shades descriptions of physical violence with sexual innuendo.

Even if she cannot describe her sexual assault, Keckley carries it with her throughout her narrative. In describing Bingham's instruments of torture, Keckley employs the language of phallic weaponry: he uses a "heavy stick" and "oak broom," to "conquer" his victim in a "shameful manner" (37). This description evokes sexual assault, as the rapist seeks to conquer both the body and the psyche of his victim, eliciting from her shame and fear. In utilizing physical violence to testify to sexual assault, Keckley reminds her readership that the experiences borne by bondswomen are even worse than one may realize. The narrative incites readers to attend carefully to scenes of violence and witness secondarily what the narrator struggles to witness primarily—in this case, the reality of rape in American slavery.

Keckley, however, does not sustain even these veiled gestures to sexual abuse. Instead, several chapters into her narrative, she ceases to testify to the immorality of slavery at all, glossing over her experiences as a bondswoman, in order to "hasten to the most interesting part of [her] story" (43): her time spent working for Mary Todd Lincoln. Conceivably exhausted by her witnessing efforts, Keckley may wish to narrate more agreeable accounts, such as tales of dressmaking instead of floggings. In doing so, she undermines her initial portrayal of slavery as an unjust system and adopts what she calls a more "objective" approach whereby she explores both the "dark side" and "bright side" of the institution (xi), the latter of which is hard to see after one has read Keckley's depictions of assault. The author clarifies that "notwithstanding all the wrongs that slavery heaped upon" her, she can still "bless it" for its "important lesson in self-reliance" (19–20). Though living as a slave was agonizing, Keckley claims to have benefitted from enslavement, as it taught her self-sufficiency and the value of hard work. This assertion may affront those, such as Jacobs, who suffered slavery's traumas without ever discovering the institution's "bright side" or "blessings"—and rightly so. However, Keckley's dramatic shift in attitude, while problematic, is also psychosocially explicable. Psychically, preserving the myth of the good system allows Keckley to cease brooding over her trauma and the struggle to witness it—a process that can feel traumatizing. Socially, the rhetorical shift allows Keckley to speak not only to her traumas or personhood but also to her American identity. By professing that slavery instilled in her a strong work ethic, Keckley exemplifies the American Dream, emphasizing, through her ascension from slavery to the White House, how one can achieve success through hard work alone. In this way, *Behind the Scenes* transitions from a text that witnesses trauma to one that testifies to American citizenship.

For a black woman and an ex-slave to claim to embody the American Dream (and thus "Americanness" itself) was a radical move that alienated many of Keckley's white readers. As a postbellum emancipated narrator, however, Keckley was granted certain narrative luxuries that antebellum narrators, such as Jacobs, were not. Foster explains that postbellum female former slave narrators "could claim a greater freedom for themselves and their literature" than the bondswomen who testified before them (*Written* 121). Because postbellum ex-slaves no longer had to convince their readers that slavery was evil in order to secure emancipation, they could choose whether or not to witness slavery's traumas without worrying as much about the sociopolitical ramifications of doing so. They could also elect, as Keckley does, to highlight their successes instead of their traumas since they no longer felt the pressure to underscore the terrors of slavery to galvanize anti-slavery sentiment. Accordingly, Foster expounds, postbellum emancipatory narratives often "downplayed the horrors of the slave experience" to focus instead "upon the contributions of the blacks to American society" (*Witnessing* 61). Texts such as Booker T. Washington's *Up from Slavery* (1901) and Keckley's *Behind the Scenes* confine the slave years to their introductory chapters, reserving the rest of their narratives to speak to the potential for racial progress. However, in shifting from trauma to citizenship, Keckley risks a-witnessing the abuse suffered by her and others—other enslaved persons who did not secure her successes and thus lacked the same venue through which to tell their stories.

Even so, as she transitions from trauma to triumph, Keckley continues to promote dual-witnessing, inciting readers to witness secondarily whatever she witnesses primarily. Like Jacobs and Truth, Keckley models this mutuality through interracial female dual-witnessing with Mary Todd Lincoln. As she presents their relationship in *Behind the Scenes,* Keckley served not only as the First Lady's dressmaker but also as her secondary witness. Perhaps to model for readers how to dual-witness, Keckley witnesses Mrs. Lincoln's ordeals as much as—if not more than—her own.[14] After President Lincoln's assassination, Keckley's first impulse is to engage the First Lady's trauma. She confesses: "I wanted to go to Mrs. Lincoln, as I pictured her wild with grief" (187). Keckley later learns from the First Lady that, upon hearing of her husband's murder, she also wished to dual-witness with her modiste, instructing those around her to "send for Elizabeth Keckley. I want her just as soon as she can be brought here . . . to have with [me] . . . in this terrible affliction" (188). In describing Keckley's wish to minister to Mrs. Lincoln and Mrs. Lincoln's corresponding need for Keckley, *Behind the Scenes* suggests that Mrs. Lincoln valued Keckley as her secondary witness, a function Keckley was keen to fulfill. In this manner, the narrative underscores the rich potential of interracial female dual-witnessing.

Keckley not only witnesses secondarily to Mary Todd Lincoln but also secondarily by proxy for her. Typically, female slave narrators witnessed to free white women on behalf of enslaved black women. It may thus seem counterproductive for Keckley to witness secondarily by proxy for Mrs. Lincoln who, due to race, station, and circumstance, possessed more power and privilege than her promoter. A radical power dynamic, however, works through *Behind the Scenes* when an Afra-American ex-slave asserts the agency to advocate for a white woman of prominence. In doing so, Keckley subverts racist and classist hierarchies by displaying a psychosocial savvy equal to (and sometimes surpassing) that of the First Lady of the United States. Specifically, Keckley defends Mrs. Lincoln's motives and decisions regarding the "Old Clothes Scandal of 1867," in which the First Lady—seventy-thousand dollars in debt due to compulsive shopping—attempted to sell and exhibit her clothes and jewels to repay her creditors (Keckley 286). The plan backfired when potential buyers refused to purchase her wares, and the press censured her for squandering money while the nation was at war and for parading evidence of her extravagance about New York (where her clothes were displayed) (Turner and Turner 432–33). Keckley was Mrs. Lincoln's defender against such censure. As self-elected secondary witness by proxy for the former First Lady, Keckley defended her employer to the media and even dedicated her own autobiography to the "attempt to place Mrs. Lincoln in a better light before the world" (286). Keckley's support is earnest, but her advocacy of another's life narrative prevents her from witnessing her own. In witnessing secondarily by proxy for Mrs. Lincoln, Keckley forgoes the opportunity to witness further for herself primarily.

Another danger of attempting to witness for Mrs. Lincoln is that Keckley may empathically anti-witness Mrs. Lincoln instead. In supporting Mrs. Lincoln, she risks treating the First Lady's trials as if they are her own. In her preface, Keckley asserts: "I have been her confidante, and if evil charges are laid at her door, they also must be laid at mine ... To defend myself I must defend the lady that I have served" (xiv). Here, Keckley conflates Mrs. Lincoln's life with her own. That Keckley is Mrs. Lincoln's confidante (or secondary witness) does not necessitate that Mrs. Lincoln's transgressions become her own. That Keckley professes this to be the case suggests that she has co-opted Mrs. Lincoln's narrative, empathically anti-witnessing the First Lady in attempting to witness her secondarily and secondarily by proxy.[15]

Additionally, in narrating the First Lady's story, Keckley risks portraying Mrs. Lincoln in a negative light, even as she appropriatively anti-witnesses Mrs. Lincoln by publishing her stories for profit. In *Behind the Scenes,* Keckley depicts Mrs. Lincoln as a well-meaning albeit immature and self-indulgent woman. In one scene, Keckley delivers a gown to Mrs. Lincoln later than her employer expected it. Though "plenty of time" remains to dress, the First Lady wails: "I have no time now to dress, and, what is more, I will not dress and go downstairs. ... I will stay in my room. Mr. Lincoln can go down with the other ladies" (87). Keckley may quote Mrs. Lincoln accurately, but, by including this scene in her narrative, the modiste paints the First Lady as an overindulged mistress. Later, Keckley depicts Mrs. Lincoln as a financially flighty woman who once justified her prodigality by asserting, "To keep up appearances, I must have money ... Consequently I ... have no alternative but to run in debt" (149–50). Here, the First Lady underscores the pressure placed on women to "keep up appearances" and the corresponding strain this mandate presents to those who lack the means to comport themselves as society dictates. However, the defense that Mrs. Lincoln offers for herself—that she had "no alternative but to run" a deficit—seems aristocratically irresponsible and conceivably offensive to many parties, even to Keckley, who, as a slave, was denied ownership of everything, including her own person; who is still denied the privileges of the upper classes; and who, nevertheless, manages to live within her means. Mrs. Lincoln's perspective could also affront those self-reliant readers who struggled to survive the war years, while the First Lady lived a life of extravagance. In presenting Mrs. Lincoln thus, Keckley provokes readers to anti-witness the First Lady voyeuristically and accusatorily, while Keckley, as (appropriative) narrator, stands to benefit from her unflattering portrayal and the anti-witnessing it wreaks.

A biographer is not obligated to portray her subject in a positive light or to avoid the appearance of anti-witnessing. Keckley, however, does not write exclusively as a biographer but also as a primary-turned-secondary witness. As such, her anti-witnessing runs counter to her efforts to witness primarily and secondarily. Keckley seems aware of this prospect and works to protect against it. In her preface, she anticipates that readers may accuse her of anti-witnessing Mrs. Lincoln. Against this "charge," Keckley rejoins that she has "been prompted by the purest motive"; that Mrs. Lincoln "forced herself into notoriety" and thus "invited public criticism"; and that, since her readers know "nothing" of the First Lady's "secret history," Keckley's exposure of her "private life" will help them "judge her more kindly than she has been" (xiv). Several problems accompany this justification. First, pure motives do not prevent anti-witnessing; "I meant well" amounts not to "I did well." Second, to claim that Mrs. Lincoln made a spectacle of herself, opening herself to voyeuristic anti-witnessing, reads as accusatory anti-witnessing, contravening Keckley's other attempts to witness her employer secondarily. Third, in attempting to justify Mrs. Lincoln's actions by disclosing their "secret history," Keckley may not only break the bond of privacy but also anticipate too sympathetic of a readership. Given the prejudices of the nineteenth century, those quick to censure Mrs. Lincoln would not have been inclined to accept the contexts and justifications offered by an Afra-American ex-slave. Instead, combined sexism and racism may have interfered with (white) readers' ability to witness either Mrs. Lincoln or Mrs. Keckley. They were more prone to dismiss the First Lady as a fickle woman and to disparage her modiste as an uppity negress who presumed to speak on behalf of the (white) First Lady of the United States. Consequently, while Keckley wards against anti-witnessing, she also incites it, underscoring the challenge dual-witnessing presents even to those "prompted by the purist motives."

Although motive does not equal action, the likelihood remains that Keckley did not in fact intend to anti-witness Mrs. Lincoln, that she sought to witness her secondarily, and that the anti-witnessing in and inspired by *Behind the Scenes* is largely due to Keckley's editor, James Redpath, who marketed the memoir as a "LITERARY THUNDERBOLT" and "Great Sensational Disclosure" (qtd. in Ryan "Kitchen Testimony" 151), both appropriatively anti-witnessing Keckley's text and stimulating voyeuristic anti-witnessing. The starkest instance of editorial appropriation is when—without Keckley's knowledge or consent—Redpath published as an appendix to *Behind the Scenes* a private collection of letters Mrs. Lincoln had written to her dressmaker. Keckley had been reluctant to allow her editor to read her personal correspondence, but Redpath maintained that he had to review Mrs. Lincoln's letters to help Keckley select appropriate excerpts to integrate into her narrative and to substantiate the amity Keckley claimed existed between the women. Redpath never returned the letters to Keckley and published them instead. The scandal of the appended letters—which revealed the accuracy of Keckley's rendering of Mrs. Lincoln as fragile, fickle, and also her friend—eclipsed the witnessing potential of the narrative, enabling Redpath to anti-witness both Mrs. Keckley and Mrs. Lincoln and to inspire readerly anti-witnessing as he turned a profit (Santamarina 517).

The result was that, like Truth and Jacobs before her, Keckley was anti-witnessed by her readership. In outraged reviews, critics refuted Keckley's assertion that her relationship with Mrs. Lincoln entitled her to witness on her behalf (Santamarina 517). The *New York Citizen* lambasted *Behind the Scenes* as "grossly and shamelessly indecent," characterizing an "offense of the same grade as the opening of other people's letters, the listening at keyholes, or the mean system of espionage which unearths family secrets with a view to blackmailing the unfortunate victims" (qtd. in Foster *Written* 130). The *New York Times* agreed, arguing that Keckley's "disclosures" represented "gross violations of confidence," and *Putnam's Magazine* affirmed that the "sensational" text "ought never to have been written or published" (qtd. in Baker 280). Keckley was accused of having voyeuristically and appropriatively anti-witnessed Mrs. Lincoln, when, though the author's witnessing efforts were inconsistent, the narrative had been voyeuristically and appropriatively anti-witnessed by Redpath. As readers recoiled at the thought of an African American woman (anti-)witnessing a prominent white lady, the majority of the blame lay with her white male editor, who appropriated the text of a black woman and tarnished the reputation of a white woman in order to profit from both. In doing so, Redpath severed the existing goodwill between the women, ending their ability to dual-witness across race and class. Following the publication of *Behind the Scenes,* Mary Todd Lincoln refused to associate with Elizabeth Keckley. As Baker reports, the former First Lady read the narrative in early May and "thereafter renounced the 'colored historian' as friend and confidant" (280). This rupture suggests how anti-witnessing divides those who could have united through shared experience.

The virulence of readers' response to *Behind the Scenes* reveals intersecting racism, sexism, and classism. Though readers framed their critique of Keckley as support for Mrs. Lincoln, the acrimony directed at author and text is likely due to Keckley's subordinate status and the shock and offense she afforded white readers when she presumed to represent the actions of America's upper echelons. Xiomara Santamarina suggests that Keckley "transgressed the law of tact" and refused to "meet the rules of gentility" (517) in exposing the First Lady's private life. Keckley's transgression, however, seems less one of tact than of station—that is, of subverting her triply marginalized position in order to comment on those, such as Mrs. Lincoln, who ranked above her. The *New York Times'* critique that Keckley should have "stuck to her needle" (qtd. in Baker 280) carries a racist, sexist, and classist charge, implying that the former bondswoman is best served by adhering to her socially assigned subservient position, which she eventually lost when her narrative was a-witnessed by the Lincolns' son, Robert, who ordered the text's suppression, resulting in *Behind the Scenes'* removal from circulation (Washington 241). Keckley received no royalties from her narrative's publication and was unable to secure future work as a modiste. (Perhaps fearing social repercussions, no white woman would hire her. The *Times'* advice that Keckley "stick to her needle" was no longer an option.) Thus, though self-reliant, Keckley followed Mrs. Lincoln into debt (Ryan 150), suggesting that she did not appropriatively anti-witness her employer after all, at least not for profit. In this way, a narrative that (inconsistently) witnessed incidents in both Keckley's and Mrs. Lincoln's lives was aggressively and co-optively anti-witnessed by its editor and readership and then a-witnessed, largely because an Afra-American deigned to write above her station.

The anti-witnessing of Keckley is most evident in the 1868 parody inspired by her text: *Behind the Seams; by a Nigger Woman Who Took in Work from Mrs. Lincoln and Mrs. Davis*[16] and signed with an "X," the mark of "Betsey Kickley (nigger)." This satire appropriately anti-witnesses the publicity surrounding Keckley's narrative, in order, as Santamarina observes, "to indulge in pernicious race-baiting" (517). While the tone of the parody is more virulent than that of Keckley's more "objective" critics, the substance is tantamount, revealing a fear of (and hatred for) *Behind the Scenes'* destabilization of social hierarchies. As Baker notes, the parody undercuts Keckley's (now Kickley's) personhood and citizenship by submitting that, even if she is no longer a slave, she will forever be a "nigger" (280)—a slur that appears twice in the title and six times in the first paragraph alone. The satire's anti-witnessing is clearly aggressive, particularly when it celebrates the physical and sexual violence Kickley confronts. The parodist, for instance, dubs Kickley's abuse a "polishing off" (6), as if the woman is incomplete or unfinished until assaulted. The author then accusatorily anti-witnesses Kickley for the rape she suffers, attributing her assault to her "beauty and developments," as if Kickley is responsible for "attract[ing] the attention" of her rapist" (7). The satirist negatively a-witnesses Keckley's argument that white men consistently used Afra-Americans' "fairness" as a weapon against them. The author writes instead (as Kickley): "He vowed that he ... would marry me, ... but as I was a nigger, ... he proposed ... to marry me without any ceremony ... [and] I—I—I—I—I—I—became a mother" (7). In this passage, the parodist equates rape to marriage (or to the "best" sort of union a black woman can expect to have). By turning Keckley's "I—I" into a series of stuttered "I's," the author attacks the bondswoman's articulation and eloquence. When the parodist signs the narrative with an "X," he or she attacks her literacy. Chortling at Kickley's unceremonious rape,[17] the satirist tonally indicates that her repeated assault is humorous.

Such anti-witnessing may appear so overblown as to be ineffectual, but, unfortunately, this is not the case. As recently as August 2013, a reviewer on amazon.com praised *Behind the Seams* as a "powerful . . . piece of history" that witnesses Keckley's story "from her point of view." Lest one dismiss this reader as simply ignorant, he or she also claims to have "read other books about Mrs. Lincoln and Mrs. Keckley" but "none . . . [so] powerful" as the racist parody, which he or she recommends unreservedly. Amazon.com is not a scholarly or an authoritative source, but its reviews can reflect how the average (i.e., nonacademic) reader interprets a text. While this commentator represents but one reader, his or her unqualified praise also reflects the systemic racism and white ignorance that pervade the twenty-first century.[18]

Keckley continues to be anti-witnessed in contemporary renderings. Stephen Spielberg's *Lincoln* (2012) a-witnesses Keckley as perpetually silent. When Keckley, portrayed by Gloria Ruben, appears in the film, she sits silently in the balcony of the House of Representatives as white male representatives below debate whether or not to ratify the Thirteenth Amendment to the Constitution. Keckley's sustained silence and marginalization to the gallery could represent the historical suppression of Afra-Americans, but her silencing also a-witnesses her voice and agency. When Fernando Wood contends, for instance, that "Congress must never declare equal those whom God created unequal," opponents to passing the amendment cheer. Keckley blinks and swallows. When the amendment passes and its champions celebrate, Keckley maintains her silence. Whether her citizenship is attacked or affirmed, she is mute and passive. She is thus silenced—and a-witnessed—by a film that spotlights the era's white male leaders, erroneously depicting white men of power to be, as Kate Masur suggests, the "primary movers of history" and "the main sources of social progress" in America.[19] African American characters, such as Keckley, are correspondingly reduced, waiting "passively . . . for white men to liberate them" (Masur)—their agency, personhood, and citizenship collectively ignored and negated, even as *Lincoln* professes to celebrate them.

As Keckley is a-witnessed in Spielberg's *Lincoln,* she is also co-optively anti-witnessed in Jennifer Chiaverini's *Mrs. Lincoln's Dressmaker,* a 2013 novelization of *Behind the Scenes.* Billed by the *Library Journal* as "absorbing," "compelling," and "accurate," Chiaverini's novel purportedly "takes readers through times of war," as "seen through the eyes of an extraordinary woman," Elizabeth Keckley.[20] *Mrs. Lincoln's Dressmaker,* the *Library Journal* contends, provokes readers to encounter and engage exceptional historical figures. The review, however, overlooks Chiaverini's appropriation of Keckley's life and work. What the journal lauds as "meticulous research" is in fact plagiarism, as many of *Dressmaker's* passages (and nearly all of its dialogue) are transcribed verbatim from *Behind the Scenes* without citing Keckley's source text. Moreover, whatever work Chiaverini does contribute changes the tenor and content of the original narrative. *Dressmaker,* for instance, mischaracterizes the relationship between Keckley and Mrs. Lincoln. Chiaverini does not seem to appreciate the interracial female dual-witnessing at work in *Behind the Scenes,* and, thus, though she reproduces Keckley's dialogue, she does not demonstrate understanding of what she has appropriated. After President Lincoln's funeral, Chiaverini quotes Mrs. Lincoln as wailing: "Did ever a woman have to suffer so much? . . . Alas! All is over with me!" (Chiaverini 233; Keckley 200). Chiaverini then supplements: "Although Elizabeth desperately wished to give her solace, she knew nothing she could do would suffice, nothing she could say would bring her peace" (233). Here, Chiaverini embellishes Elizabeth's reaction to Mrs. Lincoln's grief, but the way she does so ignores the strength of their historical relationship and minimizes the women's ability to transcend race to dual-witness. Though Keckley herself does not disclose how she felt when the First Lady witnessed her grief, she does stress that she was the only person to whom Mrs. Lincoln wished to confide and that they found solace in one another. By revising these details, Chiaverini not only co-opts Keckley's narrative but also negates the dual-witnessing the modiste depicted.

Chiaverini also appropriates Keckley's narrative to make the seamstress appear more of an activist than *Behind the Scenes* suggests she was. Although *Dressmaker* omits Keckley's years in slavery (thereby a-witnessing the traumas she suffered as a bondswoman), the novel repeatedly adds anti-slavery and feminist rhetoric to her discourse, transforming her postemancipatory treatment of slavery into that of an abolitionist and a suffragist. When Keckley attends one of Lincoln's speeches in *Dressmaker,* Chiaverini writes:

> Elizabeth . . . muffle[d] a gasp. . . . The president had just told the world that he approved of enfranchisement for black . . . men of color. . . . Perhaps that would be only the beginning. Perhaps . . . suffragists would finally have their way too. . . . First colored [men] would be allowed to vote, and then . . . white women, and . . . finally, women of color like her . . . She had already witnessed . . . many remarkable events. . . . Might not universal suffrage be another? (213)

Keckley never discusses Afra-American suffrage in *Behind the Scenes*. Her excitement in *Dressmaker* over the imminent rights of women of color seems, at best, extratextual and, at worst, incongruous with the source text's treatment of slavery's "bright side" and implicit "blessings" (Keckley xi). The historical Keckley likely supported abolitionism, and she may have espoused universal suffrage, but she does not express these opinions in her narrative, adopting instead the more "objective" stance toward African American and women's rights (Keckley xi). As Chiaverini (re)writes her, Keckley is a more consistent if less complex character. In borrowing lavishly from Keckley's narrative and omitting Keckley's irregular views on slavery and its aftermath (while transforming her into a supporter of—and spokeswoman for—Afra-American legal rights), Chiaverini boldly appropriates the language of *Behind the Scenes* as she alters its content. In doing so, she negatively a-witnesses and co-optively anti-witnesses Keckley's narrative.

What Chiaverini does not appropriatively anti-witness in *Behind the Scenes*, she a-witnesses. The fact that Chiaverini excludes from her novel anything about Keckley's life before meeting Mrs. Lincoln and that she titles her text *Mrs. Lincoln's Dressmaker* suggests that her work characterizes Keckley according to her relationship with Mrs. Lincoln and her profession as Mrs. Lincoln's modiste, not according to her individual personhood, experiences, or witnessing potential. In "The Dynamics of Disclosure," Therí Pickens explains that "one of the more useful aspects" of witnessing primarily is the "control" one is able to wield over one's own narrative. "To speak on your own behalf," Pickens writes, "reorients others toward you rather than accepts their stance as correct." Chiaverini wrests control from Keckley when she revises the nineteenth-century Afra-American's testimony as per her own non-nineteenth-century, non-Afra-American vision. In using Keckley's words without Keckley's vision or intent, Chiaverini does not acknowledge this requisition but persists in a-witnessing her reconfiguration of *Behind the Scenes*. In her acknowledgments, Chiaverini thanks editors, assistants, and historians of the Civil War and of Mrs. Lincoln (but not of Keckley) before conceding, "Of course, no work was more important" to her novel's success "than Elizabeth Keckley's own memoir, *Behind the Scenes* . . . Though I regret the unhappiness its publication brought her, I am deeply grateful [she] . . . left behind such a rich and evocative account of her life" (356). While this acknowledgment recognizes the memoir's history of anti-witnessing (in the "unhappiness" its reception brought Keckley), Chiaverini participates in the selfsame pattern of anti-witnessing by reproducing an edited version of Keckley's text with reframed dialogue and excised insights that do not resonate with Keckley's own. Moreover, the racial dynamics at work in Chiaverini's appropriation (i.e., the white woman's arrogation of the Afra-American's narrative) counteract the interracial female dual-witnessing *Behind the Scenes* models, supplanting its witnessing power with more anti-witnessing. Decades after entrusting her narrative to her first editor, Keckley remains anti-witnessed by those who treat her text.

The longstanding anti-witnessing of female-penned emancipatory narratives, such as those of Jacobs, Truth, and Keckley, emphasizes the corresponding importance for contemporary readers to dual-witness these women's traumas and truths. Engaging these texts also exposes how diligently nineteenth-century female ex-slave narrators worked to witness their psychic and social, racial and gendered, and personal and collective traumas; how challenging it is to witness such traumas successfully, particularly when the primary witness is inhibited by traumatic memory, sociopolitical constraints, and readerly anti-witnessing; and how powerful such witnessing must be to overcome these obstacles and transform the ethos of one's readership. Given the concurrent difficulty and necessity of dual-witnessing Afra-American emancipatory narratives, the question for contemporary readers is how to approach these texts today. How do the memoirs of Jacobs, Truth, and Keckley speak to us in our current era, and how may we best respond to their collective call for readerly engagement and action?

One potential answer is to resist anti-witnessing the speakers' testimonies and to struggle instead to enter into their narratives without attacking, dismissing, or appropriating them. No single method to achieve this goal exists, but if each reader remains vigilant to the ways one personally is inclined to anti-witness and works to counter such tendencies in one's own readerly engagement, one may find oneself able to dual-witness, however difficult the process may be. In her work with female-authored autobiography, Braxton models such secondary witnessing when she writes: "I come to these texts as a listener with the understanding that I have everything to learn about this tradition and that it has everything to teach" (5). As does Braxton, so may all readers of Afra-American emancipatory narratives, subverting a history of anti-witnessing to witness instead those incidents most challenging to confront.

CHAPTER 2

"You Cant Understand It"

William Faulkner's Anti-Witnessing of Race and Gender

The preceding chapter argues that the former bondswomen, Harriet Jacobs, Sojourner Truth, and Elizabeth Keckley, constricted by traumatic memory and prevailing social constraints, struggle to witness their life histories through autobiography. This chapter considers the fiction of William Faulkner, exploring the degree to which Faulkner's texts (anti-)witness the intersecting traumas and oppressions of racism and sexism in America. Unlike writers of nonfiction, who attempt to narrate their own trauma, writers of trauma fiction have the advantage of being able to step outside of their own experiences to witness fictively those catastrophes they have not personally encountered.[1] In this way, fiction writers can serve as secondary witnesses by proxy for those who have suffered trauma and oppression but may not have the language or social support to testify to catastrophe. Authors of trauma fiction, however, can also be limited by their own personal experiences and sociocultural positioning, which can counteract their texts' witnessing potential. Such is the case with much of Faulkner's work.

Lauded as one of the greatest American authors of the postbellum period, William Faulkner has also been critically censured for his novels' treatment of race and gender and racism and sexism in the American South. Arnold Weinstein contends that Faulkner "can see but cannot write" the "devastated lives" of his African American characters who struggle against the specter of

American slavery (29). Bernard Bell argues that Faulkner's novels offer flat and stereotypical renderings of black personhood, from the "mammy figure" (Dilsey Gibson in *The Sound and the Fury*) to the "rebellious marginal man" (Joe Christmas in *Light in August*) to the "tragic mulatto" (Charles Bon in *Absalom, Absalom!*) (qtd. in Cooley 30). Critics such as Doreen Fowler attribute Faulkner's difficulty writing African American characters to his cultural positioning as a white Southern male. As a "great-grandson of a slave owner," Fowler contends, Faulkner struggles to enter into "black consciousnesses" and to "render accurately black lives" (vii). The white Faulkner cannot write black characters without anti-witnessing their individual subjectivities and collective racial positioning.

Similar arguments have been made about Faulkner's treatment of female characters: that his texts cannot depict women without also anti-witnessing them. Critics note that Faulkner's women exemplify patriarchal stereotypes, from the helpless nurturer (Mrs. McEachern in *Light in August*) to the fallen woman (Caddy Compson in *The Sound and the Fury*) and the bitter spinster (Rosa Coldfield in *Absalom, Absalom!*) (Clarke 143; Davis 441). Although Faulkner's texts beautifully explore white androcentric tragedies, his black and female characters rarely transcend marginalization. Read in this light, Faulkner's African American and female characters may reveal more about the author's own (white and male) attitudes toward black and female personhood than about black and female personhood itself.

In view of this critique, this chapter, first, analyzes Faulkner's fictive (anti-) witnessing of race and gender relations and, second, examines how readers can constructively respond to Faulkner's problematic renderings. Treating *The Sound and the Fury* (1929), *Light in August* (1932), "That Evening Sun" (1931), and *Absalom, Absalom!* (1936) as case studies, I conclude that Faulkner co-optively anti-witnesses marginalized race and gender in his texts by attempting to witness black and female voices through a white male consciousness. The redeeming feature of Faulkner's project is that, even as his fiction anti-witnesses race and gender, the texts themselves simultaneously work against anti-witnessing. That is, while Faulkner's fiction anti-witnesses marginalized subjectivities, it also impels readers to dual-witness where and when its author does not. As a result, Faulkner, knowingly or unknowingly, transfers responsibility from primary witness (text) to secondary witness (reader), impelling the reader-listener to enter into the speaker's testimony—the central action of dual-witnessing. A benefit, then, to reading Faulkner is that, in considering his fiction's troubled treatment of marginalized race and gender, we can learn to recognize the dangers of anti-witnessing and embark upon the process of dual-witnessing, even when his characters and storylines do not.

The Sound and the Fury: (Anti-)Witnessing Race and Gender through Dilsey Gibson

To examine dual-witnessing in Faulkner's texts, I first consider Faulkner's fourth novel, *The Sound and the Fury,* which details the dissolution of the Southern aristocratic Compson family. *The Sound and the Fury* is the first of Faulkner's novels to address explicitly the relationship between the fall of the South (emblemized in the Compson family dynasty) and overlapping constructs of blackness and womanhood (embodied in the Compsons' black maid, Dilsey Gibson). While critics such as Hodding Carter and Thadious Davis praise Faulkner for his treatment of marginalized race and gender through Dilsey, contending that she is the "strongest" of Faulkner's characters (qtd. in Martin 53), others fear that Dilsey (and her race and gender) is co-optively anti-witnessed as Faulkner appropriates Dilsey's black and female strength to serve the Compson dynasty and, through it, white Southern aristocracy (Schreiber *Subversive* 63).

Dilsey is not given a narrative voice in the novel, nor are readers welcomed into her marginalized perspective. The first three sections of *the Sound and the Fury* are each narrated in first-person by one of the white Compson brothers: intellectually disabled Benjy, suicidal Quentin, and domineering Jason. Together, these chapters witness the dissolution of the Compson dynasty. The fourth and final section of the novel, critically referred to as "Dilsey's chapter," is written in the third-person Faulknerian persona, and, although it chronicles the experiences of the Compsons' black caretaker, Dilsey's section does not witness directly her traumas and personhood, as do the earlier chapters with the Compson brothers. Instead, the chapter touches upon the maid's experiences only insofar as they pertain to her white patriarchal employers. The black female Dilsey appears to lie outside of Faulkner's narrative grasp.

Whatever we do learn of Dilsey (and whatever strength she exhibits as a black and female character) is repeatedly co-opted to serve white patriarchal needs. Readers can hardly ignore Dilsey's positioning as a stereotypical "mammy," an archetype dating back to slavery of the good-natured, heavy-set, dark-skinned, and desexualized black domestic, an archetype that perpetuates the myth that black women are naturally servile, acting in the interests of white people (White 47). Like Mammy, Dilsey is dark, corpulent, and elderly. She is maternal to her white charges; she either scolds or ignores her own children (276). She remains loyal to the Compsons, even as the family undermines her. As Philip Weinstein contends, Dilsey is "so busy mothering her 'white children'" that readers have "no sense of her" other than as a caretaker for the white (*What Else* 16). When, for example, the Compson family discusses whether or not to raise Caddy's daughter Quentin, Dilsey says, "Who else gwine raise her cep me? Aint I raised ev'y one of y'all?" (198), suggesting that her principal role in life is to raise white Compson children. Dilsey is such a mammy figure that the novel's other characters call her "Mammy" as early as page 4, several pages before the reader learns her name on page 7.

The depiction of Dilsey as Mammy co-opts the black woman's strength for white patriarchal purposes. As Diane Roberts writes of all mammies, Dilsey, in her "uncomplicated fidelity," helps endorse a racist and sexist social order that positions black women as subordinate and maintains that they take pleasure in their marginalized status (41)—a perspective with which Faulkner may not disagree. During a 1957 interview at Virginia College, a student asked the author which, if any, of his characters in *The Sound and the Fury* he considered to be "good." Faulkner answered, "Dilsey," as she alone "held the family together for not the hope of reward but just because it was the decent and proper thing to do" (237). Faulkner's answer reveals that he admires Dilsey, but his response also idealizes a mammy figure solely for her service to her white employers. Note here that Faulkner's use of "family" refers explicitly to the Compsons. Dilsey's own family is not considered in his response. Mammy's "goodness" is grounded in her fidelity to her white employers "without hope of reward." Furthermore, one may interrogate what necessitates that black and female subservience to white Southern families is "decent and proper." If what makes Faulkner's black and female characters "good" is their willingness to sacrifice themselves for their white employers, then black and female identities like Dilsey's testify not to the individual "goodness" of marginalized persons but to the co-optive anti-witnessing that reinforces white patriarchal structures.

Faulkner's text not only anti-witnesses Dilsey as a black and female character but, through her, black women collectively. The fact that Dilsey is black and female does not mean she must represent all of black womanhood, but Faulkner equates Dilsey as an individual with black women as a group in the "Dilsey" entry to his novel's appendix, written sixteen years after *The Sound and the Fury* to appear in *The Portable Faulkner* (1945). In this appendix, which Faulkner called the "fifth section" of his novel (210), the author crafts for each of his characters entries that explicate the circumstances surrounding their life experiences. Dilsey's entry consists of two words: "They endured" (215). Faulkner's shift from third-person singular to third-person plural to describe Dilsey (the only such shift his appendix makes) suggests that Dilsey, representing more than just herself, stands for a larger whole. Questions ensue: Who is the enduring "they"? What does

Faulkner mean by "endured"? And how does this entry (anti-)witness both Dilsey and the group(s) she exemplifies?

One potential reading is that Dilsey represents not only black women but all humanity, exhibiting power as a triply marginalized black female servant who typifies the human race. Still, in turning Dilsey from a "she" into a "they," Faulkner's appendix usurps her individual alterity. Why must Dilsey stand in for all others, when the novel's other characters are free to represent themselves alone? Jason and Quentin presumably do not embody all white Southern men. Benjy does not speak for all those with disabilities. In "White Privilege" (1988), Peggy McIntosh notes that a privilege that accompanies "whiteness" is the person's freedom not to be considered "a credit to one's race" (10). One with white privilege has the autonomy to be viewed as an individual subject rather than a representative. Faulkner does not grant this license to Dilsey. Instead, in requiring her to represent other persons, Faulkner co-optively anti-witnesses his character's individual (black and female) personhood.

Dilsey's entry is also problematic in its stipulation that she (or "they") *endured*. In his Nobel Prize acceptance speech (1949), Faulkner shares his hope that humanity will "not merely endure" but will also "prevail" (120). Read in this light, Dilsey's endurance may reaffirm her position as not only an individual black woman but also a representative human being. However, Faulkner's use of the term "endure" is problematized in its evocation of the author's advice to African American leaders, published in *Ebony* in 1956. Written in the *first-person appropriative,* Faulkner's article, "If I Were a Negro" asserts that if Faulkner—speaking now as "I"—"were a negro" (a refrain he repeats throughout), he would counsel "other" African Americans to oppose racism individually but to "endure" collectively: that is, to bear the racial violence of the era without complaint (109). From his title's start,[2] Faulkner co-opts the place of a black speaker in his article and then uses his appropriated racial positioning to advise actual marginalized people to suffer racism in silence. Given this context, what does "endurance" mean for Dilsey? If she endures in Faulkner's Nobel sense, she is celebrated as the "ideal" black woman and human being, presumably for her loyalty to her white employers. If she endures in the *Ebony* sense, she becomes a heroine for abiding racial bigotry. Either reading undermines Faulkner's rendering of Dilsey in particular and black women in general.

The only good to come from *The Sound and the Fury*'s anti-witnessing of Dilsey is that Faulkner's failure offered him the opportunity to admit publicly that he had not—and perhaps could not—adequately write Dilsey (or, through her, black women). *The Sound and the Fury,* Faulkner maintained, was his favorite of his novels because it represented his "most splendid failure" (233). In an interview with Jean Stein for the Spring 1956 *Paris Review,* Faulkner confesses: "I tried to gather the pieces [of Dilsey's narrative] together and fill in the gaps by making myself the spokesman [but] it was ... not complete ... I never could tell it right. I ... would like to try again, though I'd probably fail again" (233). Faulkner admits that the so-called "Dilsey section" is not in fact Dilsey's but Faulkner's and that, as "spokesman," he has co-optively anti-witnessed the identity-narrative of a black and female character through his own white and male perspective. Faulkner also recognizes his limitations as a white male author writing black female characters when he admits that, if he "tri[ed] again" he would "probably fail again."

If Faulkner anti-witnesses race and gender in his novel, the fact that he also seems aware of this failure (and struggles against it) may appear inconsequential. The benefit, however, of such authorial and textual consciousness is that *The Sound and the Fury* has the opportunity to turn to its readers for assistance: to ask those who engage the novel to witness secondarily what it does not witness primarily. Faulkner's first introduction to his novel begins: "I wrote [*The Sound and the Fury*] and learned to read" (226). His novel asks the same of its readers: to learn to read Faulkner's failures, to witness secondarily his problematic renderings of race and gender, and, in doing so, to work against his anti-witnessing. Quentin Compson asserts in *The Sound and the Fury:* "The tragedy is secondhand" (116). Quentin speaks here to the contagion of trauma, but he also suggests that traumatic and testimonial accounts not only exist primarily (in of and by themselves) but also are experienced, read, and witnessed secondarily (or "secondhand") by those who engage them. With this perspective in mind, readers may enter into Faulkner's textual world to help him witness what his novels do not: the fraught reality of race and gender relations in the American South.

Light in August: The Dangers of Anti-Witnessing

Three years after publishing *The Sound and the Fury,* Faulkner explored race and gender in *Light in August.* In this novel, Faulkner continues to (anti-) witness the "problem" of race through the figure of Joe Christmas, a man who does not know whether he is white or black but who is eventually killed for being a "nigger rapist" and murderer (344). Faulkner's treatment of race and gender is more sophisticated here than in his previous work. In *Light in August,* both ambiguously black Joe Christmas and the white woman he kills, Joanna Burden, represent more complex portrayals of blackness and womanhood than Dilsey does. Nevertheless, Faulkner's approach to race and gender is still problematic in that it continues to anti-witnesses black and female characters to address marginalized identity only as it pertains to a white male majority. In consequence, *Light in August,* like *The Sound and the Fury,* testifies more to Faulkner's difficulty witnessing blackness and womanhood than to the constructs themselves.

Light in August improves upon racial depictions in *The Sound and the Fury* by interrogating what race is before attempting to demystify American racism. While individual characters, from Christmas's racist grandfather, Doc Hines, to the supposedly impartial attorney, Gavin Stevens, believe race is biological,[3] the novel treats essentialized "blackness" as a myth disseminated by self-defining whites in order to justify racial violence against those categorized as black. Support for this reading rests in the unresolved racial ambiguity of the novel's protagonist, Joe Christmas, and in the other (white) characters' responses to his racial identity. As Ralph Watkins posits, Joe Christmas, as both white and black (and therefore neither fully white nor black), embodies socially constructed race, witnessing through his racial liminality the absurdity of racial essentialism (13–14). Although his pale skin marks Christmas as white, the protagonist is raced as black by other characters in the text. Whether Christmas is "niggerized" (238), as he puts it, by other (white) children at the orphanage (128); by his race-obsessed lover, Joanna Burden (269); or by his ex-business partner, Joe Brown (98), Christmas' race is depicted as external rather than internal. Even Christmas's term for how others "niggerize" him suggests that racial identity is a verb (something done to a subject) versus a noun (something a subject is).

The novel affirms this view by defining Christmas as definitively black only when the law suspects he is criminal. When Brown first accuses Christmas of murdering Burden, the sheriff doubts Brown's testimony, but when Brown announces that Christmas has "nigger blood" (98), Christmas becomes "that nigger murderer," guilty in the eyes of the law not only of killing Burden but of being black (346). In a moment of racist and circular reasoning, Christmas's nonwhite status is used to support Brown's claim that Christmas murdered Burden (as the law believes only black men murder white Southern ladies), and his criminality is upheld as evidence of his blackness (as the community believes all criminals are black, as being black—especially when appearing white—is a crime) (346). Through such scenes, the novel demonstrates how Faulkner views racial essentialism as a racist apparatus, used by white men in power to criminalize blacks and "niggerize" criminals.

A potential danger of this characterization of race is that it risks a-witnessing the racism white individuals perpetuate against nonwhites. If race is

socially determined, one may view racist perpetrators themselves as victims
of a system into which they too are indoctrinated. *Light in August's* white
Reverend Hightower—who has been mock-lynched (i.e., tied to a tree and left
to die) for helping black folk in his community—makes a similar argument,
professing that his racist attackers are "good people" who simply "believe
what they must believe" (74). "It is not for me to outrage their believing,"
Hightower pronounces, after they have tied him to the tree, or "to say that
they are wrong. . . . All that any man can hope for is to be permitted to live
quietly among his fellows'" (74). One can envision Faulkner offering a similar
justification for his novels' racial anti-witnessing. However much the author
may wish for his novels to indict racism, as a white male, born and raised
in the racist South, he cannot shed his racist inculcation when writing fiction. Hightower's pronouncements concerning racism cannot be taken to
be Faulkner's own, but the conclusions Hightower draws reveal the danger
in relying entirely on a socially constructed vision of race. Doing so risks
absolving racists of the violence they perpetuate.[4]

While marginalized race and gender do not unite in a central character, as
they do in Dilsey's character in *The Sound and the Fury,* overlapping constructs
of blackness and womanhood surface in *Light in August.* Just as Christmas's
race is portrayed more complexly than Dilsey's, so is Faulkner's presentation
of women and womanhood more complex in *Light in August* than in *The
Sound and the Fury.* Joanna Burden, for example, resists easy categorization.
Burden is one of Faulkner's "bitter spinster" characters, but, although older
and unmarried, she is neither asexual nor virginal. She flouts both the gender
and racial norms of her white Southern community by initiating a sexual
relationship with a man she believes to be black (Joe Christmas)—a relationship she, rather than her male partner, directs and controls.

When Christmas attempts to assert power over Burden by raping her,
Burden refuses his patriarchal control by acceding to the assault. The first
time Christmas tries to rape Burden, his chosen victim does "not resist at all"
but instead "help[s]" Christmas meet his goal "with small changes of positions
of limbs" (236). In acting thus, Burden transforms imminent victimization
into a shared rape fantasy. Although critics such as Laura Bush describe
Christmas and Burden's encounter as "one of the most horrific scenes of
sexual violence against women," which is "limited to Joe's viewpoint" (323),
more often than not, Burden, not Christmas, directs and controls their sexual
interaction. In fact, after their first encounter, Burden continues to summon
Christmas to her to act out more rape play. Faulkner writes that Burden
repeatedly "forced" Christmas "to climb into a window to come to her. . . . She
appointed trysts . . . where he would find her . . . with her clothing half torn

to ribbons upon her, in the wild throes of nymphomania" (259). The verbs "forced" and "appointed" reveal that Burden, not Christmas, dominates their sexual encounters and that she uses the would-be rapist's weapons (force, time, and surprise) against her aggressor, transforming male-perpetrated violation into female-directed collaboration.

In portraying Burden as one, to borrow from Audre Lorde, who attempts to use the "master's tools" (in this case, rape) to "dismantle his house" (in her own house yet) ("Master's Tools" 112), Faulkner complicates *Light in August*'s principal female character as well as his representation of women. The difficulty with this rendering is that, even as Burden takes control of her sexual autonomy, the implications of her "nymphomania" are problematic. In *Against Our Will: Men, Women, and Rape,* Susan Brownmiller argued for the first time (in 1975) that rape is not a crime of lust, as previously believed, but of perpetuating male dominance over women (15). This is indeed how Christmas attempts to use rape: as asserted power, not sexual desire. Christmas does not appear to be sexually attracted to Burden but professes to hate "the bitch," even as he pursues her (236).[5] Although Christmas's attitude underscores Brownmiller's contention, now widely accepted, that rape is a crime of power, not desire, Faulkner would not have been exposed to this analysis. The novel's portrayal of both rape and gender dynamics thus raise the following questions: What does the novel (anti-)witness about women and sexual assault, and what underlying messages does Burden's "power" impart?

A danger of *Light in August* is that—in grounding Burden's female agency in her decision to sleep with her assailant—it teaches readers that the principal way female victims gain power is in helping male victimizers assault them and also that women who enjoy sex—particularly those who are not "supposed" to (e.g., the unmarried and middle-aged)—are deviant "nymphomaniacs" who probably want to be raped, as—in the most troubling interpretation of the novel—all women do. Christmas, for one, thinks as he rapes Burden: "She's trying to be a woman and she dont know how" (240). This interpretation of Burden's sexual "assistance" suggests that the protagonist views all women as rape victims (i.e., what Burden is presumably "trying to be"), and what distinguishes Ms. Burden from the rest of womankind is that she does not know how to be raped—i.e., to be a woman—"properly." Again, a character's perspective (e.g., Christmas's) cannot be taken to be Faulkner's own, but the implications of Christmas and Burden's trysts reinforce a precarious view of both women (as victim-deviants who need to be raped) and rape (as the process by which womanhood is established).

Furthermore, as Karen Andrews argues, Faulkner's representation of Burden's affair with Christmas risks subverting a potentially "progressive relationship" between a white woman and a black man (10). That is, instead of deconstructing racial binaries and countering historical fears of miscegenation, the denouement of the lovers' intercourse—when Christmas murders Burden and is shot and castrated for it—helps reinforce segregationist and lynching logic, in which black men invariably rape and kill white Southern ladies and must die for it (Allen 10). As Andrews suggests, Burden and Christmas's "doomed relationship" teaches readers that interracial relationships are "fraught with racism and sexism and finally lead to violence; therefore, they cannot and should not happen" (10). Read in this light, *Light in August,* while attempting to witness race and gender relations in the American South, reinforces racist and sexist ideologies.

Why then read the novel at all? *Light in August* underscores the value of dual-witnessing. Even if Faulkner's text does not consistently witness race and gender, it works to promote readerly engagement of these constructs. Faulkner accomplishes this feat by testifying to the enduring traumas of racial and gendered anti-witnessing in the American South. *Light in August,* for example, warns against anti-witnessing through the counterexample of community gossip. When Burden is murdered and her house is set on fire, the townsfolk do not gather to help their neighbor but "crowd" together instead, as if they were at a public lynching, "to look down at" her burning house and decapitated corpse. They offer no condolences but gleefully speculate that her slaying was "committed not by a negro but by Negro," who must have "ravished [her] too; at least before her throat was cut and at least once afterward" (288). Burden's onlookers aggressively anti-witness her life and death. They voyeuristically anti-witness when they delight in the catastrophes she has borne and accusatorily anti-witness when they look not only at her but "*down* at" her, (symbolically) judging her for victimhood.

Faulkner also links the crowd's anti-witnessing to constructs of race and gender when the gossips assume that a black man must have assaulted the white woman, because the victim was known to associate with African Americans, and, presumably, only black men rape and kill white women. This aggressive anti-witnessing has voyeuristic as well as accusatory elements, as—in the bystanders' view, at least—Burden elected to socialize with black men, whom they "know, believe, and hope" prey on white women. Her gruesome death thus represents to the crowd an inevitable and a just punishment for the mixing of white ladyhood with black virility—be it miscegenation or mere social interaction (288). Burden's spectators continue to link their aggressive anti-witnessing to race when they determine that Blackness itself raped and killed their neighbor, as if the essentialized race they have constructed—what the spectators call "Negro" with a capital "N"—is evil and criminal (288). Finally, the viewers link anti-witnessing to gender and misogyny when they hope that Burden was raped before and after death. In this scene, Faulkner offers a chilling example of how communities anti-witness aggressively and how anti-witnessing can reveal racism and sexism in American culture.

In "By Word of Mouth: Narrative Dynamics of Gossip in Faulkner's *Light in August*," Ellen Goellner argues that the novel's portrayal of gossip does not represent anti-witnessing but models instead dual-and communal witnessing, in that gossip, like "psychoanalytic dialogue [dual-witnessing], is concerned with the place of the speaker [primary witness] in relation to the hearer [secondary witness], structuring the negotiations of meaning" (109). Goellner's argument overlooks gossip's destructive potential, which enables characters not to witness dually or communally (or to construct "whole" meanings out of fragmented parts, as Goellner posits) but to anti-witness catastrophe. Even if voyeurism and accusation are common responses to trauma, such aggressive anti-witnessing should not be conflated with dual-and communal witnessing. Gossip does not work through in order to abate catastrophe but amplifies trauma by sensationalizing and delighting in others' distress. In revealing how members of Burden's community unite not to help but to harm, Faulkner explicates the dangers of anti-witnessing, compelling readers not to follow his characters' counterexamples but to dual-witness instead.

Light in August also exposes the harm in co-optive anti-witnessing, evinced in the beliefs of the novel's white abolitionists. Nathaniel Burden teaches his daughter, Joanna Burden, that whites are obligated to help blacks because white Americans have profited from institutionalized racism and have a corresponding duty to establish parity for African Americans (253). Depicting American race relations as "the white man's burden" (as their family name, "Burden," implies), Nathanial Burden describes the black race as "doomed and cursed to be forever . . . a part of the white race's doom and curse for its sins" (253). Nathaniel Burden treats black existence and experience appropriatively, as a burden to which white people may lay claim and for which they are single-handedly responsible. In doing so, he reinforces the white/black hierarchy and master/slave dynamic he professes to undercut, working against, not toward, racial equality. The example of Nathaniel Burden demonstrates a danger of co-optive anti-witnessing: alleged advocates can perpetuate bigotry by appropriating others' experiences. This point is salient both to the novel and to this argument as a whole because such appropriative anti-witnessing is precisely what I charge Faulkner with when I argue that his black and female characters do not testify to their own marginalized perspectives but speak to the author's position as a white Southern male.

When Joanna Burden internalizes and acts upon her father's co-optive anti-witnessing, she embodies the contagious nature of anti-witnessing. Although she follows Nathaniel Burden's injunction to help "advance" the negro race (276), her reasons for doing so are more appropriative than productive. After speaking to her father about Southern race relations, Joanna Burden begins to see black people "not as people but as a thing, a shadow" under which all white people live (253). "I told father," she recalls, "that I must escape, get away from under the shadow, or I would die. 'You cannot,' he said. 'You must struggle, rise. But in order to rise, you must raise [black people up] with you'" (253). Joanna Burden learns that white people are so "oppressed" by their duty to blacks that they must help black folk rise up with them, so future generations of whites will no longer be burdened with black problems. This approach to race relations fails to witness in order to work through America's racial history, as one cannot overcome bigotry with more bigotry, especially when prejudice masquerades as advocacy.

Joanna Burden continues her father's tradition of anti-witnessing in appropriating Christmas's presumed blackness for personal and sociopolitical gain. She first co-opts her lover's racial identity by determining that he is black even though he has told her that he cannot determine his racial heritage (254). Christmas's admission of racial indeterminacy does not hinder Burden from moaning "Negro! Negro! Negro!" as she has sex with him, labeling her partner as black and claiming him as her personal (black) object. Burden's co-opting of Christmas persists when she erroneously announces that she is pregnant with their "bastard Negro child" (266), as if, in appropriating Christmas's blackness, she can now give birth to and possess his race, as a mother can an infant. Finally, Burden insists that Christmas also self-identify as she defines him (i.e., as absolutely instead of ambiguously black). She then appropriates this constructed personhood to help her realize her own goals for (other) African Americans. When Burden orders Christmas to "tell [other] niggers that ... [he is] a nigger too" (277), she co-opts his personhood for her advocacy work, independent of whomever Christmas feels he is or whatever he wants to do with his life and identity.

Burden is determined to appropriate Christmas. When Christmas rejects Burden's offer to pronounce himself black, attend an African American college, learn the law, and take over her business in order to help (other) black folks "up out of darkness" (276), she asks him to pray with her about her plan (280). When this request is denied, Burden threatens Christmas by revealing a "cap-and-ball revolver" hidden beneath her shawl (282). To refuse appropriation is to accept death. If Christmas will not become whomever Burden wishes him to be, she will shoot to kill, rendering him without identity. In this scene,

Burden anti-witnesses Christmas in every way possible. First, she co-optively anti-witnesses him by appropriating his subjectivity for her own purposes. Second, she a-witnesses him by refusing to recognize how Christmas may see himself (as separate from her own vision of him). Third, she aggressively anti-witnesses him through her willingness to wound him rather than to witness him secondarily. Christmas murders Burden by slitting her throat, a gruesome response that can also be read as a physical and psychic "self-defense": Christmas kills Burden only after she threatens his life by pointing a gun at him and attempts to appropriate his self for her own purposes.

Burden's co-opting of Christmas may represent her attempt to punish him for his repeated attempted rapes of her. When a man assaults a woman, he violently appropriates her body and sense of self. When Burden makes Christmas black and demands at gunpoint that he use this blackness "on [her] account" (277), she violently co-opts Christmas's identity to serve her own desires. If such is the case, Burden's treatment of Christmas is understandable, but an appreciation of her potential motivation does not justify her co-optive anti-witnessing of Christmas's personhood. Instead, *Light in August* uses this interaction to underscore how destructive anti-witnessing can be. Christmas's anti-witnessing of Burden leads to (though does not cause) her relentless anti-witnessing of him, which results in her death, an event that opens new opportunities for the community to anti-witness her through the spread of malicious gossip. Anti-witnessing effects anti-witnessing.

An irony of *Light in August* is that the woman who appropriated Christmas in life is co-opted in death. Just as Burden attempts to appropriate blacks in general (in turning their suffering into her own personal burden) and Christmas in particular (by making him black), in death, she is communally appropriated as an emblem of "white Southern ladyhood." Burden's presumed rape and death at the hands of the "nigger murderer," Joe Christmas, allow for white male neighbors to hunt and kill another black man (346). When Faulkner wrote *Light in August,* a core element of American lynching rhetoric was the myth that black masculinity represented a physical and sexual threat to white femininity (hooks *Yearning* 57). White men were taught to believe that they shared a duty to lynch black men in order to protect the sanctity of "their" white Southern women (Allen 10). This fabrication aggressively anti-witnesses black men (in assuming they are rapist-murderers) and co-optively anti-witnesses white women (in constructing "white Southern ladyhood" to justify the murder of black men). In both cases, Faulkner's novel suggests, anti-witnessing facilitates racism and sexism.

Once dead, Burden shifts in public perception from being a "nigger lover" (292) to a "nigger victim," whose death may be avenged by lynching the "nigger murderer," Christmas (346). Faulkner writes that Burden "lived and died a foreigner and outlander" (289). "While she was alive," white Southern men "would not have allowed their wives to call on her" (292), but, now that she is dead (and no longer poses an ideological threat to them), these same men kill a black man to avenge her death. When Percy Grimm, captain of the state National Guard, shoots and castrates Christmas, he seethes: "Now you'll let white women alone, even in hell" (464). Grimm offers this sentence only two paragraphs after he has dismissed Burden as an "old maid," ready to take her "pants down to the yellowbellied son of a bitch" (464). Grimm's statement makes clear he is not actually concerned about Burden's victimhood. If he believes Christmas raped Burden, then he aggressively anti-witnesses Burden alongside Christmas in blaming her for "tak[ing] her pants down to" a "yellowbellied"—or cowardly and biracial—man. But Grimm's focus is not Burden. Her victimhood merely offers him the excuse to kill Christmas. Grimm both a-witnesses Burden (in refusing to recognize her) and co-optively anti-witnesses her (in taking her over) in order to secure the prize of murdering Christmas.

Light in August skillfully testifies to the destruction anti-witnessing can wreak, whether it manifests aggressively (through gossip), co-optively (by appropriating another's life for one's own goals), or as a-witnessing (in refusing to recognize another's alterity). Paradoxically, however, the novel repeats these same receptive failings in anti-witnessing its own characters (and race and gender through them). The text a-witnesses black women in particular. As Judith Bryant Wittenberg notes, black women in *Light in August* are "totally inaccessible to the reader" (161), and, when black women do appear, they are co-optively anti-witnessed for white male purposes. Consider the role Christmas plays in the gang rape of an unnamed Afra-American. In this scene, an adolescent Christmas is invited by five white friends to enter a shed and rape a captive black woman (156).[6] As the victim neither elicits nor encourages her attack, Faulkner's depiction of sexual violence does not aggressively anti-witness the woman as it does when Burden facilitates Christmas's assault. Nevertheless, the text's portrayal of cross-racial gang rape anti-witnesses its victim by a-witnessing both her identity and traumatic experience. Philip Weinstein notes that Faulkner does not provide any details about the woman other than that she is black, young, and abused. We are not given her name ("Marginalia" 176), nor do we learn how she was captured, how she escapes, or what happens to her after her rape. The invisibility Faulkner assigns this girl aligns his text with those assailants who a-witness her in refusing to recognize her alterity and personhood.

The novel's a-witnessing of a nameless victim is further problematized by the woman's race. Since few other Afra-American characters appear in *Light in August,* the novel presents black women as either victims or nonexistent.[7] Thus, as Burden's acceptance of rape reinforces the sexist and racist message that all (white) women wish to be raped by (black) men, the appearance of an Afra-American rape victim—as one of the only black woman to surface in the novel—carries with it the sexist and racist notion that black women exist (at least textually) only to be violated by white men. In presenting cross-racial sexual assault as something white women desire and black women endure, *Light in August* anti-witnesses not only white and black women (and black men as rapists) but rape as well. In doing so, the novel reinforces Christmas's belief that a woman's purpose is to be raped (240). The text aligns with those who would anti-witness women, nonwhites, and survivors alike, and Faulkner's novel again presents race and gender from a white androcentric point of view: white women exist to be protected by white men from black men; black men exist to challenge and then be killed by white men; and black women exist to entice and then be raped by white men. All exist to be acted upon by white men, who exist to act upon all. Such is the racial and sexual world of *Light in August.*

When Christmas's turn comes to rape the black woman, the text allies with his perspective, not hers. Faulkner writes that when Christmas "entered the shed," he "could not move ... smelling the woman smelling the negro all at once enclosed by the womanshenegro" (157). This scene is written from Christmas's point of view: *He* enters the shed; *he* cannot move; *he* smells the black woman. Readers are told nothing of how his victim feels but know only that her victimizer is revolted by what he identifies as her essential blackness and womanhood. When Christmas, sickened by the sight and smell of his prey, finds he cannot rape her, he beats her instead (157).[8] Christmas may elect to use his fists instead of his phallus as a weapon to prove that he is neither black (he beats the girl for displaying the blackness he fears lies in himself) nor effeminate (he may worry that, unable to rape a woman, he is somehow not a "man"). In both instances, marginalized race and gender and victimhood are appropriated to offer Christmas the opportunity to exhibit his own anxieties about race and masculinity, and the unnamed woman is both a-witnessed (in that we never enter into her perspective) and co-optively anti-witnessed to reveal how her attacker feels about his social positioning, rather than how she feels about hers. In short, while *Light in August* begins to model the value of dual-witnessing (through testifying to the dangers of anti-witnessing), the text ultimately perpetuates the anti-witnessing it warns against, and Faulkner's project to witness marginalized identities falters again.

"That Evening Sun": The Dangers of A-Witnessing

Faulkner departs from his novels' anti-witnessing of Afra-American characters in "That Evening Sun," a story narrated by an adult Quentin Compson
(of *The Sound and the Fury*) about incidents that took place when he was a
child. Praised as Faulkner's "best" short story (Bollinger 53), "That Evening
Sun" depicts the trauma that besets Nancy, the Compson family's black cook,
when she becomes convinced that her estranged husband, Jesus, has returned
to town to kill her because she is pregnant with a white man's child. Whether
or not Jesus is in Yoknapatawpha or plans to murder his wife remains unclear,
and readers never learn whether Nancy lives or dies. Instead, "That Evening
Sun" concludes as Jason Compson Sr.[9] and his children walk away from her
cabin, abandoning Nancy (she believes) to imminent death. Since white male
Quentin narrates the story about his white family's (mis)treatment of an
Afra-American, the story's viewpoint—like that of Faulkner's other work—is
predominately white and male. However, rather than appropriating black
women's experiences to speak to white men's concerns, "That Evening Sun"
criticizes white people for the damage they inflict on black women when
they a-witness Afra-American trauma and personhood.

"That Evening Sun" emphasizes how little has changed since slavery. A
generation after the Civil War, white Southern aristocratic families like the
Compsons can no longer legally own black people, but they can treat African
Americans as less than human. Quentin reflects that, despite technological
advances such as paved streets, telephones, and electricity, Mississippi has
not progressed socially (289). African Americans continue to face antiblack
racism. When Quentin describes "iron poles bearing clusters of bloated and
ghostly and bloodless grapes" (289), he evokes bodies lynched on trees, a
reminder of the violence black people confronted in Reconstruction and
beyond. Quentin also observes that black women bear the brunt of white
patriarchal oppression: years after slavery, they cannot aspire to roles higher
than domestic servitude to white families. "The Negro women," Quentin
recounts, "still take in white people's washing after the old custom" (289).
When he watches black washerwomen carrying bundles of clothing "almost
as large as cotton bales" (289), Quentin links their current occupation to
slaves picking cotton (94). Ren Denton notes that the title of Faulkner's story
evokes the "time of day when the slaves returned to their cabins" (94). That
the story concludes openly with Nancy wailing alone in her cabin, waiting
to die, suggests that the traumas and oppressions inherent in slavery do not
end with the Civil War (or the last page of Faulkner's story) but continue
to terrorize black people—a terror evinced in Nancy's wailing. Whether ten

or fifty years have passed since slavery,[10] "That Evening Sun" suggests, the Emancipation Proclamation did not end antiblack oppression but, as Robert Penn Warren writes, "merely transferred the crime against the Negro into a new set of terms" (331).

In part, what allows the specter of slavery to endure is white society's a-witnessing of the experiences and humanity of black people in general and black women in particular. Black women, "That Evening Sun" demonstrates, are oppressed by white men and women as well as by black men—a reality that white men and women and black men continue to a-witness. A white man, Mr Stovall, impregnates Nancy. A black man, Jesus, may kill her for it. Nancy has little control over her body or her life (i.e., whether or not she becomes pregnant or lives or dies). She is preyed upon by white and black men. Mr Stovall, a bank cashier and Baptist deacon, has contracted Nancy for sex. (Nancy works as a washerwoman, cook, and prostitute.) Stovall, however, refuses to pay Nancy, even after he has impregnated her. When Nancy confronts him: "When you going to pay me, white man? It's been three times now since you paid me a cent—" (291), Mr Stovall kicks Nancy so hard in the mouth that she spits out blood and teeth (291). Nancy is arrested for prostitution, but Stovall is not punished, even though the marshal and townsfolk witness his abuse. This scene underscores the oppression impoverished black women face in a white capitalistic patriarchy. Nancy, a poor black woman, sells sex to wealthy white men to survive. Nancy's white male clients are not penalized for breaking the law (i.e., paying for sex), but she, a black female sex worker, is punished for selling what she owns (her body). When Mr Stovall refuses to pay Nancy for her labor, he treats her like a slave. (During slavery, black bondswomen were repeatedly penetrated and impregnated—without pay or recourse—by wealthy white men [White 34].) When Nancy advocates for herself and demands payment, she is kicked in the teeth and imprisoned. This attack is then a-witnessed by the white people who observe it, a negative response that compounds Nancy's mistreatment.

When Nancy attempts to hang herself in her jail cell, this act is also anti-witnessed by white men in authority. A white male jailor unties Nancy's noose, saving her from suicide, only to whip her for trying to take her own life (291). The message is clear: Nancy's body is not hers to sell; her life is not hers to take. Both belong to the white patriarchy. The jailer suspects that Nancy tried to kill herself because she is addicted to cocaine since "no nigger would try to commit suicide unless he was full of cocaine" (291). In voicing this theory (for which no textual evidence exists), the jailer a-witnesses the reasons Nancy may actually wish to die: lack of agency; fear of bodily harm from Mr Stovall or Jesus; desire to save her unborn child from a life of subjugation; and/or hatred of the white man's child growing within her. The jailer also aggressively anti-witnesses Nancy when he beats her and calls her a "nigger" for attempting suicide (291). If Jesus murders Nancy for having sex and becoming pregnant without his permission, he will join Mr Stovall and the jailor in aggressively anti-witnessing her. Through such scenes, Faulkner helps readers witness secondarily what his characters do not: the difficulty of existing as a black woman in a white patriarchy—a difficulty white people and black men compound by a-witnessing black women's experiences and personhood.

Nancy is anti-witnessed not only by white men, such as Mr Stovall and the jailor, but also by white women, such as Mrs Compson. In the story (as in reality), white women join with white men to subjugate black women instead of uniting with black women over shared patriarchal oppression. When Nancy fears that Jesus will murder her, Mrs Compson does not empathize with her but expresses resentment that Mr Compson will leave her side to take Nancy home. "Is her safety more precious to you than mine?" (293), she asks her husband. When Nancy begs to sleep on the floor of the Compson children's bedroom rather than to be killed in her cabin, Mrs Compson coldly replies: "I can't have Negroes sleeping in the bedrooms" (299). In posing such a question and making such a statement, Mrs Compson a-witnesses Nancy's fear and co-optively anti-witnesses her jeopardy, acting as if she is somehow more at risk than Nancy is. Mrs Compson evokes those white mistresses of plantations who would a-witness black bondswomen's trauma and aggressively anti-witness their pain when white masters expressed too much "interest" in (or raped) them.[11] Mr Compson has not assaulted Nancy, but she has been mistreated by other (white) men. Rather than expressing concern or offering to help, Mrs Compson aligns with the white patriarchy to a-witness Nancy's trauma and redirect attention to herself. In doing so, she exposes what Ayesha Hardison identifies as "white women's investment in whiteness, which makes them complicit in black women's multivalent oppression" (87). In an effort to align with white privilege and power, Mrs Compson anti-witnesses Nancy.

Nancy is also anti-witnessed by black men in the story. Jesus bemoans the fact that white men have more power and privilege than black men do. As a black man, Jesus "can't hang around a white man's kitchen, but a white man can hang around" his (292). White men can usurp black men's goods but not vice versa. Because Jesus makes this statement while discussing the paternity of Nancy's unborn child (292), his complaint has a gendered charge: While a black man could be lynched for looking at a white woman (White 177), white men were free not only to enter black men's kitchens but also to impregnate black women—as Mr Stovall has Nancy. A grim irony exists in Jesus' phrasing: while a white man can "hang around" a black man's kitchen (or woman) without incident, a black man could be hanged for "hanging around" a white man's. This racial double standard enrages Jesus. However, when Jesus links the word "kitchen" to "woman" and refers to both in the possessive (e.g., a "white man's kitchen"), he treats Nancy, women, and black women in particular as white men treat him (and all black men): as property. Through such scenes, Denton argues, Faulkner positions Nancy as a "double victim of white patriarchy and black males" (105). Nancy witnesses this double victimhood when she tells Quentin that she is "nothing but a nigger" (293), oppressed by white people and black men alike.[12] However, the other characters do not acknowledge Nancy's double marginalization. When she witnesses to Quentin, he gets up and leaves the room (293). The others either a-witness or aggressively anti-witness her experience or both.

Faulkner's characters consistently a-witness Nancy's experiences, as she attempts to witness primarily. Nancy tells Quentin that being treated like a "nigger" is "not her fault" (293). She is aggressively anti-witnessed anyway. She testifies to her marginalization, trauma, and fear by explaining her situation and seeking assistance from white people. They a-witness her plight. Even the Compson children—Quentin, Caddy, and Jason Jr.—a-witness Nancy's suffering. When, for instance, Nancy and the children walk down the street, she pretends to speak to Mr Compson as if he is present, though he is not. The reader understands what the children do not: Nancy fears Jesus is waiting for her in the dark and believes he is less likely to jump out and attack her if he thinks Mr Compson is with her. Nancy knows the power of white patriarchal authority and attempts to use it to protect herself from Jesus when the actual white patriarch, Mr Compson, has declined to do so. Caddy finds it odd that Nancy is talking as if "father was here too" (301), but none of the children cease bickering long enough to engage Nancy's fear or to ask her why she is speaking to someone who is not there (301). The children's a-witnessing of Nancy's behavior could be dismissed as childhood innocence, but it also betrays what Charles Mills calls "white ignorance," when white privilege insulates white people from having to confront the race-related traumas and oppressions nonwhite people face (22). The children's a-witnessing of Nancy's psychic state reveals how white privilege empowers white people, from an early age, to ignore and negate the experiences of nonwhite people.

"That Evening Sun" also demonstrates that such a-witnessing does not diminish as white children grow older but develops into habits that are passed on to future generations. Mr Compson a-witnesses Nancy's trauma and then teaches his children to do likewise. Although Mr Compson initially shows kindness to Nancy by offering to walk her home, he does not witness her trauma secondarily. He repudiates her. Four times, Mr Compson calls Nancy's fear of being murdered "nonsense" (307, 308). When he cannot convince her that her terror is unwarranted, he stops talking to her, rounds up his children, and leaves (308). In doing so, he a-witnesses Nancy's trauma and instructs his children to do the same: "Ah, damnation," he grumbles, "Come along, chillen. It's past bedtime" (308). When Caddy—more attentive to Nancy's pain than her father or brothers—asks Mr Compson, "What's going to happen?," he dismisses Nancy's fear and his daughter's question: "Nothing" (308). When Caddy asks if Jesus is hiding in the ditch, her father asserts: "He's not there … He went away a long time ago" (309). Mr Compson negatively a-witnesses Nancy's distress and trains his children to do the same. In insisting Jesus will never return, he also perpetuates the anti-black-male stereotype that men leave black women and do not come back. Mr Compson has no way of knowing where Jesus is. He simply assumes black men do not return to their wives and that Jesus is thus not close enough to pose a threat to Nancy. Black women, such as Nancy, who question Mr Compson's judgment are a-witnessed and abandoned. Girls, such as Caddy, who distrust his assessment are also a-witnessed: They are told they are wrong and to be quiet. The Compson children thus learn to align with the white patriarch against the terrified black woman. They a-witness Nancy, abjuring her concerns and leaving her to face catastrophe alone.

Some critics contend that Mr Compson's decision to leave Nancy is justified. In taking his children home at night, he does not a-witness Nancy's trauma but acts logically since her peril is imagined, not actual (Lee 49). Faulkner's story suggests otherwise. Jesus poses a physical threat: He keeps a razor blade on a string around his neck to use as a weapon (295). Mr Compson has told his children "not to have anything to do with Jesus" and will not allow him near their house (290). Mr Compson may simply be a racist who does not want his children to interact with a black person who does not serve them (as Nancy does). He may also realize that Jesus poses harm and thus separates his children from him in an effort to keep them safe. Even when Mr Compson tells Nancy that she has nothing to fear from Jesus, he never says Jesus is not dangerous. He argues instead that Jesus is not close enough to hurt her. The implication is that, if Jesus were nearby, Nancy would be at risk.

The story's title also suggests imminent death. "That Evening Sun," is taken from the song, "Saint Louis Blues,"[13] which begins: "Lordy, how I hate to see that evening sun go down" (qtd. in Bennett 339). Ken Bennett explains that the evening sun is a trope in black religious music, such as "Saint Louis Blues," portending death and judgment (340). Though the song appears only in the story's title and is not referred to again in the text, it frames the story's tone and substance. Both the singer of "Saint Louis Blues" and Nancy fear the evening sun, which foretells death and destruction. Within the story, when the Compson family wonders why Nancy has not yet returned to her cabin, Caddy suggests: "Maybe she's waiting for Jesus to come and take her home" (293). The "Jesus" Caddy refers to is Nancy's husband, not Jesus Christ, but her phrasing evokes such black spirituals as "Swing Low, Sweet Chariot," whose lyrics, "Coming for to carry me home" refer to death (i.e., when Jesus Christ takes the speaker home to heaven). Symbolically, as established through Faulkner's title and Caddy's comment, when the Compsons leave Nancy's cabin after the sun has set, they abandon her to death.

Nancy's wailing can even be read as singing the "Saint Louis Blues." To witness her trauma, she sings the blues that foreshadow death. In dismissing her song and leaving her to die, the Compsons a-witness the traumatic narrative in Nancy's song. Her wailing also exhibits hyperarousal, the "persistent expectation of danger" that plagues those with posttraumatic stress disorder (Herman 35). During a traumatic experience, Herman explains, "the human system of self-preservation" enters a state of permanent panic, as if "danger might return at any moment" (35). As a result, trauma victims are often hyperactive and hypersensitive (20). They startle easily (35) and scream and weep hysterically (20). Since Nancy exhibits these symptoms, she can be read as traumatized—both by the threat Jesus poses and by the anti-witnessing she confronts when attempting to witness primarily. (The more Nancy is anti-witnessed, the louder she wails.) Instead of dismissing Nancy's trauma, characters and critics should witness her blues secondarily and communally.

Because Nancy resurfaces as a character in Faulkner's *Requiem for a Nun* (1950), some conclude that Mr Compson was right: Nancy's fears were unfounded, and Jesus never murdered her (Kuyk, Kuyk, and Miller 34). These critics, however, overlook that Faulkner's timelines do not always cohere. While the same characters appear throughout his works, chronology from text to text is inconsistent. A character may die in one work and reappear in another. Quentin, for example, kills himself at age nineteen in *The Sound and the Fury* and narrates "That Evening Sun" at age twenty-four. Accordingly, Nancy could have been killed at the end of (or immediately following) "That Evening Sun" and still appear, alive and well, in *Requiem for a Nun*. Chronological discrepancies in Faulkner's canon may reveal more about his desire to return to certain characters and spend more time with their storylines than about whether they live or die. Critics who negatively a-witness Nancy's fear, simply because Mr Compson dismisses it as "nonsense" (307,

308), risk accepting the uninformed viewpoint of a white patriarch over a black woman witnessing her pain. Numerous contemporary studies reveal that, when women describe physical and psychic pain to men in authority, their experience is ignored and negated (Epstein, Fasler, Kieslel). The a-witnessing of women's pain is compounded by race: black women are less likely to be believed than white women, especially when they describe pain to white men (Chawla, Lawson, Spataro, Thorbecke). To counteract such racial and gendered a-witnessing, readers can choose to believe black female speakers, such as Nancy, when they insist they are in pain.

Mr and Mrs Compson anti-witness Nancy and encourage their children to follow suit. Caddy, however, deviates from her parents' model and begins to witness where and when they do not. Caddy engages Nancy's narrative by posing questions. When Nancy tells Jesus her "watermelon" did not come off his "vine," Caddy attempts to understand: "What vine?" (292). She is ignored. She persists in asking: "Are you asleep, Nancy?" (296), "Can you see us, Nancy?" (297), "Why is Nancy afraid of Jesus?" (299), and "What're we going to do?" (301). Caddy is inquisitive, but her questions also reveal an interest in Nancy, a desire to understand (and perhaps to witness secondarily) what the terrified woman is trying to communicate. In ignoring Caddy's questions and commanding her to be silent (309), her parents a-witness her. Caddy learns to stop asking questions and resumes a-witnessing with the rest of her family. Such textual moments reveal how the white patriarchy (embodied in the Compsons) silences white girls, such as Caddy, alongside black women, such as Nancy, inhibiting dual-witnessing. The Compsons' a-witnessing of Caddy does not have the same negative effects as their abandoning of Nancy. Caddy, though female, still has white and class privilege. Thus, she is not as marginalized as Nancy, and her family's a-witnessing of her does not result in her death (as it likely does for Nancy). In *The Sound and the Fury,* however, Caddy, like Nancy, will also become pregnant by a man who is not her husband. As a vulnerable young woman, she will also be anti-witnessed by a white capitalistic patriarchy. She may not be murdered (as Nancy presumably is), but she does go nearly mad with grief. Through Caddy and Nancy's narratives, Faulkner underscores the damage white patriarchal anti-witnessing wreaks against women and girls in general and black women in particular.

In returning to Nancy's story as an adult, Quentin may attempt to witness secondarily and secondarily by proxy what he a-witnessed as a child. He finds he cannot. Whatever Nancy was trying to witness registers in Quentin's memory only as wailing: "It was not singing and it was not crying," he recollects. "It was like singing and it wasn't like singing, like the sounds that Negroes make" (296). Even so, in recalling Nancy's story (and what her wailing both did and did not sound like), Quentin proves a better secondary witness than the story's other characters. Denton argues that the "sound's ambiguity" of Nancy's wailing "echoes the cultural fact that whites such as the Compsons are often dismissive of"—or negatively a-witness—"black concerns and lack the understanding"—or commitment—"to decode black emotive energies" (102). Quentin works against this tendency when he acknowledges, first, that Nancy has witnessed something and, second, that he cannot understand what she has witnessed. He also recognizes that Nancy's wailing sounds like that of other black people, an allusion to the fact that many African Americans witness their oppression, whether or not white people engage it. Moreover, by ending the story openly (we do not learn what happens to Nancy), Quentin ensures that he does not co-optively anti-witness Nancy's narrative: he bears witness only to what he can remember. This approach separates Quentin from the rest of the Compsons, who refuse to witness dually and communally. Caddy starts well by asking questions, but she does not follow through. Jason Jr. either a-witnesses Nancy or aggressively anti-witnesses her when her terror threatens to ruin his childhood "fun" (306). Mr and Mrs. Compson consistently anti-witness. Quentin stands apart in returning to Nancy's story in order to attempt to witness secondarily what he once did not. Through his example, Faulkner may encourage readers to re-engage (in order to witness secondarily) narratives we too have previously anti-witnessed.

Faulkner prompts readers to engage his work multiple times in order to understand it. When an interviewer asked him: "Some people say they can't understand your writing, even after they've read it two or three times. What approach would you suggest for them?" Faulkner replied, "Read it four times" (qtd. in Rieger). Faulkner's retort may seem egotistical, but he also takes his own advice. As a writer, he returns to the same characters and storylines, perhaps in an attempt to witness what he previously has not. For example, Faulkner originally wrote "That Evening Sun" from Nancy's perspective but revised the story before publication to be narrated by Quentin. Faulkner's decision to write in Quentin's voice instead of Nancy's could be read as appropriatively anti-witnessing Nancy's narrative by selecting a white man to tell her story instead of letting her do so herself. However, following his struggle to witness Dilsey Gibson in *The Sound and the Fury* and the "womanshenegro" in *Light in August,* Faulkner may have realized that, as a white Southern male, he could not witness secondarily by proxy Afra-American characters and experiences. In "That Evening Sun," Faulkner may thus have attempted to witness instead the damages white people inflict on black women when they a-witness Afra-American trauma and personhood. Denton suggests that, in writing in Quentin's voice versus Nancy's, Faulkner "positions himself as an outside author . . . who is unknowing but sympathetic" (102). He may ask readers to follow his example: to approach the text, like the adult Quentin, as one who does not fully understand but would like to, who is willing to dual-witness what once registered only as wailing. The succeeding question is: How? How does one cross identity construct and experience to witness dually and communally? Faulkner's *Absalom, Absalom!* provides an answer.

Absalom, Absalom!: Learning to Dual-Witness

Faulkner's propensity to (anti-)witness race and gender shifts in *Absalom, Absalom!*, a novel that chronicles the rise and fall of the Sutpen dynasty and the central cause of that fall: the murder of partially-black Charles Bon by his white half-brother, Henry Sutpen, to prevent Charles from marrying their white sister, Judith. Like Faulkner's other fiction, *Absalom, Absalom!* explores constructions of race and gender, the crumbling of the American South, and the intrusion of the past on the present. Like Joe Christmas, Charles Bon is killed only when white characters determine his blackness, and, like Faulkner's earlier work, *Absalom, Absalom!* presents the reactions white characters have to black characters, suggesting that this text may witness race from a white and male perspective, reducing the novel's ability to speak to the complexities of race and gender in American literature and history.

Absalom, Absalom! differs, however, in teaching readers, independent of race and gender, how to engage another's testimony, that is, how to dual-witness through Venn liminality. While "That Evening Sun" improves upon Faulkner's earlier work in witnessing white patriarchal America's tendency to a-witness Afra-American trauma and oppression, *Absalom, Absalom!* goes farther, teaching readers how to dual-witness across race, gender, and experience. As if to emphasize this reciprocity, Faulkner does not select a single, reliable narrator to impart *Absalom, Absalom!*'s plot. Instead, concealed traumas and hidden histories surface out of a series of intergenerational, interregional conversations, held between Henry and Judith's aunt, Miss Rosa; her Harvard-bound neighbor, Quentin; and his college roommate, Shreve. This narrative structure—wherein a story is witnessed through dialogue— marks a communal form of witnessing into which the reader is also invited. Even the use of Quentin Compson as the primary perspective of the novel transforms *Absalom, Absalom!* into a secondary witness to both *The Sound and the Fury* and "That Evening Sun," in which Quentin is also a main character. This intertextuality implies that Faulkner's modeled dual-witnessing is not contained within a single work but extends out of a given novel into the histories of other narratives, fostering a mutual conversation in which the reader participates. In this light, Faulkner's novel models the process of dual-witnessing, teaching readers—through the (counter)examples of its protagonists—how to respond to others' testimony.

Absalom, Absalom! explores how racism is learned and disseminated in order to testify to the devastation racial prejudice wreaks. From the start, the novel exposes how the national ethos of the American Dream (symbolized in Sutpen's grand design) instills racism and classism in those white adherents willing to subjugate nonwhites to secure their own prosperity. The novel's antihero, Thomas Sutpen, learns to associate black subjugation with white upward mobility. When he watches "the country flatten ... out ... with good roads and fields and niggers working in the fields" (182), Sutpen correlates social and commercial progress (e.g., roads, towns, and cotton fields) with institutionalized racism ("niggers working in the fields"). When he observes wealthy white men—"with a different look in the face from the [poor] mountain men" among whom he was raised—sit "in fine clothes" upon "fine horses" to watch the slaves work (182), he learns the "difference not only between white men and black ones but ... between white men and white men" (183). Sutpen discerns that white privilege, epitomized in the finely dressed white men and their finer white plantations, is rooted in the systemic racism that sustains slavery. Finally, Sutpen assimilates intersecting racist and classist hierarchies when he realizes that wealthy white men (by virtue of their class) exert power over impoverished white men, who (by virtue of their race) wield power over black men. (Women do not enter into Sutpen's consciousness). At this point, Sutpen embraces racism and classism, resolving to pursue his model of the American Dream so that he may attain the status of those wealthy white landowners who subjugate poor whites and nonwhites alike.

Sutpen's determination to rise above others begins when, as a boy, he is told by a senior house slave, wearing "better clothes" than he, that he cannot enter a plantation by the front door but must use the servants' back entrance (186). Sutpen, whose racism and classism are already entrenched, is doubly affronted by his refused entry. In his view, a black man has thwarted racial hierarchies by asserting authority over a white caller and has upset class hierarchies by appearing better dressed than his visitor. In recalling this event, Sutpen cannot remember what message he wished to convey to the plantation's owner. What he takes from the encounter is a mounting racism against all "monkey nigger[s]" (186) and a corresponding obsession to become wealthy himself so he can never again feel marginalized by those he believes exist beneath him in the social order. After this perceived insult, Sutpen flees to the West Indies, where he secures his fortune through unpaid black labor (189). The novel reveals the racism and classism implicit in Sutpen's interpretation of the American Dream, which teaches him, first, that the wealthy are superior to the poor, as whites are to nonwhites, and, second, that an expedient way for white people to find success is to subjugate poor and nonwhites.

Absalom, Absalom! does not celebrate the bigotry implicit in Sutpen's Dream but testifies instead to how prejudice harms not only those discriminated against but also those who perpetuate discrimination. In the case above, Sutpen becomes the overseer of a sugar plantation, subdues a slave revolt, and marries the landowner's daughter, who bears his son, Charles Bon (212). Sutpen's design appears complete, but his racism undercuts his prosperity. When he discovers that his wife and son have "negro blood," he "repudiates" them, preferring to dismantle his dynasty than to allow biraciality to contaminate his Dream (305). Sutpen next uproots one-hundred slaves to America, raises a plantation in Mississippi (Sutpen's Hundred), and becomes a member of the Southern aristocracy. When his new white wife gives birth to their son and daughter, Henry and Judith, Sutpen has twice achieved his grand design, first as a plantation owner in the West Indies and second as one in Mississippi. Sutpen's racism, however, threatens his sovereignty. When Bon returns decades later to court Judith, Sutpen induces Henry to kill his biracial brother in order to protect the white Sutpens from miscegenation and incest (216). In doing so, Sutpen cements his family's downfall: Henry runs away, Judith resolves never to marry, and his dynasty dies with Bon (220). In this way, *Absalom, Absalom!* reveals how racism both sustains and spoils Sutpen's American Dream. Racial prejudice may help Sutpen's design flourish (the patriarch uses slave labor twice to erect his plantations), but it thwarts Sutpen's mission when his fear of miscegenation wrecks what he achieved.

In addition to narrating the rise and fall of Thomas Sutpen, *Absalom, Absalom!* speaks to the rise and fall of the American South, suggesting that the racism that once allowed the region to prosper (through institutionalized slavery) also brought about its downfall by instigating the conflicts that led to the Civil War and the collapse of white Southern standards of living. However well-intentioned, this outlook has two fundamental problems. First, the stance implies that racism must inherently end of its own accord and should be allowed to do so uninterrupted. Against this reasoning, one may query: How much trauma must nonwhites endure (and for how long) before racism works against its perpetrators too? Historically, the answer has been "too much" and "for too long." Second, the implication that racism destroys those who perpetuate it continues to align the reader with a white male and racist perspective. Throughout *Absalom, Absalom!,* white characters discuss the fate of Thomas Sutpen. In these conversations, the viewpoints of Sutpen's nonwhite slaves, his first wife, and his murdered son are elided, except when appropriated to illuminate the role of Sutpen as white patriarch. In this way, Faulkner a-witnesses and co-optively anti-witnesses his nonwhite characters' lives and experiences to speak from a white androcentric perspective.

Despite *Absalom, Absalom'*s tendency to (anti-)witness race from a white and male point of view, the novel's message that racism is both learned and destructive is effective, as is—in keeping with *Light in August*—the text's treatment of race as socially constructed. Throughout *Absalom, Absalom!,* Faulkner's narrators repeatedly testify to how those in power (i.e., wealthy white patriarchs) create strict racial distinctions in order to justify continued prejudice. Nowhere is this point more clearly evinced than in the white characters' fear of miscegenation. Sutpen's concern over mixing races disrupts the racial hierarchies upon which he builds his dynasty: if he cannot decipher who is white from who is not, then he cannot determine whom to step on and over in his pursuit of the American Dream. Accordingly, Bon's race becomes the novel's central "trauma" that must be witnessed by multiple speakers. The revelation that arises from these conversations—that Henry murders Bon not only because he is his brother but also because he is black (286)—is treated by *Absalom, Absalom'*s white narrators as so momentous that it derails several of them. Quentin Compson's discomfort with miscegenation (and incest) shatters him completely (386), precipitating his suicide in *The Sound and the Fury.* Such instances reveal the degree to which miscegenation threatens *Absalom, Absalom!'*s white men as well as the effort these patriarchs devote to maintaining racial distinctions and hierarchies.

Although such scenes speak to the social construction of race, they again a-witness and co-optively anti-witness nonwhite and nonmale perspectives by narrating from a white androcentric point of view. *Absalom, Absalom!* reveals how anti-black racism also destroys white men (exemplified both in Thomas Sutpen and those "readers" like Quentin who are both enthralled and devastated by Sutpen's chronicle). The novel does not witness—except in the incidence of Bon's death—how racism harms people of color. As Barbara Ladd attests, Bon "never speaks except through the mouths of those [white men] who tell his story" and thus has "no identity independent of their projection" (535). Such textual a-witnessing and co-optive anti-witnessing, Ladd recognizes, "leads the reader to ask not only who or what Charles Bon was . . . but . . . who and what the [white] speakers are with respect to the Charles Bon they construct" (535–36). In other words, Bon's murder teaches us more about those white men who execute and discuss his death than it does about Bon himself.

Absalom, Absalom! also omits female perspectives in witnessing the unraveling of Sutpen's design. While Sutpen worries that Judith and Bon's biracial children will pollute his lineage, he does not concern himself with how his daughter may feel to learn that Bon is her biracial half-brother. Nor does he seem to care what Judith will suffer when her (other) brother kills her fiancé. He does not consult with his daughter about these matters but discusses them with white male Henry alone (215–16). As patriarch, Sutpen demonstrates care only for his white, male line. This focus is confirmed when, in a final attempt to maintain his dynasty, an elderly Sutpen impregnates fifteen-year-old Milly and then abandons her when she gives birth to a female child (234). Faulkner does not side with Sutpen, but, in witnessing from his perspective instead of Bon's or Judith's—both of whom disappear entirely after the fateful shooting—*Absalom, Absalom!* aligns with a white, androcentric perspective, a-witnessing the novel's marginalized characters and co-optively anti-witnessing their narratives to speak to white and male incidents.

The novel's overall treatment of marginalized race and gender is still more nuanced than that of *The Sound and the Fury* and *Light in August. Absalom, Absalom!* includes in its character list several nonwhite and nonmale characters. Although not central narrators, these African American women help witness the myriad hardships that accompany double marginalization. When Henry discovers that Bon, like Thomas Sutpen before him, has a biracial ex-wife, he is horrified, not because his future brother-in-law once had a "nigger mistress"—this the racist and sexist Henry expects of every white "man grown up and living in" the American South—but because Bon bothered to marry her at all (87). This moment speaks to the intersecting prejudices women of color face in the antebellum South and America at large.

In considering the "offense" of Bon's previous marriage, Henry begins to categorize "the other sex" into three "sharp divisions" (87), uniting marginalized race, gender, and class into a trifecta of bigotry. The highest class of women, Henry determines, is composed of wealthy white "ladies," the "virgins whom gentlemen someday married" (87). Next, he ranks white "women," the "courtesans to whom they went while on sabbaticals to the cities" (87). Last in line are black "females," those "slave girls and women" to whom white ladies "owed" their virginity (87). According to Henry, white men sleep with—or rape—this third caste of black "females" as a gift to white women in order to preserve the commodity of their virginity. Otherwise, Henry reasons, Southern gentlemen would not be able to resist the temptation of raping white ladies as well. Henry celebrates white men's victimization of black women (in the "present" of leaving white virginity intact), while treating black "females" like animals that "he and his kind" are "forced to pass time away with" (87). Henry continues to demonstrate racism and sexism by bemoaning the "fact" that he and his friends are "forced" to rape women of color, as if white male aggressors are somehow the victims of their own privilege instead of those nonwhite women they assault. In this scene, *Absalom, Absalom!* reveals the myriad oppressions marginalized women face when hierarchies of race, gender, and class combine to victimize.

The fact that Henry freely admits that he and his friends rape black women brings the question of miscegenation to the fore, revealing how sexism intersects with racism. When white men rape black slaves, Henry implies, even if the women become pregnant as a result of their victimization, interracial breeding is not a matter of concern—at least not to the white male attackers. Biracial babies born to slave women increase white landowners' property by creating more slaves. Biracial babies born to white Southern ladies (as would be the case if Judith and Bon copulated) topple racial and gendered hierarchies and, through them, the dynasty of white men like Sutpen. By way of example, Sutpen's biracial daughter, Clytie, lives her life at Sutpen's Hundred as a perceived threat to no one. Since Clytie cannot inherit Sutpen's dynasty due to her race and gender, she does not imperil his design. Although *Absalom, Absalom!* presents these ruminations through Henry's white and male perspective, the novel—in explicating Sutpen's racist, sexist thoughts—bears witness to the difficulties nonwhite American women have faced.

Further evidence that *Absalom, Absalom!* witnesses women more successfully than Faulkner's previous work is that the novel treats its female characters not only as victims of a patriarchal system but also as powerful in their own right, despite the marginalizing structures that work against them. *Absalom, Absalom!* is the only one of Faulkner's novels to offer its readers a strong and sustained female narrator.[14] Henry and Judith Sutpen's aunt, Rosa Coldfield, spends the first half of the novel witnessing to Quentin not only the story of her own life but that of Thomas and Henry Sutpen and Charles Bon as well. In this way, the narratives of three men are shaped and shared by a woman—a reversal (and hierarchical upheaval) of Faulkner's usual process in which white men co-opt and (anti-)witness the lives and experiences of women. Nor does Rosa witness her story in a void; she summons the white male Quentin to witness her tale secondarily. Rosa upsets patriarchal dynamics by imparting a story predominately about white men to another white man.

Absalom, Absalom! also witnesses how women of color can subvert racist and patriarchal power dynamics and shape white men's narratives. Sutpen's biracial daughter, Clytie, upholds her familial claim and personhood by occupying Sutpen's plantation longer than any other character. In this way, the non-white daughter of a slave subverts race, gender, and class conventions by becoming, if not owner, overseer of one of the grandest estates in Mississippi. Furthermore, when Rosa visits Sutpen's Hundred after Bon's murder, Clytie thwarts the social codes that dictate that slaves must address white people as "Master" or "Mistress." She calls Miss Rosa "Rosa" to her face, blocking the white woman's entrance to her house (111). In doing so, Clytie crosses racial divisions to relate to Rosa as a woman and an equal (actually as a superior, in forbidding Rosa access to Sutpen's plantation). Finally, in *Absalom, Absalom!*'s closing pages, Clytie burns Sutpen's Hundred to the ground, revealing how a triply marginalized black slave woman can bring a fiery end to a white man's dynasty (299).

The novel portrays Sutpen's biracial ex-wife, Eulalia Bon, as equally savvy. Quentin and Shreve surmise that Eulalia purposefully sends Charles to court Judith, knowing that Sutpen's fear of his son and daughter's miscegenation will cause him to destroy his design. In this way, Eulalia wreaks revenge for Sutpen's original abandonment of her and Bon, as the racism that led Sutpen to desert his first family now destroys his second one. In a reversal of racial and gendered hierarchies, a woman of color uses a white man's bigotry against him to destroy all he holds dear. One possible reading of Eulalia's action is that Faulkner's powerful women are aggressively anti-witnessed as conniving and criminal. If Quentin and Shreve are correct that Eulalia sends Bon to Judith to ruin Sutpen, then Bon's mother exhibits no more concern for her son (and how he feels about his ordained courtship) than Sutpen does for his daughter (and how Judith feels about the identity of her chosen partner). Eulalia demonstrates so little care for Bon that, in plotting to ruin Sutpen, she orchestrates her son's murder. Whether Eulalia's agency is read as malicious or not, the power she wields as architect of Sutpen's downfall is evident. And since the racist white patriarch is clearly more malevolent than his ex-wife, Eulalia's toppling of intersecting racial and gendered hierarchies does not register as exceedingly offensive.

In keeping with its (anti-)witnessing of marginalized race, *Absalom, Absalom!* does not sustain its rich portrayal of women. Even if Quentin and Shreve rightly speculate that Eulalia orchestrates Sutpen's downfall, the book is not about her as a woman of color but about the white man she plots to destroy. We learn nothing of Eulalia's life before or after Sutpen; she exists merely to explain how he fails. The same is true of Clytie, who, compared to Bon, occupies hardly any narrative space. As Philip Weinstein notes, Sutpen's biracial daughter is "sparingly represented" (*What Else* 52). Her status is elided to make room for her white male family. We also learn nothing of

Clytie's mother, who is not even given a name but is identified exclusively by her race and gender as the "negress" (272). Charles Bon's first wife, the "octoroon," is also defined by her biraciality. Compare these women's namelessness to the elaborate names given to their sons and husbands: Charles Bon's son, Charles Etienne de Saint Velery, is married to a "negro wife," who, in contrast to her husband, is defined by her blackness and womanhood and her relative position to a man (as his wife) (306). The narrative gaps written around nonwhite women suggest that Faulkner cannot enter fully enough into black and female perspectives to witness out of them. Despite its proliferation of women of color, *Absalom, Absalom!* still uses black and female characters to speak to the standpoints of white men.

One potential reading of Faulkner's anti-witnessing of his nonwhite and nonmale characters is that the author, as a white male author, wished to avoid co-optively anti-witnessing his marginalized characters by presuming to speak out of their unique and foreign (to him) perspectives. He thus kept his focus on white Southern men, hoping to witness how racism destroys even those members of society who perpetuate it. The irony of this decision (if this is in fact what happened) is that in attempting not to anti-witness marginalized characters, Faulkner's novels do so anyway, both by a-witnessing marginalized characters and perspectives and also by appropriating nonwhite and nonmale speakers and stories to testify to those tribulations faced by the most privileged members of society.

Nevertheless, a benefit to reading *Absalom, Absalom!* is that, even when it fails to witness primarily and secondarily by proxy, the novel still prompts readers to witness secondarily. Faulkner's earlier fiction speaks to the treatment of race and gender in the American South. *Absalom, Absalom!* builds upon this foundation (and then enriches it), by passing its authoritative voice over to its readers, prompting us to witness where and when the text does not. In this light, the novel can be read as a story not only about race and gender but also, as David Minter recognizes, about the "circumstances of its own telling" (98). I would add that *Absalom, Absalom!* transcends even the "circumstances of its own telling" (or primary witnessing) to model and impart, first, the process of reading (or secondary witnessing) and, second, how intersecting practices of telling and reading (i.e., primary and secondary witnessing) can work together in dual-witnessing.

An irony of *Absalom, Absalom!* is that a novel that teaches us how to read (or witness secondarily) is itself difficult to read. Although Faulkner pronounced his work "the best novel . . . written by an American" (qtd. in Gray *Life* 204), others appraise the text as "overwhelmingly complicated" and "unintelligible" (Sullivan). *Absalom, Absalom!* is indeed a challenging text, but

Faulkner does not make it complex for complexity's sake. Instead, the book's inscrutability underscores the near-impossibility of entering into another's testimony. However necessary theorists may deem primary witnessing, they also stress the effort required to convey one's history through language. The same can be argued for those who receive another's narrative: if primary witnesses struggle to speak the unspeakable, secondary witnesses endeavor to comprehend the incomprehensible. Fittingly, even as *Absalom, Absalom!*'s primary witnesses seek engaged listeners to testify to, they distrust their hearers' ability to witness secondarily. Rosa repeatedly interrupts her account to ask Quentin, "*Can you see?*" (136), exposing her fear that she is testifying to an addressee who cannot "see"—or witness—her past. Quentin exhibits a similar anxiety when he—in answer to Shreve's edict: "Tell me about the South"—imparts Rosa's tale, in which he now figures (290). As the roommates work through Sutpen's decline, Quentin doubts that Shreve, a Canadian, can ever witness secondarily Southern catastrophes. He dismisses his friend's attempts to engage his narrative, proclaiming, "You cant understand it. You would have to be born there" (290): only Southerners can work through their history; outsiders cannot witness what they were not born into.

If Rosa and Quentin question their listeners' capacity to witness secondarily, how can *Absalom, Absalom!* model dual-witnessing? First, as stated above, the novel highlights the difficulty of dual-witnessing, as even those who wish to witness can fail in the attempt. Second, when Rosa and Quentin's addressees cannot "see" or "understand," the role of secondary witness falls to their readership. This prospect is evinced in the "you" of both Rosa's "*can* you *see?*" (136) and Quentin's "*you* cant understand" (290). In both instances, an inclusive "you" extends out of and beyond the narrators' listeners to include those readers who also struggle to engage Faulkner's narrative. In this manner, Faulkner offers readers the opportunity to witness where and when his novel does not. To accentuate this process, he discloses the Sutpens' trauma in *Absalom, Absalom!*'s first chapter. As early as page 6, Quentin divulges that the dynasty collapses when Henry murders Judith's fiancé. What prompts Henry to shoot Charles remains veiled, but the key players and events are identified from the start. In structuring his novel thus, Faulkner encourages readers not to read passively for information but to enter actively into a text, so we may witness secondarily those facts we believe we already know.

Critics have not yet focused on the mutuality inherent in *Absalom, Absalom!*'s dual-witnessing, but they have discussed Faulkner's characters' compulsion to witness primarily. Faulkner underlines this importance when he maintains that "every character in [my] book is telling"—or witnessing— "his biography" (qtd. in Cullick 48). In *Absalom, Absalom!*, the drive to witness is illustrated most clearly in Rosa, who testifies to the Sutpens' tragedies as well as to her own traumas entangled in their history. When she recounts the details of Bon's murder, for instance, Rosa interrupts her narrative to testify to her shame at having once consented to marry "ogre"-patriarch Thomas Sutpen, only to suffer his subsequent verbal abuse (132). In fact, Rosa reveals, Henry's shooting of Charles does not vex her as much as Sutpen's insult does, an affront so grievous she feels compelled to witness it and so shattering she cannot. Every time Rosa tries to repeat Sutpen's *"bad outrageous words"* (136), she becomes traumatically constricted, turning the burden of witnessing over to her listener. *"I will . . . let you be the judge"* (134–35), Rosa concedes—a "you" that includes both her immediate addressee, Quentin, and the novel's potential secondary witness, the reader.

Such textual moments underscore the significance of dual-witnessing in *Absalom, Absalom!*. In the scene above, Rosa sends for a secondary witness to help her work through her narrative. Even if readers overlook Rosa's need for an addressee, we find ourselves already allied with her selected witness, Quentin, who also initially fails to see why Rosa has called him to her. "'Why tell me about it?'" Quentin wonders. "'What is it to me?'" (6–7). After listening to Rosa, he comes to appreciate the urgency of his role. "If she merely wanted her story told," Quentin reflects, she "would not have needed to call in anybody" (6). That Rosa invites Quentin to hear her story betrays her need for an active listener. Perhaps for this reason Faulkner calls their conversation not just a day of telling but also a day "of listening" (23), of relationality. As Quentin begins to apprehend his role as secondary witness, *Absalom, Absalom!* offers its readers this same opportunity: to realize both the necessity of dual-witnessing and the potential to become secondary witnesses.

Absalom, Absalom! does not claim dual-witnessing is simple or easy but indicates that Miss Rosa and Quentin are right to interrogate their addressees' engagement, as even receptive listeners find secondary witnessing difficult, requiring time, energy, and emotional effort. Quentin often only "half-listens" to Rosa, preferring to let her voice "vanish" (8) than to attend to her "grim, haggard" speech (7): He cannot sustain the empathic attention secondary witnessing demands. Quentin, though, does not abandon secondary witnessing altogether. He remains enmeshed in Rosa's account, envisioning his own version of the Sutpens' demise. Even as he tunes Rosa out, Quentin pictures Henry storming into Judith's room and declaring that she cannot marry Charles, as he has killed him (114). Lost in thought, Quentin continuously asks Rosa to repeat herself (128). This exchange marks an odd instance of dual-witnessing: On the one hand, Quentin does not secondarily at all; he does not even pay attention. On the other, as potential secondary witness,

Quentin enters so deeply into Rosa's reminiscence that he can no longer listen as he once did. Her chronicle has taken on a vitality to which Quentin now belongs, and he will not disregard this new, incarnate testimony to focus on Rosa's other ramblings.

In trying to witness Miss Rosa's testimony secondarily, Quentin risks anti-witnessing it by co-opting her narrative as his own. Still, the fact that Quentin interrupts both his dream vision and Rosa's tale to pose clarification questions indicates that, even as he flounders, he still attempts to witness secondarily. Quentin may not be an ideal listener, but he is not a failure either. Whether equipped or not to serve as secondary witness, he takes up Rosa's mantle and continues to work through her narrative with his room-mate, Shreve. The fact that Rosa and Quentin's witnessing does not conclude with their "day of listening" suggests that the undertaking cannot be realized hastily. As Rosa and Quentin's and then Quentin and Shreve's interactions demonstrate, dual-witnessing is a prolonged, painstaking process.

In Quentin and Shreve's case, Shreve facilitates Quentin's psychic develop-ment by prompting his roommate to elucidate where he comes from geo-graphically but also—as Quentin interprets the question—psychologically. By asking his friend to explain his feelings about the South, Shreve (offering himself as a secondary witness) invites Quentin to witness primarily his own repressed trauma (i.e., his mutual love of and hate for his homeland). When Quentin offers Rosa's story in answer to Shreve's question, he shifts from Rosa's secondary witness to her secondary witness by proxy, testifying on her behalf. Shreve's directive "Tell me about the South" (178) enables Quentin to work through the Sutpens' history as a secondary witness by proxy while testifying primarily to his own feelings about the South.

Possibly because Shreve (the listener) initiates dual-witnessing with Quentin (the speaker), the roommates at first appear more successful at collective sharing than Miss Rosa and Quentin. Quentin was a reluctant secondary witness; Shreve is a willing participant. The roommates' interaction thus appears more reciprocal than Quentin and Rosa's, in which he tunes her out to visualize his own version of her story. When Quentin and Shreve dual-witness, they enter mutually into their narrative, so that, as Faulkner writes, "either of them" could witness the Sutpens' history, and, "in a sense, both" do: "both thinking as one . . . the two of them creating between them" (243). Here, the roommates transcend the physical space of their bedroom to enter the psychic space of dual-witnessing. Faulkner writes: "Now neither of them was there. They were both in Carolina . . . forty-six years ago, and . . . both of them were Henry Sutpen and both . . . were Bon, compounded each of both yet either neither" (280). This scene marks a prime example of dual-witnessing, as Quentin and Shreve enter into each other's experiences (and those of Henry and Bon) without sacrificing their own alterities.

Through dual-witnessing with Shreve, Quentin comes to understand the Sutpens in a way he never could with Miss Rosa. "It seemed to Quentin," Faulkner writes, that, with Shreve, "he could actually see" the figures in Rosa's story (154). Through dual-witnessing with a receptive listener, Quentin begins not only to fantasize about the Sutpens (as he did before) but also to enter into their history, enabling their narrative to come to life for him in a way it previously did not. "He could see it," the narrator reflects: "[H]e might even have been there. Then he thought *No. if I had been there I could not have seen it this plain*" (155). Quentin's recognition that he must both engage with the story and preserve some distance from it makes him a more successful secondary witness for, as he implies, if he had personally suffered with the Sutpens, he would not now have the perspective that allows him to witness their history without co-opting it. As Joseph Urgo and Noel Polk argue in *Reading Faulkner: Absalom, Absalom!*, only when Quentin and Shreve "dissolve the separateness" between them and "become twinned"—that is, when they learn to dual-witness—do they "resolve the crucial question of why Henry killed Bon" (7). Note that we do not learn this information from Henry (who is alive to witness his own story). The Sutpens' history unfolds through the efforts of secondary witnesses, underscoring the power of dual-witnessing.

If Quentin is not an ideal secondary witness to Miss Rosa, neither is Shreve to Quentin. At first, like Quentin before him, Shreve does not listen attentively, and when he does enter into his roommate's narrative, he risks co-opting the speaker's tale. Quentin repeatedly reminds Shreve that Rosa is not a relative but a neighbor: "Miss"—not "Aunt"—Rosa (143–44). Shreve, however, dismisses Rosa's prefix, persistently calling her "Aunt" over Quentin's protests. The difference between "Miss" and "Aunt" may seem minor, but Shreve's inability to address the character properly reveals a corresponding unwillingness to pay attention to her narrative, a form of a-witnessing. Another possibility is that Shreve has entered so deeply into Henry and Bon's story that he feels as if he is one of them. He thus refers to "Aunt" Rosa, as if she—as she is to Henry and Bon—is his own aunt, not a stranger he has never met. Thus, as Faulkner both a-witnesses and co-optively anti-witnesses race and gender, Shreve does with Sutpen's tale: he a-witnesses Rosa by treating her as an "Aunt" instead of a "Miss," and he co-optively anti-witnesses Henry and Bon by confusing himself as secondary witness with those primary witnesses to whom the actual story belongs.

In keeping with his tendency to anti-witness co-optively, once Shreve begins to shape the Sutpens' saga, he also appropriates their narrative, conflating his presumptions with their truths. Shreve deduces, for example, that Sutpen's insult was to propose that he and Miss Rosa copulate premaritally, then wed only if they produced a male heir. Sutpen and Rosa's son, Shreve theorizes, would revive a dynasty cut short when Henry shot Charles, then fled, leaving no one to carry on the family line (234). Shreve also presupposes that Henry killed Charles because he was both Judith's brother and black, though no one can substantiate this conclusion. Shreve's assumptions may be correct (and critics tend to privilege his readings), but nothing Rosa has said definitively supports his conjectures. That Shreve remains convinced he has unearthed the Sutpens' secrets suggests he may cling to the infallibility of his own interpretations. In writing over instead of entering into *Absalom, Absalom!*'s structured blanks, he falters as a secondary witness. Nevertheless, Shreve's coinciding tendencies sometimes to dual-witness and other times to anti-witness do not undermine his overall potential to witness secondarily. His shortcomings expose the fine line between dual- and anti-witnessing. Faulkner may even exhibit these competing responses in a single character to highlight the involvedness dual-witnessing requires. Faulkner never reveals which of Shreve's theories are correct because an aim of reading *Absalom, Absalom!* is not to uncover facts but to wrestle with the process of witnessing.

Faulkner's call to dual-witness is not without personal risk, as sharing in another's traumatic testimony can itself feel traumatizing. *Absalom, Absalom!* captures the incapacitating secondary effects of trauma in Quentin, who finds himself shattered from grappling with the Sutpens' catastrophes. Thus, when Shreve suggests that, having put the Sutpens' trauma to bed, they too retire for the evening, Quentin lies awake, shivering uncontrollably, not only physically cold in his New England dorm room but psychically destabilized from having witnessed trauma secondarily (287–88). Shreve connects Quentin's quivering to his conflicted feelings about the Sutpens in particular and the South in general. Eager to dual-witness (or to pry into Quentin's psyche), Shreve prompts his roommate to explain why he "hate[s] the South" (386). But Quentin is so constricted—both by what he has witnessed in the Sutpens' history and what he fears to examine in his own—that he cannot reply. He dismisses Shreve's inquiry, crying, "I don't hate it," and then repeating internally, "*I dont. I dont! I dont hate it! I dont hate it!*" (386). Quentin's disavowal is his and Faulkner's last word on the subject (at least in this book) as the refutation constitutes *Absalom, Absalom!*'s final lines. For a work that heralds dual-witnessing, this conclusion seems regressive, as Quentin, curled fetally on his bed, is able to witness neither secondarily (having come unglued in the process) nor primarily (trying to convince both Shreve and himself that he does not hate his own un-witnessable "it").

Even so, Quentin's undoing need not be that of his readers. Despite the difficulties of dual-witnessing, the novel upholds the practice as an effective means of working through the traumatic past. Instead of fixating on the degree to which Faulkner's characters (anti-)witness, readers can embrace their collaborative process, learning to witness where and when they do not. In *Absalom, Absalom!*'s oft-quoted "ripple passage"—in which the past's invasion of the present is likened to ripples spreading across the surface of a pool—Quentin muses that "*maybe nothing ever happens once and is finished*" (290). He is speaking of the relationship between past and present, but he could also be addressing the reciprocity of dual-witnessing, which also spreads rhizomatically outward—like ripples over the water's surface—to include readerly participation in its broadening scope. And if dual-witnessing does extend out of Faulkner's pages to engage his readership, then its promise cannot be judged solely on the basis of his characters' successes and failures but also on the quality of his readers' responses.

When Quentin tells Shreve that one "cant understand" the South without having been "born there" (209), he uses the dismissal to deflect Shreve's questions. His response to his roommate's queries, however, is also correct: A secondary witness can never completely understand a primary witness's testimony. Even if one feels traumatized from having witnessed secondarily (as Quentin does), that addressee still has not suffered the speaker's experiences primarily. However, if we take Quentin at his word and accept that dual-witnessing requires us to try to understand what we can never understand, we may learn to enter into a narrative without co-opting it, to witness secondarily without anti-witnessing. In "The Stakes of Reading Faulkner," Warwick Wadlington queries: "What's at stake in reading Faulkner?" (197). One answer is that we read Faulkner to learn how to read, to struggle to witness characters secondarily, to risk dual-witnessing even unreadable texts. Ideally, this process also extends out of and beyond Faulkner's pages into the realities of our everyday lives. Thus, a benefit of reading Faulkner (despite his continued [anti-]witnessing of marginalized race and gender) is that, in doing so, we may find the courage to dual-witness even the incomprehensible texts of our own life narratives, so that we—in the spirit of Faulkner's Nobel prize acceptance speech—may "not merely endure" alone, as members of a given class, race, or gender, but may "prevail" together (121).

Arthur Kinney observes that Faulkner's racism—and, I would add, sexism—is "profoundly subtle and profoundly deep" (qtd. Cooley 311). I agree. I also believe that Faulkner's shift from privileging speaker and text (as primary witnesses) to readers (as secondary witnesses) may help compensate for his novels' anti-witnessing. While such a move could be read as Faulkner's shirking his duty as writer (by asking readers to accomplish what he and his works cannot), the gesture is itself emblematic of dual-witnessing, in which a primary witness, struggling to testify, asks a secondary witness to engage his story in order to witness the narrative together. As Rosa invites Quentin to witness her story secondarily, Faulkner prompts readers to do the same: to dual-witness, where he does not, the intersections of race and gender in American (literary) history. And, if this is indeed the case, what we should take from reading Faulkner is not only how well his novels (anti-)witness race and gender but the degree to which we do the same.

CHAPTER 3

"You Got Tuh Go There Tuh Know There"

Dual- and Communal Witnessing in
Zora Neale Hurston's *Their Eyes Were Watching God*
and Margaret Walker's *Jubilee*

This chapter examines how African American literature models and promotes dual-witnessing by underscoring the necessity of primary witnessing, while impelling the reluctant reader to witness secondarily. To explore this doubly testimonial orientation, the chapter analyzes Zora Neale Hurston's *Their Eyes Were Watching God* (1937)—in which the life narrative of the protagonist, Janie Crawford, is witnessed secondarily through conversation with her friend Pheoby Watson—and Margaret Walker's *Jubilee* (1966), which also embraces dual-witnessing and then advances the conversation from two speakers of the same community, race, and gender (Janie and Pheoby in *Their Eyes*) to many speakers who partake in epic-scaled multiethnic, multigendered, and multiclassed communal witnessing. In reading the novels together, the chapter considers how *Their Eyes* witnesses primarily to *Jubilee*, which witnesses the earlier work secondarily and intertextually.

"To Kiss and Be Kissed": Dual-Witnessing in *Their Eyes Were Watching God*

When *Their Eyes Were Watching God* was published in 1937, readers dismissed the novel as "overly sentimental" and not "serious" enough to contribute to the African American literary canon (Bloom 15). Black male reviewers critiqued Hurston for her unwillingness—or inability—to write fiction in the black protest tradition.[1] Sterling Brown dismissed the novel as "not bitter enough" and denounced Hurston's "easygoing and carefree" depictions, which he believed elided the "harsher side of black life in the South" (20). Alain Locke critiqued the text for being "out of step" with the "more serious trends" of black protest fiction (18), and Richard Wright condemned Hurston for writing a novel in the minstrel tradition, which emboldened white readers to laugh at—not with—black characters and voyeuristically to anti-witness black personhood and culture (22). Perhaps due to this critical censure, *Their Eyes* remained out of print for nearly thirty years following publication and was largely "unknown, unread, and dismissed" by the literary establishment (Washington ix).[2]

In their appraisal, Hurston's black and male critics take too narrow a view of both protest literature and Hurston's contribution to it. While her reviewers rightly recognize that *Their Eyes* does not expose American racism as explicitly as do novels such as Richard Wright's *Native Son* (1940) or Ralph Ellison's *Invisible Man* (1952), their critiques overlook the testimonial nature of Hurston's novel, which witnesses to its readers, first, the role dual-witnessing plays in enabling a speaker to work through her life narrative and, second, the ability of African American literature to model this dual-witnessing through fiction, both of which work to further goals of black protest literature, as defined by Trudier Harris: to bring "redress to the secondary status of black people" and to attempt "to achieve the acceptance of black people into the larger American body politic." In the way it functions, *Their Eyes* does in fact serve as black protest literature in contesting the racial and often gendered anti-witnessing of the white patriarchy—evinced even by Hurston's black male critics—and in witnessing (and celebrating) black womanhood and inspiring dual-witnessing.

Despite its apparent lack of racial militancy (Wall 724), *Their Eyes* engages the racial politics of Hurston's era, witnessing "with sharp accuracy," as Katie Geneva Cannon notes, "the positive sense of self" that flourishes among "the Negro farthest down" (37)—that is, those African Americans who live "farthest down" the US coast in the all-black town of Eatonville, Florida, and who also subsist (in the case of the protagonist, Janie Crawford, and her friend, Pheoby Watson) "farthest down" the ladder of social hierarchy due to their marginalized race, gender, and class. In depicting underprivileged Afra-Americans not as absent, subordinate, and victimized (as they are so often portrayed by white and black male authors) but as present, principal, and resilient, Hurston writes a new kind of protest literature that witnesses and acclaims the fullness of black and female life, independent of—and without the need to invoke—dominant (white male) culture and privilege. As June Jordan attests, "affirmation of black values and lifestyle within the American context is, indeed, an act of protest" (6).

Hurston witnesses the vitality of African American life and culture through her novel's use of Southern black dialect. Although her contemporaries expressed concern that Hurston's utilization of African American Vernacular English (AAVE) reduced *Their Eyes* to minstrelsy, appropriatively anti-witnessing black language for the entertainment of white readers (Bloom 15), the novel emphasizes the multifaceted beauty inherent in African American figurative language, witnessing Sothern black culture through the idioms and discourse of its people. The inclusion of what Hurston calls "new force words," such as "ham-shanked," "battle-hammed," "bodaciously," and "muffle-jawed"; metaphors, such as "cloakers" for deceivers and "syndicating" for gossiping; double descriptives, such as "high-tall," "low-down," "chop-axe," and "sitting-chairs"; and verbal nouns, such as "put the shamery on him" ("Characteristics of Negro Expression" 25) helps animate Southern black language and culture, particularly for those non-Southern, nonblack readers unacquainted with the diverse voices of Janie's world. As a folklorist and anthropologist who claimed Eatonville as home, Hurston was in a unique position to witness, in the words of Stephen Spencer, both as an "educated observer" (or secondary witness by proxy) and also as "one of the folk" (or primary witness) (18). In her mutual capacity as both secondary witness by proxy and primary witness, Hurston employs Southern black dialect to exalt and enliven both the language and culture of her characters and the historical rural Southern black people they represent.

In addition to celebrating what Doris Davis calls "the beauty of the black voice," Hurston's use of dialect increases the witnessing potential of her protagonist. In reading Janie's story, readers sense that Janie is speaking authentically in a manner that feels right to her. When Janie promises Pheoby that she will do her best to "give [her] de understandin' to go 'long wid" the story she narrates (7), readers are inclined to believe her. Furthermore, because the book is framed more as an act of telling than of writing—or of witnessing than of documenting—*Their Eyes* becomes what Henry Louis Gates Jr. in *The Signifying Monkey* calls a "speakerly text," a text that emulates the "phonetic, grammatical, and lexical patterns of actual speech" in order to produce the "illusion of oral narration" (181). Accordingly, engaged readers may feel as if Janie, in her own authentic voice and style, is narrating her story directly to them alongside Pheoby. As a speakerly text, Hurston's novel does not simply record Janie's personal history but facilitates dual-witnessing, offering a readerly experience in which the protagonist witnesses primarily and directly to her secondary witnesses (e.g., to Pheoby within the text and to readers without it).

Moreover, through engaging Janie's vernacular, readers can learn (how) to dual-witness. Readers unfamiliar with the novel's dialect may initially approach Janie's language as foreign, confusing, and a barrier to engaging the novel. Similarly, readers and listeners unaccustomed to dual-witnessing may at first regard a primary witness's imparted experiences as alien, disconcerting, and an impediment to mutual understanding. However, once readers enter into Janie's dialect and begin to identify its common features, the novel becomes increasingly comprehensible.[3] Likewise, addressees willing to sustain secondary witnessing, despite the difficulty of doing so, may find themselves better able to dual-witness. The initial difficulty of encountering an unfamiliar dialect thus has the added advantage of transforming passive readers into active interpreters and co-creators of meaning, prompting those outside Janie's community to engage with her narrative, to read in her voice, and, in doing so, to join her in witnessing. When Janie tells Pheoby, "You got tuh go there tuh know there" (285), her advice possesses multiple meanings: just as a speaker must "go there," not only physically, as Janie has in her travels, and not only psychically and emotionally, but also linguistically, in order to "know there" (to witness one's own life events), so too must the listener. Pheoby (and the reader through her) must "go there" into Janie's language and narrative in order to witness her secondarily, to "know" the "there" of Janie's self and history. In reading *Their Eyes,* readers may discover, alongside Janie and Pheoby, a way to "go" and "know there" through dual-witnessing.

The fact that Hurston does not use Janie's dialect consistently throughout her novel but divides the presentation of the story between Standardized American English (SAE) and AAVE models a linguistic dual-witnessing in which Janie discloses her experiences with the help of a narrator who witnesses the narrative secondarily and secondarily by proxy. Hurston's split-style narrative has been critiqued as often as her characters' vernacular. The early readerly consensus seems to have been that *Their Eyes* should not have been written in dialect and that, if Hurston were to use AAVE in her text, no other writing or speaking style (e.g., that of the narrator) should appear. Robert Stepto argues that Hurston's use of both a third-person and a first-person narrator suggests that Janie never learns to witness at all, since "her author (who is, quite likely, the omniscient narrating voice) cannot see her way clear to giving Janie a voice outright" (166). Stepto contends that Hurston repeatedly disrupts her character's narrative in order to insert her own voice and views into the text. He concludes that Janie can witness neither to Pheoby nor to her readership.

While critics such as Stepto interpret the narrator's third-person SAE voice as an authorial intrusion, the double-voiced structure of *Their Eyes* models intratextual witnessing. Not only does Janie witness for herself, but the narrator also serves not as a substitute for Hurston but as Janie's secondary witness by proxy: one who imparts the novel's story in conversation—not competition—with the protagonist-as-primary-witness. Chapter 2, for instance, is witnessed jointly by the narrator and Janie. The narrator begins in SAE: "Janie saw her life like a great tree in leaf with the things suffered, things enjoyed, things done and undone. Dawn and doom was in the branches" (8) to which Janie adds, in AAVE, "'Ah know exactly what Ah got to tell yuh, but it's hard to know where to start at" (8). Janie then witnesses in AAVE childhood memories to Pheoby before the narrator reemerges to recount in SAE the start of the protagonist's "conscious life," when she first began to contemplate her future (8). When Janie discusses her newfound aspirations with her grandmother, Nanny, Hurston's language returns to AAVE, even as the narrator continues to interpose her own SAE interpretations into the characters' conversation (10–11). In this manner, Janie's spring awakening is linguistically dual-witnessed between narrator and protagonist. Note too that the narrator's contributions surround Janie's admission that she does not know how to begin witnessing. One could thus read the narrator's interjections as the endeavors of a secondary witness by proxy to help disclose to secondary witnesses (e.g., to Pheoby and the novel's readers) what the primary witness, Janie, struggles to convey. In this way, Hurston's multivernacular, multivoiced novel embodies and models the careful cooperation witnessing requires, as speakers and listeners—both within and without the text—work together to witness a single narrative.

Also underlying the narrative is Hurston's witnessing of America's history of racial oppression. The novel's introduction lyrically depicts Janie's return to Eatonville after an extended absence, but harrowing racial imagery simmers beneath lilting romanticism. Laura Dubek notes that the words and phrases that appear in the novel's first five paragraphs—"ships," "distance," "death," "burying the dead," "sick," "ailing," "bloated," "mules," "brutes," "skins," "bossman," "nations chewed up," "killing tools," "mass cruelty," and "masters"—evoke the terrors of the Middle Passage and the traumas of slavery. Add to this list the novel's subsequent allusions to bloodhounds (10), trees

(7–8, 10–14, 18, 21, 24), and lynching (89), and *Their Eyes* invokes not only the depravity of the slave era but all that followed, from Reconstruction through Jim Crow. In this respect, the text functions as a protest novel, underscoring America's legacy of racial violence.

Hurston's novel does more than gesture to racial oppression through figurative language; it also witnesses the traumas black women face due to combined racism and sexism. Janie begins her story, as secondary witness by proxy, by testifying to what her grandmother suffered in slavery. Nanny, Janie discloses, was raped by her white master (17). When his wife discovered that Nanny's daughter, Leafy, had her husband's gray eyes and blonde hair, she threatened to "take [Nanny] to de whippin' post . . . and cut de hide offa [her] back" (18), thereby accusatorily anti-witnessing the slave woman and rape victim for her own victimization. Such abuse, Janie discloses, did not end when Nanny escaped from slavery but continued to hound future generations of black women, including Leafy and Janie herself. Leafy was raped at seventeen by her schoolteacher (19), a man Nanny entrusted to educate her daughter, not to subject her to violence. As in Elizabeth Keckley's *Behind the Scenes,* published before *Their Eyes* (in 1868), and Toni Morrison's *Beloved,* published subsequently (in 1987), the rape of black women by male school teachers suggests that Afra-Americans' societal education includes the brutal lesson that black women will suffer both racial and sexual violence.

Nanny makes this very point when she teaches Janie that "[d]e nigger woman is de mule uh de world" (14), oppressed by white and black men alike. Janie experiences "muledom" directly when all three of her husbands subjugate her. Her first husband, Logan Killicks, evokes Nanny's theory when he orders Janie to work the fields alongside actual mules (27) and, when she resists, rebukes her for failing to appreciate his "good treatment" (30). Janie's second husband, Jody Starks, would rather "trample and mash [her] down" than cultivate an equitable relationship (86), and Janie's third husband, Tea Cake, beats her to prove "who is boss" (148). All three of Janie's husbands strike her at various points in the novel. Through each relationship, Janie learns that black women are subjugated both by white men and women (as Nanny and Leafy were) and by black men (as she has been).

The novel, however, does not portray black women only as oppressed persons, deserving of readerly pity; it also witnesses the vivacity and tenacity of Afra-Americans through characters such as Janie. Unlike the victimized women in the novels of such contemporaries as Richard Wright, Hurston's black female characters, Davis recognizes, evince a "vitality of spirit that refuses to be muted" (271). Janie, for example, exhibits what Davis calls a "formidable spunk" and "reliance on vocal, verbal power" (282)—or testimony—that enables her not only to survive her husbands' oppression but to prevail over it, that is, to flee Logan (33), to stand up to Jody (86), and to kill Tea Cake to save herself (184). Through scenes such as these, Valerie Boyd suggests, *Their Eyes* testifies that (African American) women are the "equals of men in every way" and that their life narratives are "infinitely rich and worthy" of expression and appreciation (303), that is, of primary and secondary witnessing.

Above all else, Hurston celebrates the process and promise of dual-witnessing. While her depiction of Janie, as Bertram Ashe suggests, speaks to the author's understanding of gender roles (29), the novel's principal focus is the transformative power of collaborative storytelling. To testify to the value of dual-witnessing in her novel, Hurston's narrative issues out of a reciprocal conversation held between Janie (as primary witness) and Pheoby (as secondary witness). Readers meet Janie after the tale she wishes to impart is over, once she has been "tuh de horizon and back" (284) and is able to witness primarily her adventures and heartbreak. But Janie does not divulge her tale in a vacuum. To work through her history, Janie must first witness her story to an engaged secondary witness, Pheoby. In framing the text this way, *Their Eyes* both contains an example of dual-witnessing (when Janie and Pheoby witness Janie's life story together) and models dual-witnessing itself (illustrating, through Pheoby's reception of Janie's testimony, modes of secondary witnessing).

Their Eyes demonstrates the transformative power of dual-witnessing by emphasizing Janie's quest to witness primarily. Janie tells Pheoby that, as a young girl living in a predominately white community, she did not initially realize she was black. Only when she saw a photograph of herself among a group of white children did she realize she was "colored" and not "like de rest" (9). This scene speaks to the social construction of race and the corresponding marginalization of African Americans. Presumably, Janie has looked at her body and seen her reflection before this point, but she has not yet perceived how she is different from, and othered by, white society, until she sees a photograph in which she stands literally apart from (and figuratively below) those who are white. The question Janie poses to the children's parents—"Where is me? Ah don't see me"—and their response—"Dat's you . . . don't you know yo' ownself?" (9)—epitomizes her quest to discover and witness herself. When Janie asks the white adults where and who she is, they do not acknowledge the significance of her question but laugh instead at the little girl who does not know she is "colored." When Janie shares this story with Pheoby, she incites her friend (and readers through her) to respond as her first listeners do not: to witness secondarily and, in doing so, to help

Janie witness primarily the answer to her question, "Where and who am I?," in order to "know"—and witness "[her] . . . ownself."

To help readers witness secondarily, *Their Eyes* offers counterexamples of characters who, by anti-witnessing Janie, impede her ability to witness primarily. As early as the first page of the novel, readers are introduced to Janie's former neighbors as collective anti-witnesses. When Janie returns to Eatonville after an extended absence, she is not welcomed home but is met by those who "sit in judgment" (1) and aggressively anti-witness her for anticipated failures. The porch-sitters jibe: "What dat ole forty year ole 'oman doin' wid her hair wingin' down her back lak some young gal?—Where she left dat young lad of a boy she went off . . . wid? . . . Betcha he off wid some [young] gal" (2). In offering this commentary, Janie's neighbors reveal their voyeuristic and accusatory desire that Janie, who eloped with the younger Tea Cake, has been abandoned and shamed and is now crawling back home to judgment. As the townspeople gossip "with relish," they make "killing tools out of laughs" (2), underscoring the "mass cruelty" (2) inherent in communal anti-witnessing. Later, the narrator describes anti-witnessing as a weapon, portraying those who anti-witness aggressively as wielding tongues that, like guns, are "cocked and loaded" (185). Such scenes warn readers against anti-witnessing's violence and encourage them not to anti-witness with the Eatonville gossips but to dual-witness with Janie instead.

Janie is anti-witnessed not only by her community but also by individuals. The male predominance of these individuals signifies the patriarchal nature of black women's oppression. Although all of Janie's husbands mistreat her, her second husband, Jody, provides the starkest example of (patriarchal) anti-witnessing when he negatively a-witnesses his wife's alterity and personhood. Jody's anti-witnessing of Janie begins from the moment they meet. When Janie expresses concern about leaving her first husband, Logan, Jody rejoins: "Leave de s'posin' and everything else to me" (29). While Jody's statement seems to reassure Janie, the remark represents an instance of anti-witnessing: Jody usurps Janie's agency—her own independent "s'posin'"—along with "everything else" for personal (and primarily selfish) reasons (i.e., to own and objectify her, ostensibly for her own benefit). This anti-witnessing persists throughout their marriage. When Jody is named mayor of Eatonville, the townspeople ask Janie to make a speech as the mayor's wife, but Jody prevents her from doing so, thereby silencing—and a-witnessing—her (43). "Thank uh fuh yo' compliments," Jody declares (as if the town has complimented him, not Janie, by asking her to speak), "but mah wife don't know nothin' 'bout no speech-makin'. Ah never married her for nothin' lak dat" (43). Jody married Janie not for her ability to witness primarily but in order to have someone over whom to wield patriarchal control. That Janie may have something to say (let alone witness), does not occur to Jody.

The result of Jody's anti-witnessing is the erasure of Janie's personhood and a corresponding inability to witness primarily. When Jody silences Janie, a "feeling of coldness and fear" washes over her; she feels "far away" and "lonely" (46). The consequences of anti-witnessing are separation and loneliness, the antitheses of the cooperation and camaraderie established through dual-witnessing. As the years pass, Jody's anti-witnessing takes its toll on Janie. From this moment forward, she silently submits to Jody's imperious nature and performs her duties as she a-witnesses her own opinions and personhood. Jody has anti-witnessed Janie for so long that she closes herself off by "pressing [her teeth] together and learning to hush" (72). As a result of Jody's anti-witnessing, Janie becomes constricted, shutting her mouth to prevent herself from witnessing.

The climax of Jody's anti-witnessing of Janie is when he publicly and accusatorily anti-witnesses her for making a mistake at his store (78). Finally, Janie releases the antipathy she has sublimated and insults her husband, announcing that he looks like "de change uh life" or a naked, menopausal woman (79). Janie's outburst could indicate that she has finally begun to witness, but her retort is more indicative of pent-up resentment than of psychosocial testimony. Janie's willingness to defend herself after years of silent submission represents a personal breakthrough, but the way she chooses to do so—by comparing her aging husband to a mature woman—also suggests that maturity and womanhood are undesirable and humiliating traits. In attempting to attack the patriarchal power embodied in Jody, Janie aligns with it, debasing womanhood. The result is further anti-witnessing. After the confrontation, Jody moves to another room in the house and avoids all contact with Janie. When Janie tries to make amends, Jody gives her a "ferocious look . . . with all the unthinkable coldness of outer space," and Janie realizes that nothing can bridge the gap between them, that she "must talk to a man who was ten immensities away" (84). This scene underscores the distance that develops through anti-witnessing and the increased difficulty of dual-witnessing when supposed partners are alienated from one another.

In contrast to Jody's chronic anti-witnessing, Tea Cake initially cultivates intergendered dual-witnessing with his wife. When Tea Cake and Janie meet, Tea Cake invites her to play checkers with him. In extending this invitation, Tea Cake distinguishes himself from men such as Jody (who instructed Janie to "leave . . . everything" to him) by inviting Janie to join him in a game that metaphorically connotes dual-witnessing in granting equal status to both player-participants. Following their checkers match, Tea Cake does not suppress Janie's efforts to witness (as Logan and Jody have) but continues to encourage her not only to play checkers but to fish, shoot, and attend the Eatonville picnics (a form of communal witnessing Jody denied Janie when he isolated her from the community). Tea Cake builds a relationship with Janie grounded in reciprocity instead of dominance. Janie seeks this same mutuality with him, inviting him to share openly with her so that each partner witnesses primarily to—and secondarily for—the other. When Tea Cake is bit by a rabid dog and begins to suffer in silence, Janie reminds him: "You got tuh tell me so Ah kin feel widja. Lemme bear de pain 'long widja, baby" (174). Janie reminds Tea Cake that their relationship is predicated upon dual-witnessing: both partners "tell" (or witness primarily) to the other, so that the other can "bear de pain" along with (or witness secondarily) his or her partner. Janie does not offer to bear Tea Cake's pain for him (or to anti-witness co-optively) but to bear it alongside him—to serve as Tea Cake's secondary witness, as he so often has as hers.

Just as Jody's anti-witnessing impedes Janie's ability to witness, Tea Cake's secondary witnessing inspires Janie to witness not only dually but also communally. Whereas Jody separated Janie from Eatonville's porch talk, Tea Cake brings communal witnessing to their home in the Everglades. Their house in the wetlands is "full of people every night," who come "to talk and tell stories" (or to witness communally), and Janie, for the first time in her life, is able both to "listen" (or to witness secondarily) and to "talk" (to witness primarily) (134). Accordingly, Ashe notes, Janie becomes a "fully-integrated audience-member and teller-of-tales" (34). She becomes an embodied dual-witness, serving simultaneously as a "fully-integrated audience-member" (or secondary witness) and a "fully-integrated teller-of tales" (or primary witness). In literature, the wetlands can symbolize a moral morass in which characters struggle to distinguish right from wrong. Here, the "muck" of the Everglades signifies not only moral ambiguity but also a space of Venn liminality that nurtures, through sustained witnessing, individual and communal growth.

Unfortunately, even in the fecund soil of the Everglades, Tea Cake abandons his initial commitment to dual-witness, asserts his patriarchal power, and begins to anti-witness Janie. In doing so, he underscores both the blurred boundary between secondary and anti-witnessing and the difficulty of sustaining intergendered dual-witnessing in a patriarchal society. Thus, although critics such as Shawn Miller celebrate Tea Cake as Janie's "liberator" (80), he eventually exhibits the same patriarchal and anti-witnessing traits of her previous husbands. Tea Cake a-witnesses Janie by not inviting her to the party he hosts with money he has stolen from her (124), and he anti-witnesses her by beating her to "[reassure] him in possession" and "show he [is] boss"

(140). As Deborah Plant notes, by the close of Tea Cake's role in the novel, "the reciprocity"—or dual-witnessing—"characterizing their early relationship is glaringly absent" (168). Although Tea Cake presumably wants to maintain an equitable partnership with Janie, his obsession with patriarchal control, his need to demonstrate to Janie and the surrounding community that "it's uh man heah" (248), interferes with his ability to dual-witness with his wife.

Janie's marriage to Tea Cake suggests that, notwithstanding the daydreams of her youth (exemplified in the scene during which a teenaged Janie gazes up into the branches of a pear tree and determines that she will find plea-sure, equality, and fulfillment—her own vision of dual-witnessing—in het-erosexual marriage [11]), heterosexual love and marriage neither equal nor guarantee dual-witnessing. While male and female spouses may witness with each other (as Janie and Tea Cake initially do), the patriarchy can also disrupt the reciprocity of heterosexual romance. Dual-witnessing is not cir-cumscribed to heterosexual marriage but is nurtured through a variety of relationships, such as the friendship sustained between Janie and Pheoby or the collaboration cultivated between the narrator and the protagonist and the novel and its readership. Carla Kaplan gestures toward this expansive potential of dual-witnessing when she suggests that, while "at the emotional register," Tea Cake's death functions as a "tragedy," it also "liberates Janie to continue her quest to satisfy her 'oldest human longing . . . [for] self revela-tion'"—or primary witnessing—"with someone who can listen" or witness secondarily (132). Though heartrending, Tea Cake's death, like Jody's before him, frees Janie to pursue what she has sought all along: dual-witnessing with a receptive partner.

Janie establishes this mutuality with her friend Pheoby, a model secondary witness. (Pheoby is, after all, the only one [besides the reader] with whom Janie openly shares her tale). Before Janie returns to Eatonville, the narrator reports that another woman, Mrs. Turner, "sought out Janie to friend with" (140). Mrs. Turner, an Afra-American who exhibits racism against other black people, does not elicit Janie's friendship to dual-witness but to align herself with the status Janie's light skin affords. The narrator explains: "She didn't cling to Janie Woods the woman. She paid homage to Janie's Caucasian characteristics as such. And when she was with Janie she had a feeling of transmutation, as if she herself had become whiter" (145). The narrator's use of the term "friend with"—in addition to signifyin(g) on AAVE⁴—suggests that, like "witness," the word "friend" is not only a noun (something one is) but also a verb (something one does). While Mrs. Turner does not ever friend—or witness—with Janie, Pheoby does. For this reason, critics celebrate Pheoby as a "successful *storylistener*" (Ashe 45) and an "ideal tale-bearer" or secondary witness (Kaplan 118). What differentiates Pheoby from Mrs. Turner and Janie's three husbands is that she fosters a relationship with Janie without agenda, facilitating the protagonist's ability to witness primarily. Pheoby's "hungry listening" (or secondary witnessing) enables Janie "to tell" (or witness primarily) her story (10).

Pheoby first demonstrates this "hungry listening" (and her corresponding commitment to dual-witness with Janie) when she refuses to contribute to Eatonville's communal anti-witnessing. When the porch-sitters begin to gossip about Janie, Pheoby rejects their conversation by getting up, walking over to Janie's house, and inviting her friend to tell her story. In encouraging Janie to witness in her own home, Pheoby facilitates dual-witnessing in a space in which Janie feels both comfortable and agent. Judith Herman underscores the necessity of establishing a safe environment in which to witness (162). Pheoby and Janie also seem to recognize the importance of witnessing in a comfortable psychic and physical space. In fact, Janie criticizes the Eatonville gossips not only for anti-witnessing her but also for failing to invite her, as Pheoby has, to witness primarily to them in a manner and environment in which she feels comfortable. "If they wants to see and know," Janie asks Pheoby, "why they don't come kiss and be kissed?" (6). If her neighbors wish to "see and know" her, that is, to witness her secondarily, they need to seek her out, as Pheoby has, in "kissin' friend[ship]" (7) and as the reader has, in engaging Hurston's novel.

Contrast Pheoby's engagement of Janie's story with the scene in which Janie, on trial for having killed Tea Cake, is asked to testify to the events surrounding her husband's death. Although the jury ultimately finds Janie not guilty of murder, the courtroom is not depicted as a safe environment in which to witness, suggesting that testifying at trial is not equivalent to primary witnessing. Perhaps to distinguish the evidence Janie offers from her witnessing with Pheoby, Hurston does not share Janie's testimony directly with the reader but summarizes her trial statements indirectly: She "sat there and told and when she was through she hushed" (187). Janie's narrative silence during her trial has raised critical controversy. At the 1979 MLA convention, Stepto voiced concern that Janie was "curiously silent" in a scene that required her to preserve her life and liberty (qtd. in Washington xiv). Stepto is right that Hurston's narrator dominates the trial scene, but he does not note the distinction between Janie testifying in court and witnessing with Pheoby. As Hurston may appreciate (and Stepto may not), the legal system does not automatically facilitate dual-witnessing. As Kaplan suggests, regardless of her testimony, Janie knows that her listeners lack the necessary "understandin' to go 'long wid it" (Hurston 19) and that, without that understanding, "self revelation" just "tain't worth de trouble" (Hurston 19; Kaplan 129). Howsoever Janie explains the circumstances surrounding Tea Cake's death, the white male judge and jury will struggle to witness her narrative secondarily, and, if she cannot help her listeners to witness secondarily, little reason exists for her to witness primarily. Hurston writes that what Janie "had to remember was she was not at home" in a safe space but "in the courthouse fighting . . . lying thoughts" (220), that is, anti-witnessing. Scenes such as this one suggest that, when the primary witness is removed from a comfortable environment and placed in a potentially hostile one, anti-witnessing is the probable result.

In contrast to those who anti-witness Janie's testimony, when Pheoby witnesses secondarily, she does not sit passively but actively engages her friend's story. "Pheoby held her tongue for a long time," the narrator writes, "but she couldn't help moving her feet. So Janie spoke" (7). Pheoby listens quietly and attentively (she "h[olds] her tongue") for as long as Janie wishes to witness primarily ("for a long time"), but she also enters directly into the narrative and dialogues with its speaker and text ("she couldn't help moving her feet"). This sustained secondary witnessing enables Janie to continue to witness primarily: "So Janie spoke." In this passage, *Their Eyes* instructs readers how to read as secondary witnesses: select the text (as Pheoby seeks out Janie); immerse oneself in its narrative as unobtrusively as possible (hold one's tongue); and travel with the novel, move one's feet. Dual-witnessing, like reading, is not a static process but an active one. Pheoby's position as secondary witness helps model for the reader not only how to respond to Janie (and, through her, all primary witnesses) but also how to respond to Hurston's novel in particular and speakerly texts in general.

Although *Their Eyes* promotes the importance of dual-witnessing, Hurston does not maintain that the process is effortless. Instead, as Kaplan writes, the novel "deliberately figures" Pheoby's active listening as a "hard act to follow" (132), while the textual inclusion of anti-witnessing suggests that a reader may as easily emulate Jody Starks (the archetype of anti-witnessing) as Pheoby Watson (the paradigm of secondary witnessing). In considering what (and how) Pheoby teaches readers, Kaplan queries rhetorically: Is anyone actually capable of witnessing as Pheoby does? Are not most readers more likely to respond "antagonistic[ally]," "inaccessib[ly]," and "incompetent[ly]"—that is, aggressively, ignorantly, and co-optively—to narratives such as Hurston's? (131). The answer to both questions is "yes": readers are capable of witnessing with and like Pheoby. To do so, however, they must also recognize the likelihood that, even in attempting to dual-witness, they may anti-witness. "Only by including oneself in Hurston's blanket indictment," Kaplan explains, by "assuming that one is, for whatever reason, a different reader than Hurston's idealized ... projection, can one learn to listen differently" (136). Only by recognizing that (and how) one may anti-witness can one learn to dual-witness. If the reader remains cognizant of the intersecting ways one can anti-witness, one can learn to situate oneself at the liminal core of a Venn diagram of secondary witnessing, a space where one may perceive (and then continuously position oneself against) the reader's coinciding roles as aggressor toward, bystander outside, and appropriator of the text. In engaging narratives with this Venn consciousness, one can join Janie and Pheoby in dual-witnessing.

Dual-witnessing is nearly impossible to sustain. However, the practice, as Ryan Simmons recognizes, is "crucial because, given enough time and enough readings, it can change the world, one reader—one connection—at a time" (190). Such is the case for Janie and Pheoby. As primary witness, Janie finds the "peace" that has long alluded her (193). As secondary witness, Pheoby is likewise reformed and renewed. After engaging Janie's narrative, Pheoby announces that she is no longer satisfied with her life. "Ah done growed ten feet higher from jus' listenin' tuh you, Janie," she affirms. "Ah ain't satisfied wid mahself no mo'" (226). The resolutions she takes from their conversation are two-fold. First, "nobody better not criticize [Janie] in [her] hearin'" again (192). As secondary witness, Pheoby will not allow others to anti-witness Janie in her presence. Second, Pheoby determines to "make" her husband, Sam, "take me fishin' wid him after this" (193). Inspired by Janie's example, Pheoby seeks also to witness an independent self, nurtured through equitable relationships (i.e., by partners fishing together). By the end of the novel, Janie has witnessed the traumas she has endured and the triumphs she has achieved, both as an Afra-American "mule of the world" and as a unique individual with her own experiences. In witnessing primarily to Pheoby, Janie completes her quest. In witnessing Janie's story secondarily, Pheoby and Hurston's readers' begin their own.

"I Has Listened ... and I Has Learned": Communal Witnessing in *Jubilee*

Like *Their Eyes,* Walker's *Jubilee* (1966) models the importance of dual-witnessing. To do so, the novel witnesses not only the life of one individual woman (the protagonist, Vyry) but also the experiences of other slaves in the South; the fierce realities of the American institution of slavery; and the victims, victimizers, and bystanders who stood—and fought—on both sides of the American Civil War. As a result, *Jubilee* does not witness primarily from a single perspective or even show that perspective in conversation (as Hurston does in *Their Eyes*); instead, it witnesses primarily and communally from multiple, contradictory positions, encouraging readers to enter into not just one person's perspective but (through our Venn liminality) all perspectives collectively. In witnessing not just one protagonist's perspective but America's as a whole, Walker chronicles daily life in the South, treating *Jubilee* as a novel of historical record. In entering into the narrative, readers learn how antebellum Southern Americans farmed, cooked, and ate at every level of society. We are introduced to slaves' religions and superstitions and voodoo; to the Underground Railroad; to how slaves escaped and how they were punished if caught. And although the heroes and heroines of Walker's epic novel are predominantly black, *Jubilee* does not witness exclusively from the perspective of African Americans. Instead, Walker enters into the psyches and situations of all characters: female and male; black and white; child and adult; Southerner and Northerner; civilian and soldier; slave and free, so that readers may witness secondarily not just one perspective but many. Thus, in five hundred pages of epic fiction, Walker plums the truths of pre- and postbellum America so that her readers may witness secondarily both the depth of an individual's experience (as we learn to do in *Their Eyes*) and the breadth of familial, cultural, and historical American traumas and triumphs.

Critics celebrate Walker as the foremother of neoslave narratives and the first to utilize fiction to witness the historical truths of American slavery (Graham and Whaley 4). *Jubilee*'s fictive witnessing is enriched by the fact that the novel represents not only the workings of Walker's imagination or the results of her research but also the particulars of her family history. Walker explains in her acknowledgments and dedication that *Jubilee* is the semifictional account of "Vyry Brown" or Margaret Duggans Ware Brown, Walker's great-grandmother. As the novel's back cover indicates, *Jubilee* developed out of a series of true bedtime stories that Walker "heard as a child from her grandmother, the real Vyry's daughter." Serving as both family historian and secondary witness by proxy, Walker's grandmother, Elvira Ware Dozier, refused to a-witness America's racial history but testified instead to the truth of her nation's past and her own family's experience of it. Although Walker's father reproached his mother-in-law for telling his daughter "all those harrowing . . . tall tales," Dozier persisted: "I'm not telling her tales; I'm telling her the naked truth" (Walker "How I Wrote Jubilee" 50). In responding thus, Walker's grandmother impressed upon her the importance of witnessing the past and the corresponding potential for narrative not only to delight and entertain but also to educate and transform. As an adult, Walker embraced this example, writing a novel that witnesses both historical and familial truths.

In shaping her narrative, Walker spins her great-grandmother's history into a masterpiece of historical fiction that seeks to witness in its entirety the experience of the South in the American Civil War. Walker wrote *Jubilee* from the intersecting perspectives of granddaughter, novelist, and historian, immersing herself in the antebellum, Civil War, and Reconstruction eras by engaging "the entire sweep of nineteenth-century history" and literature from Southern historical collections through emancipatory narratives (Carmichael 4). The extensive research Walker conducted to supplement her grandmother's stories underscores her authorial resolve to witness American history not exclusively from one standpoint but simultaneously from many. Maryemma Graham explains that Walker viewed fiction as a means to witness what historians sometimes could not: all conflicting sides of an issue at once ("Introduction" *This Is My Century* xxx). She also attempted in *Jubilee* not merely "to answer questions about slavery, as [S]outhern historians had been doing" but to witness the experience as "fully," "truthfully," and "artfully" as possible ("Introduction" *This Is My Century* xxx). That is, in writing *Jubilee,* Walker (successfully) sought to witness from many perspectives, not to report from one viewpoint. Perhaps as a result, *Jubilee* speaks both to the need to witness the traumatic legacy of American slavery and to the unique ability of fiction to do so.

Because both novels concern the same era and subject matter *Jubilee* is often compared to Margaret Mitchell's 1939 *Gone with the Wind*. Whereas Mitchell's work anti-witnesses black personhood[5] and Southern culpability and romanticizes racism and white supremacy,[6] Walker's witnesses American history as it was and is. Accordingly, *Jubilee* is sometimes called a "Civil War novel in the reverse tradition of *Gone with the Wind*" or "*Gone with the Wind* from a black point of view" (Condé 217). When asked in an interview to compare their works, Walker suggested that she and "the other Margaret" approached American slavery and Civil War history from disparate positions: "She was coming out of the front door, and I was coming out of the back door" (Roswell 23). Remarkably, however, *Jubilee* witnesses not exclusively "from a black point of view," as Mary Condé suggests, but from multiple (and often hostile and conflicting) positions: for example, black and white, male and female, slave and free, child and adult, North and South, antebellum and postbellum, and all the possibilities in between.

To achieve this expansive vision, *Jubilee* witnesses the cruelty inherent in American slavery. Vyry suffers, as Claudia Tate notes, "all the pain, degradation, and loss common to slavery" (47). She is orphaned as a toddler (17), victimized by a cruel mistress (37), denied legal marriage to her children's father (182), auctioned for public sale (162), and flogged for attempted escape (172). Vyry's whipping represents one of the most vicious scenes in the novel. After attempting to flee slavery with her children to unite with their free father, Vyry is stripped naked and tied to the whipping post. Walker writes:

One of the guards . . . took the whip in his hands. It was a raw-hide coach-whip used to spur the horses. He twirled it up high over his head, . . . wrapped it all the way around her body and cut neatly into her breast and across her back . . . The whip . . . cut the blood out of her and stung like red-hot pins sticking in her flesh . . . It hurt so badly she felt as if her flesh were a single molten flame, and before she could [breathe], . . . he had wrapped the whip around her the second time. . . . She opened her mouth to scream, but her throat was too dry to holler and she gritted her teeth and smashed her head hard against the post in order to steel herself . . . When he . . . whip[ped her] the third time . . . everything went black; . . . When she came to . . . she saw blood splattered and clotted around her . . . Fever parched her lips and eyes and her bruised hands and ran through her brutalized flesh . . . [W]hen she was able to examine herself she saw where one of the lashes had left a loose flap of flesh over her breast like a tuck in a dress. It healed that way. (172–74)

In providing a comprehensive description of Vyry's flogging (of which the above quotation is a mere fragment), Walker helps the reader visualize—and thereby enter into—the protagonist's torment. One can see and hear the crack of the whip that the guard twirls above his head like a ringmaster at the circus. One can feel, if only secondarily and to a small degree, the bondswoman's agony, which almost instantaneously constricts her (when, as if caught in a living nightmare, she screams only silence). Nor does Vyry's suffering cease when she loses consciousness. When she wakes, her back is in shreds. Her breast has been whipped off her body. In engaging such a passage, readers are asked to witness the dehumanizing cruelty of Vyry's individual punishment and of institutionalized slavery as a whole. The line that concludes the scene, "It healed that way," suggests that, although America may heal from slavery, its citizens—from Vyry to *Jubilee*'s readers—remain psychically shredded and emotionally scarred. Through her description of Vyry's whipping, Walker provokes those who would a-witness the enduring traumas of slavery instead to confront its undeniable aftermath.

In presenting its picture of slavery, *Jubilee* not only speaks from Vyry's point of view but also testifies, in the tradition of nineteenth-century eman-cipatory narratives, to the cruelty suffered by all black slaves. When, for example, the bondswoman Lucy (and Vyry's half-sister on her mother's side) is caught fleeing the plantation, her cheek is branded with the letter "R" for runaway (113). Like Vyry's flogging, the violence in this scene is graphic. In fact, Walker describes not only the branding itself but also every detail lead-ing up to the incident so that her readers, alongside the victimized Lucy (and the traumatized-through-witnessing Vyry), begin anxiously to anticipate the impending violence. As the iron moves toward Lucy's face, the captured slave becomes hyperaroused, "twitching all over and foaming at the mouth" in anticipation of the pain to follow (114). Watching from the kitchen, Vyry exhibits secondary traumatization, becoming physically constricted, "her whole body . . . tightening like a drum" (114). When readers encounter this scene, they too may tense their bodies and hold their breath as they wait for the inevitable description of abuse. In doing so, they enter simultaneously into Lucy's victimhood and Vyry's position as empathic bystander, thereby learning (how) to witness secondarily as a survivor-in-solidarity, as a reader who witnesses with the victim, Lucy.

The same scenes that prompt readers to witness secondarily also acknowledge how painful this process can be. Vyry, readers are told, does "not see when they actually brand" Lucy (although readers do, since Walker includes its description in her narrative) (114). She does "not hear the hissing sound of the iron on the sizzling flesh" but, at the moment that iron touches cheek, "drop[s] in a dead faint . . . while somewhere back in her consciousness there [is] a terrible bellowing sound like a young bull or calf crying out in pain" (114). In depicting Vyry's constricted response to Lucy's trauma, *Jubilee* highlights how distressing (and even traumatizing) secondary witnessing can be. In persisting in detailing Lucy's branding—and compelling the reader to witness secondarily what Vyry cannot—the novel emphasizes the importance of dual-witnessing despite its difficulty, prompting readers to continue to witness when and where its characters do not. Moreover, *Jubilee* suggests that those who refuse to witness secondarily do not automatically escape the traumas they a-witness; they may find themselves plagued by traumatic intrusion. In the scene above, Lucy's "terrible bellowing" pervades Vyry's constricted consciousness. Even as she lies unconscious on the floor, Vyry cannot ignore Lucy's primary witnessing (her "crying out in pain") (114). In much the same way, the national trauma of slavery continues to haunt American citizens even as they a-witness its legacy of racial violence.

In addition to Afra-American trauma (embodied in Vyry's whipping and Lucy's branding), the tenacity of black women is meant to be engaged and celebrated by *Jubilee*'s readers. In "Willing to Pay the Price," Walker extols the indomitability of Afra-Americans: "The white man has . . . tried to dehumanize us, but we have nevertheless maintained our own integrity in the face of brutalizing conditions" (23). This refusal to submit or crumble in the face of oppression must be witnessed—a task Walker takes up (through Vyry) in *Jubilee*. If Vyry is a victim of institutional slavery (and of a white capitalist patriarchy), she is also, as Graham notes, "a black everywoman" ("Introduction" *This Is My Century* xxx), a heroine who not only survives but prevails. Following the outbreak of the Civil War, when a group of (black and white) women are left to fend for themselves, Vyry, "to the amazement of the whole household," plows the field herself (276). Inspired by her initiative, the other women join her, planting corn, collards, peas, tomato plants, potatoes, and onions (277). Due to Vyry's resourcefulness, the group survives. Later, when Vyry's children lie ill with malaria, she nurses them back to health, while her second husband, Innis, stands by helplessly. "Innis was alarmed over the children's illness," Walker writes, "but Vyry remained calm and refused to be alarmed. She fought through three nights without taking off her clothes" (339). In scenes such as these, *Jubilee* prompts readers to witness secondarily not only Vyry's victimhood but also her resilience.

Jubilee upholds Vyry as the prototype of Afra-American agency: her combined strength and spirit frequently surpass that of those who rank above her socially, such as the novel's white women (e.g., Vyry's mistress, defenseless on the plantation during the war) and its black men (e.g., her husband, powerless to save their children). What makes Walker's fictive witnessing even more remarkable is that the novel does not testify exclusively to black and female traumas and triumphs but broadens its narrative scope to speak to—and speak out of—other multicultural experiences. *Jubilee,* for example, witnesses not only the oppression of Afra-Americans but that of all women, irrespective of race. In one harrowing scene, Vyry's white half-sister, Lillian (and the future mistress of the plantation) is sexually and physically assaulted by Union soldiers (289). The trauma of Lillian's attack is so marked that she remains psychically constricted for the novel's duration (294). She ceases to recognize her own daughter, extended family, friends, or environment and requires the assistance of others to eat, dress, and bathe. For the rest of her life, Walker writes, "Lillian was like a ghost who ... seemed to leave half her mind and soul with the dead" (294). Novels that witness the horrors of American slavery do not typically uphold Southern belles as mutual victims of the Civil War. *Jubilee,* however, demonstrates, in the words of the doctor who examines Lillian, how the war "affected everybody some way or other" (300). The systemic violence, inherent in institutionalized slavery, has contaminated all Americans, irrespective of race, gender, and class. A message implicit in Lillian's plotline may be that, while contemporary Americans have survived slavery and its aftermath, we too are altered by our nation's history, whether we recognize it or not. The way to recover from shared trauma, *Jubilee* suggests, is—contra Lillian—to witness rather than to forget.

Despite the inclusivity of the claim that all Americans are affected by slavery, *Jubilee* does not purport that all Americans (or even all women) have suffered equally or that they all mutually care for one another (as Lillian and

Vyry seem to do). Instead, the novel underscores how the patriarchal, racist, and classist systems that conspire to oppress American women also divide them from one other, promoting fraught relationships between women of differing races and classes rather than fostering the connection and sense of sisterhood that facilitates dual-witnessing. Lillian's mother, Salina, does not relate to Vyry but tortures the black slave girl for "daring" to resemble her husband, John, who is both master of the plantation and Vyry's biological father. Indeed, when Salina—or "Big Missy," as the slaves call her—discovers that her white husband has raped Vyry's enslaved mother, Hetta, she does not empathize with her husband's victim (Hetta) or direct her anger where it belongs (at John, the embodiment of racist patriarchal violence) but punishes their innocent daughter, Vyry, by throwing a pot of urine in the child's face (32) or hanging Vyry by her wrists in a locked closet and leaving her there long after she has lost consciousness (32). Through such scenes, *Jubilee* reminds readers that, even when they are mutually oppressed by the patriarchy, women are not oppressed equally, and they do not always unite over their shared oppression. Instead, intersecting factors, such as race and class (and in Salina's case, jealousy), intrude to divide women from one another and to oppress further those marginalized by multiple forms of difference, such as the biracial slave girl, Vyry.

Jubilee also demonstrates how race and gender constructs intersect with those of class to marginalize and oppress the impoverished (both black and white, slave and free) and to prevent members of the lower classes from subverting divergent identity constructs to connect with one another. Vyry, for example, recognizes as a child that her race, gender, and class all separate her from her master-father and his white family. She observes that "even in the midst of plenty in the Big House there was want in the Quarters, and while Marster and Big Missy were feasting and rejoicing there was misery among the suffering slaves" (59). As she "gr[ows] older," Vyry also "beg[ins] to realize" that wealth does not always accompany whiteness and that "the poor whites" could suffer even "more than the black slaves, for there was no one to provide them with the rations of corn meal and salt pork which was the daily lot of the slaves" (59). The result, Vyry discerns, is racial division among the impoverished. "Black people were taught by their owners to have contempt for this 'poor white trash'" (60), she notes, and poor "white people did not work well with slaves. Each group regarded the other contemptuously and felt that the other was his inferior" (61). The overseer's wife, Janey, maintains: "I hate niggers worsener poisonous rattlesnake. We'uns is poor, but thank God, we'uns is white" (63). As Vyry intuits and *Jubilee* testifies, the racist capitalist patriarchy divides poor blacks from poor whites, just as it divides black women from white women. The unspoken solution to such segregation is intersectional and multicultural dual- and communal witnessing.

To help foster witnessing across race, gender, and class, *Jubilee* testifies not only against racist, sexist, and classist systems of oppression but also from the perspective of their perpetrators. In doing so, the novel impels readers to enter into the mindset of both victims and victimizers, so we may witness secondarily a spectrum of American difference and domination and, in doing so, learn to witness with the oppressed against their oppressors. To accomplish this feat without sacrificing the depth of a character's interiority, Walker writes *Jubilee* in a third-person limited narrative mode, unifying the novel through her sustained use of the third person but plumbing the depths of individual consciousness through the narrator's limited—or intimate—perspective. In this way, readers may secondarily witness not only the viewpoints of the ex-slave Vyry but also, for example, those of her white master and father, John Dutton.

Consider the novel's opening scene in which Vyry's mother, Sis Hetta, lies dying in childbirth, and Marster John ambles across his plantation's grounds, reflecting on his long-standing relationship with her. Walker writes:

> He began to think through the years when Hetta was a young girl and there was no thought of her dying, ever. His father gave him Hetta when he was still in his teens and she was barely more than a pickaninny. He remembered how she had looked growing up, long legged like a wild colt . . . Her small young breasts tilted up, . . . her slight hips and little buttocks . . . set high on her body. . . . They titillated him and his furious excitement grew . . . watching her walk. It was all his father's fault. Anyway it was his father who taught him it was better for a young man of quality to learn life by breaking in a young nigger wench than it was for him to spoil a pure white virgin girl. And he wanted Hetta, so his father gave her to him, and he had satisfied his lust with her. . . . He still remembered her tears and her frightened eyes and how she had pleaded to be left alone, but he had persisted. (8–9)

This quotation not only witnesses John's individual psyche and history but also reflects that of the patriarchal culture to which he belongs. From John's reflections, the reader discovers a culture in which black slave girls are gifted to teenage white boys as a rite of passage, presumably to temper the boys' lusting after white women. John reflects: "His father . . . taught him it was better for a young man of quality"—read: wealthy, white adolescent—"to learn life by breaking in a young nigger wench than . . . to spoil a pure white virgin girl" (8). The messages implicit in this "lesson" are that white men cannot control their sexual desire; that white female virtue is somehow in jeopardy; and that "life" to wealthy, white adolescent males is that state of being in which they should not be forced to forsake their sexual appetites to protect white ladyhood but instead should "master-bate" by raping or "breaking in" black girls.

John's father's phrase "breaking in" also teaches the reader the patriarchal view of black female life, suggesting that if the learned "life" of white men is one of sexual appetite, then the life of black girls and women is one of rape. Explicitly, every black slave woman is going to be raped anyway, so the sooner she is "broken in" to sexual abuse, the better. John starts raping Hetta when she is "barely more than a pickaninny," a child. (We learn several pages later that he begins assaulting her before she reaches sexual maturation [10].) In this same passage, Walker also uncovers how white women are objectified for white patriarchal purposes: the purity of the white woman's body, her sanctified "ladyhood," is appropriated by white males as an excuse to rape black females. White women are thus also exploited by men—turned into objects of purity instead of lust—so that men may continue to disguise (to themselves, even) their own victimizing attitudes and actions.

In addition to the societal lessons and clues that grow out of John's meditation, the passage witnesses phenomena unique to Dutton's individual psyche. John's act of blaming his lust for—and raping of—Hetta on his father (attempting to justify: "It was his father's fault") gestures to how the patriarchy teaches future generations of white men to objectify women. John's treatment of Hetta is, to a degree, his father's fault for modeling this behavior in the first place. But the anger John directs at his father may also betray his shame surrounding his treatment of Hetta, a need to blame his victimizing of her on someone else. John's shame could stem from the fact that he is attracted to a black woman in the first place, whom he also describes as an animal (e.g., his need to "break [her] in" like a horse or his direct comparison of Hetta to a "wild colt"). But maybe Dutton is also ashamed that he has repeatedly raped a woman who is now dying as a result of his rape and her subsequent pregnancy. In addition to recalling Hetta's "small young breasts tilted up" and "little buttocks," John also remembers—with guilt or sorrow?—"her tears and ... frightened eyes" as he rapes her (9). This last line in particular is remarkable in its ability to immerse readers at once in the individual victimizer's psyche (John's); the widespread victimizing oppression of the patriarchy; the individual victim's consciousness (Hetta's); and the widespread victimization of black and white women together. Textual moments like these, in which readers are prompted to witness secondarily multiple and conflicting viewpoints, reveal the witnessing potential of trauma fiction and provoke readers to extend dual-witnessing out of the novel in which they are immersed and into the world in which they live.

Walker continues her third-person limited narration throughout *Jubilee*, so that, as we work through its pages, we enter deeper into the conflicting consciousnesses of disparate characters. When Vyry discovers that Lillian has been raped by Union soldiers, the narrator recounts: "Vyry saw what damage the soldiers had done . . . She saw molasses all over the floor, walls dirtied, . . . chairs broken. She could hardly pick her way . . . up the stairs to Miss Lillian's room, where she found her. 'Oh, my God,' said Vyry, 'I ain't never seen sitch a mess in all my borned days'" (289). Vyry's statement—"I've never seen sitch a mess" before—seems salient, coming from a woman who has witnessed lynchings; seen a man brand a runaway slave on her face; and been beaten so viciously that a mere flap of skin remains where her breast should be. Multiple meanings extend out of Vyry's "mess." The house is in shambles, and Lillian has been raped and lies constricted on the floor, but Vyry is also facing the whole "mess" of slavery, of the war, of Reconstruction, of a country—supposedly born in freedom—that could allow this "mess" to transpire in the first place.[7] Thus, out of a single scene, Vyry walking up the stairs to her sister, Walker witnesses the mess that is America, a mess to which we all belong and to which we must all bear witness.

In witnessing from a multitude of perspectives, *Jubilee* provides readers with the opportunity to enter into the South so thoroughly that we are taught about blacksmithing and carpentry and healing with roots and herbs; about the economics of plantation life and sharecropping; and about what the rich and poor wore. Before we reach the end of the epic, we have the chance to witness secondarily the life and thoughts of Vyry, Lillian, Marster John, Salina, Sis Hetta, various house and field servants, black freemen, two of Vyry's husbands, three of her children, the plantation's overseer, and soldiers from the Confederate and Union armies.

In her detailed depictions, Walker most often takes up the perspective of African Americans, struggling to survive through the nineteenth century. She does not, however, portray all Northerners as saviors, not even Union soldiers. Instead, *Jubilee* makes clear that American (racial) oppression is not limited to the South. The men who fight to preserve the union and emancipate the South also burn Southern plantations, steal food and farm stock from ex-slaves and ex-owners alike, and rape Southern women (280). When Union soldiers visit the "Big house" to read the Emancipation Proclamation and free the slaves, they wreak violence on Lillian's body and across the plantation. When Vyry tries to make herself breakfast, she finds the kitchen "overrun with soldiers" who have eaten, stolen, or destroyed everything in the house, smokehouse, barn and barnyard, and adjoining property (280). As their revelries become increasingly spirited (and violent), the soldiers "turn loose" the horses, give the hogs "a merry chase with sticks," "set the cotton on fire," and beat and rape Lillian (281). They treat domestic space like a war zone. These Northern soldiers seem less committed to a cause (such as Emancipation) than to the destruction of the Southern enemy and anyone connected to it, including those African Americans they supposedly arrived to free. In such portrayals, Walker refuses to glorify unequivocally those who fought to end slavery but witnesses instead how members of the white patriarchy, independent of geography, oppress and violate social subordinates. Slavery, *Jubilee* implies, is not just a "Southern" problem about which Northerners can feel retrospectively self-satisfied. Its blood memory stains us all.

Finally, *Jubilee* demonstrates that the racism, sexism, and classism inherent in institutional slavery did not cease when the Civil War did but persisted through Reconstruction, perpetuated by the national rampages of the Ku Klux Klan and embodied in those white proprietors who entrapped black families into working the land for free (365–66). The physical novel itself testifies to the scope and magnitude of American violence and oppression. After the Emancipation Proclamation is read, over two-hundred pages of text remain, signifying that, however many years have passed (or pages turned) since institutional slavery, Americans still have many more to go before they can close the book on the subject. Walker was writing a sequel to *Jubilee* when she passed away in 1998, suggesting that the narrative history of American racism, sexism, and classism does not end with *Jubilee* but continues to be witnessed in novels yet to be completed. In this case, Walker's unfinished project speaks to the need for readers to witness secondarily what the author no longer can: our nation's dark history and violent heritage.

By testifying (from any and all perspectives) to the systemic racism, sexism, and classism in and across America, *Jubilee* details not only the single life narrative of one African American woman (i.e., the actual Margaret Duggans Ware Brown or her fictive counterpart, Vyry Ware Brown) but also American culture and history as a whole, grounded in the particular experiences of an Afra-American who lived, survived, and died in the American South. Walker explains that when she conducted research for *Jubilee,* the available historical records explained the Civil War and its aftermath exclusively from the "[S]outhern white point of view," the "[N]orthern white viewpoint," or the "Negro viewpoint" ("How I Wrote Jubilee" 52). In *Jubilee,* Walker testifies to and through all three conflicting viewpoints, situating her novel's narrative voice at the liminal core of a Venn diagram of witnessing in order to align not only with Southern whites, Northern whites, and Negros but all Americans at once. Perhaps for this reason, Graham describes *Jubilee* not only as a Civil War epic or African American novel but also as "a memoir of the nation" ("Preface" *How I Wrote Jubilee* x), a work of fiction that witnesses intersecting "Afro-American" and "Anglo-American" (and ultimately human) truths (Graham "Introduction" *How I Wrote Jubilee* xix).

From this Venn perspective, *Jubilee* testifies to the transformative power of witnessing. In an interview with Graham, Walker underscored her belief that the "right and responsibility" of the writer-artist are to "show the way," to witness primarily and secondarily by proxy and to teach others (such as her readership) to dual-witness (Graham "Fusion" 280–81). Fittingly, the novel's climax centers around Vyry's first extensive act of primary witnessing. When her first husband, Randall Ware, returns at the end of the novel to reclaim his former wife (now remarried to Innis Brown), Vyry relays the details of Lillian's assault and her ensuing posttraumatic stress. Instead of witnessing Lillian's trauma secondarily (or acknowledging Vyry's secondary traumatization at the suffering of her half-sister), Randall anti-witnesses Vyry for continuing to care about a white woman after Emancipation. To this, Vyry retorts: "All I got to say, Randall Ware" (482)—a phrase that launches six pages of witnessing and signifies the enormity, the "all," that Vyry "got to" witness.

Vyry explains that Randall's accusatory response fits into a larger pattern of anti-witnessing. "You done called me a white folks' nigger," she responds, "cause my daddy was . . . white" (482), as if Vyry is to blame for her parentage or racial heritage. While Randall's criticism is hurtful, Vyry testifies, his censure is not unusual, as those closest to her have often anti-witnessed her. "Old Marster was my own daddy," she confirms, but "never did own me for his child" (483). Instead, John Dutton a-witnessed his daughter both by ignoring their familial relationship and also by negating her personhood (i.e., by counting her as property instead of as family). Vyry explains that she "begged" her father-master to let her "marriage with" Randall and to "go free" herself, but "he said no" (483), anti-witnessing her by forbidding her to live an autonomous life. Moreover, John "stripped" his daughter "naked" and put her "on the auction block for sale," anti-witnessing her body and personhood and inspiring voyeuristic anti-witnessing among those who gathered to ogle and bid for her. Finally, Vyry witnesses, her father "ain't punish nobody when he stand to see them beat me" (483). Worse even than her own whipping is the fact that her father a-witnessed the torture of his daughter. Through witnessing her history of being anti-witnessed and placing Randall's comments in conversation with her experience, Vyry teaches her first husband (and the reader through him) that when one responds to a survivor in a destructive manner, one contributes to her trauma. In anti-witnessing Vyry, Randall—who also abhors those such as John Dutton who have mistreated her—aligns with her abusers in victimizing her. Vyry's testimony thus illuminates not only her past history but also the responsibility respondents have to the speaker-survivor. When readers blame, ignore, or appropriate another's testimony, they join in her victimization and help perpetuate her trauma.

Through Vyry's climactic testimony, *Jubilee* underscores the difficulty of witnessing primarily, particularly when the one who testifies, like Vyry, has been repeatedly anti-witnessed. Thus, when Vyry divulges that her father a-witnessed the trauma of her whipping, she suddenly "stop[s]" and "look[s] . . . frightened, almost panic stricken" (484), realizing that she has begun to witness a trauma she has never yet disclosed. This moment takes on added significance when Vyry continues to witness her narrative despite the difficulty of doing so and when her husbands, moved by her testimony, begin to dual-witness. "They caught her words," Walker writes, "and suddenly they were both standing over her" (484). In carefully attending to Vyry's story, the men perceive nuances they had previously overlooked. For perhaps the first time, they "catch" her words, a type of active listening that enables dual-witnessing. They move physically closer to her (or "stand over her") and, instead of listening passively, invite her to continue witnessing: "'What did you say?' asked Innis. 'Who stood to beat you?' asked Randall Ware. Then both of them together said, 'When?'" (484). In engaging her narrative, Randall and Innis signal their support for Vyry and their investment in her narrative. By asking questions such as "What?," "Who?," "When?," they encourage the speaker to testify. In this pivotal scene, *Jubilee* underscores the difficulty and necessity of witnessing what has long been anti-witnessed and the call to witness secondarily (as Randall and Innis do when they express outrage at—and empathy for—Vyry's suffering).

When Randall and Innis engage her trauma, Vyry finds the strength to continue to witness. In answer to their questions and expressed concern, Vyry "snatch[es] at her clothes, t[ears] them loose, and bare[s] her back" (484). In doing so, she witnesses her traumatic history through her body, transcending the inefficacy of language to witness both physical and psychic catastrophe. "That's what they done to me that morning when I was trying to meet you at the creek," she testifies. "That's how come I got them there scars" (484). In tearing off her clothes and baring her back, Vyry recalls both the trauma of her whipping (when she was stripped to be flogged) and also that of her sale on the auction block (when she was stripped to be sold). Here, however, no one disrobes Vyry against her will. Instead, Vyry resolves to undress before the engaged and empathic—versus appropriative and voyeuristic—gaze of her husbands and readers. In doing so, she wields control of her body, her narrative, and her trauma, witnessing primarily what has, until now, been anti-witnessed.

Vyry's husbands respond to her testimony in kind, witnessing secondarily despite the difficulty of doing so. When Vyry tears open her dress, Randall and Innis are appropriately "horrified" at the "sight of her terribly scarred back" (484). However, they do not allow their horror to interfere with their ability to dual-witness but continue to engage Vyry's narrative. Accordingly, not only primary but also secondary witnessing (and, read together, dual-witnessing) marks the climax of Walker's epic novel. The narrator imparts that when Innis beholds Vyry's back, he "knew and understood" (484): He not only "knows" the details of Vyry's traumatic history but also "understands" or witnesses them secondarily. *Jubilee* invites a similar response from its readers: not only to know (or to read about) the history of American slavery but also to understand and bear witness to it. Randall impels this readerly reaction when he swears: "Oh ... my God! ... Look at what those bastards have done" (484). Randall's excited utterance compels *Jubilee*'s readers not to look away (or to a-witness Vyry's trauma) but to engage the text in order to witness what the protagonist (and countless other African Americans) have endured. Vyry herself incites Innis's promise to "know and understand" and Randall's call to "look" when she testifies to her husbands and readers: "I wants you to bear me witness" (485). Vyry's charge to witness secondarily (or "to bear [her] witness") is particularly significant, considering that Innis and her readers already know about her past abuse. As her husband of several years, Innis has presumably seen Vyry's naked and scarred body. Likewise, her readers have read the scene detailing her whipping and know the circumstances surrounding her trauma. When Vyry impels her addressees, therefore, to "bear [her] witness," she elicits more than mere knowledge. She impels Innis' understanding, Randall's refusal to look away, and character-driven and readerly-fulfilled dual-witnessing.

As a result of such dual-witnessing, Vyry begins to heal. Her secondary witnesses are likewise altered. Although Randall has returned to retrieve Vyry, after witnessing her history, he knows "they could never go back to what had been before" (485). Whereas he once abandoned Vyry because he refused to sacrifice his freedom for their love, he now sacrifices his desire (to keep Vyry as his wife) in recognition of her self-sufficiency. Randall knows Vyry is not a slave to be claimed but an independent individual who demands to be witnessed. Innis draws closer to Vyry through dual-witnessing. When he witnesses her trauma secondarily, he sees not only her lacerated body but also her soul, "touched with a spiritual fire" and "forged in a crucible of suffering"

(485). He also recognizes how Vyry can transcend her own individuality to become "a living sign" of "all the best that any human being could hope to become," an "assurance that nothing could destroy a people who sons had come from her loins" (485). In witnessing Vyry secondarily, Innis appreciates his wife not only as a single person but also as a representative of the collective strength of all (Afra-)Americans. He is thus moved to testify: "I has listened to, and I has learned from listening to what yall has to say" (486). He has listened and witnessed, known and understood, and learned from having done so. Innis's use of "yall" suggests that he addresses not only Vyry as an individual but also the collective group of persons she exemplifies. If Vyry becomes in this scene a representative primary witness, Innis becomes a consummate secondary witness. Together, they signify the revolutionary potential of primary and secondary witnesses who unite in—and are transformed by—dual-witnessing.

Jubilee emphasizes the transformative power of dual-and communal witnessing through Vyry and Innis's concluding characterizations of marriage and family. Vyry portrays marriage as a form of dual-witnessing when she testifies that "Innis and me has got a marriage . . . We has been through everything together, birth and death, flood and fire, sickness and trouble" (489). Vyry defines marriage not as a legal contract but as a mutual relationship fostered between two individuals who are dedicated to witnessing "everything together" (489). Innis builds upon Vyry's (re)definition of marriage when he likens family interaction to communal witnessing. He discloses that what initially attracted him to Vyry was her demonstrated commitment to family—an intimate community structure that he sensed would prove restorative. "Here," he testifies, "was the first time I ever seed a colored family what looked like they was a loving wholeness together, a family what slavery hadn't ever broke" (487). The characterization of family as "a loving wholeness together" evokes the process of communal witnessing during which multiple persons, empathizing with—or "loving"—one another, unite "together" in "wholeness" to work through one another's life narratives. Like Vyry's depiction of marriage, Innis's characterization of family does not evoke legal language but celebrates the decision of individuals who unite to witness trauma together. In both Vyry and Innis's affirmations, the quality of the relationship is emphasized above its legality, suggesting that one can make one's own marriages and families with anyone who is equally willing to witness mutually.[8] In this light, the proposal to "marriage with" (483) Vyry and Innis—and all of *Jubilee*'s characters and plotlines—extends out of the text to the novel's readership. When readers engage a novel such as *Jubilee*, we have the opportunity to "marry" the text and form a "family" with its characters, storylines, and author as well as the actual people and historical narratives the work fictively represents.

By concluding a novel that testifies to the multifarious traumas inherent in institutional slavery with an extended scene of successful dual-witnessing (and induced communal witnessing among the novel's readership), *Jubilee* suggests that the way to prevail over trauma in general (and over institutionalized slavery in particular) is to witness it dually and communally. Only by witnessing the truth of America's original sin, *Jubilee* suggests, can the nation's readers work through a shared traumatic history. The novel ends fittingly with Vyry, having witnessed primarily (and having been witnessed both secondarily and communally), "feeding her own chickens and calling them home to roost" (497). As Vyry calls her chickens home, so too does the novel invite readers "home" to witness (through fiction) the truths of American slavery, which continue to affect and inform not only the descendants of African American slaves but also (and to varying degrees) all Americans, independent of race, gender, class, and geography. The first line of Walker's acknowledgments reads: "Many people of different races, colors, and creeds have given me material assistance in the creation of this story" (ix). *Jubilee* testifies to and for them all, speaking to the power of fiction—and its readers—to witness the traumas of an individual, a people, and a nation.

CHAPTER 4

"This Thing We Have Done Together"

Haunted Witnessing in the Novels
of Toni Morrison and Jesmyn Ward

The preceding chapter explores how Zora Neale Hurston's *Their Eyes Were Watching God* and Margaret Walker's *Jubilee* promote multiethnic and multigendered dual- and communal witnessing. This chapter analyzes Toni Morrison's Pulitzer Prize–winning *Beloved* (1987) alongside Jesmyn Ward's National Book Award–winning *Salvage the Bones* (2011) and *Sing, Unburied Sing* (2017) to investigate how these contemporary works witness the traumatic aftermath of American slavery as well as the mutual jeopardies of blackness, womanhood, and poverty to impel even reluctant readers to engage the individual and collective histories of impoverished African American women in particular and marginalized Americans in general.

"Not a Story to Pass on": (Anti-)Witnessing in *Beloved*

In *Beloved,* the former slave Sethe murders her infant daughter rather than allow her "Beloved" to become enslaved. Eighteen years later, the embodied spirit of her dead daughter surfaces to reconcile with its mother. In their analyses of the text, critics focus on *Beloved's* ability to witness primarily the traumas of slavery and its aftermath (Bouson *Quiet* 136; McDowell "Negotiating" 144). Readers note that the novel witnesses secondarily by proxy a historical life-narrative (Rody 93).[1] They explore how the novel's stream of consciousness and fragmented form mirrors the shattered and circuitous style of traumatic testimony, when voiced by a primary witness, struggling with posttraumatic stress disorder (Bouson *Quiet* 136; Wyatt 2).[2] Critics also contend that *Beloved* uses the individual voices of strong but shattered black protagonists to testify to the pervasive haunting of institutionalized slavery (Mobley 358). To this conversation, I add an analysis of how Morrison's text shapes our readerly response to her novel's testimony. *Beloved*, I argue, teaches readers about the danger of anti-witnessing and the promise of secondary witnessing. Through myriad counterexamples, *Beloved* warns readers that we may anti-witness in any number of ways—aggressively, ignorantly and negatively, and/or co-optively—and must thus work together to (re)position ourselves at the core of a Venn diagram of secondary witnessing. This Venn liminality, *Beloved* suggests, enables witnesses to work through personal and cultural traumas, making the reading of trauma fiction psychosocially productive. Without the support of a secondary witness (an individual reader willing to delve into *Beloved*) or group of communal witnesses (collective readers who witness together the effects of American slavery), we may not prevail over traumatic pasts. *Beloved* thus demonstrates the extent to which historical and fictive speakers need the support of witnessing communities in order to survive.

Beloved speaks to the unspeakable horrors and enduring traumas of American slavery. The fact that Morrison sets her seminal novel about slavery in 1873, ten years after the Emancipation Proclamation was issued, suggests that the psychosocial violence of slavery did not end with the freeing of the slaves but persisted—whether for another ten years (when the novel is set) or for over 110 years (when *Beloved* was published). Accordingly, *Beloved* asks readers to confront not only the vast devastation slavery wrought through the nineteenth century but also how its aftermath persists today. "Slavery," Sherryl Vint attests, "remains an open wound in American culture" (242). For Morrison, Nellie McKay argues, publishing *Beloved* represents a "conscious act toward healing" this "painful wound" (3)—an attempt to witness the enduring traumas of slavery and to prompt readers to witness them in return. Perhaps for this reason, Yvette Christiansë identifies *Beloved* not only as Morrison's "most testimonial work" but also as "*the* most powerful novel of its generation to 'bear witness'" to the trauma of slavery and, I would add, to impel its readership to do the same. Moreover, Morrison does not restrict herself in *Beloved* to illustrating the broad scope of American slavery but, as Linda Krumholz notes, also "constructs a parallel between the individual processes of psychological recovery and a historical or national process" (395). That is, *Beloved* testifies to the dangers not only of systemic anti-witnessing (emblematized in institutional slavery) but also of anti-witnessing on an individual level (exhibited through the narratives of her richly developed characters). In doing so, *Beloved* provokes readers (via counterexample) to engage those collective and particularized traumas we may otherwise ignore or negate.

To guide readers through this process, *Beloved* speaks first and foremost to the violence anti-witnessing wreaks. The novel's clearest illustrations of anti-witnessing are aggressive, as when schoolteacher, the overseer of the Kentucky plantation "Sweet Home," violently punishes the pregnant Sethe for reporting his nephews' abuse of her when the two men stole Sethe's breast milk by forcibly nursing from her (81). When schoolteacher learns that Sethe has disclosed this assault to her mistress, Mrs. Garner, he anti-witnesses the slave woman aggressively, instructing his nephews to whip her for attempting to witness her trauma primarily. Sethe's resulting wounds are so severe that, when they heal, her back is covered in a cluster of knotted scars, a mutilation Sethe later describes as a "tree" that "grows" on her body even after eighteen years. The phrase Sethe uses to describe her physical trauma—"it grows there still" (20)—underscores the lasting effects of aggressive anti-witnessing. Sethe's suffering does not end when schoolteacher and his nephews stop abusing her or when her opened back closes. Instead, as Sethe confides to Paul D (the only other slave to survive Sweet Home), she continues to suffer the aftermath of schoolteacher's anti-witnessing. The scars that grow on her back represent the way anti-witnessing continues to affect traumatized subjects, literally scarring Sethe for life.

Readers also experience the augmented effects of aggressive anti-witnessing in Sethe's "rough response" to schoolteacher's pursuit of her: her attempted murder of her children (201). When Sethe escapes slavery to find freedom with her mother-in-law, Baby Suggs, schoolteacher follows her to return her to slavery. Preferring death to a life of enslavement and anti-witnessing, Sethe endeavors to kill her four children (and presumably herself) but is successful only in slaying her toddler daughter, whose throat she cuts with a handsaw (176). Sethe's visceral reaction to schoolteacher's return—itself a form of internalized aggressive anti-witnessing, in aligning with the victimizer (schoolteacher) against his victims (her children and herself)—emphasizes the lasting damage aggressive anti-witnessing provokes. Schoolteacher's original anti-witnessing of Sethe continues to "grow" not only over her back but into her psyche as well, so that, when her abuser returns to collect her, she responds not as a primary or secondary witness but as an aggressive anti-witness, acting not against her victimizer but—now as a victimizer herself—against his innocent victims. In engaging this passage, readers discover how aggressive anti-witnessing begets anti-witnessing, compounding trauma.

Not all of *Beloved*'s examples of anti-witnessing are aggressive. Just as one can aggressively anti-witness by aligning with a victimizer, one can co-optively anti-witness by appropriating another's life narrative. Mr. Garner, the master of Sweet Home, co-optively anti-witnesses his black male slaves when he classifies them as men. "Y'all got boys," he brags to his white neighbors: "my niggers is men" (12). Here, Garner appears to validate his slaves' humanity, but he actually co-opts their personhood. In taunting the other slave owners that his slaves are "men" while theirs are merely "boys," Garner shifts attention from his slaves' humanity to his own (false) generosity in recognizing their personhood as well as to his uber-masculine status as man-maker. Garner's supposedly progressive vision of black personhood is revealed to be co-optively corrupt and, in some respects, worse than that of his white audience, since Garner recognizes (where his friends do not) that the black men he owns are human beings, and yet he is still capable—man-enough—to enslave them. One may also question whether Garner considers his female slaves to be "women" in the same way his "niggers is men." Posing this inquiry exposes the co-optive paternalism implicit in Garner's assertion: his black males become "men" because he decrees it; his black females are not "women" because their humanity has never occurred to him. This passage exposes the co-optive anti-witnessing inherent in the master-slave bond, deconstructing the myth of the "good master" and underscoring the injustice that ensues when one human being appropriates (by claiming to own) another.

As if to recognize the anti-witnessing intrinsic to institutionalized slavery, the white abolitionist siblings, Mr. and Miss Bodwin, inform Baby Suggs that they "don't hold with slavery, even Garner's kind" (167). The Bodwins, however, also exhibit their own co-optive tendencies, suggesting that the propensity to anti-witness is not restricted to Southern slave owners but is a fault found throughout humanity. Mr. and Miss Bodwin appropriatively anti-witness Sethe when they help her and her daughter Denver, so that they can—at least in part—feel pleased with themselves. Rather than entering into Sethe's trauma, Mr. Bodwin appropriatively anti-witnesses her trials to relive the "heady days" of his abolitionism (306). When he has the chance to advocate for Sethe, following her murder of her daughter, Mr. Bodwin intercedes, not necessarily because he sympathizes with the slave mother's plight but because "nothing since" the "good old days" of abolitionism has proved as "stimulating" (307), as if anti-slavery efforts represent an adventure to divert white progressives instead of a socio-ethical imperative. Likewise, Miss Bodwin fantasizes about sending Denver to college, anticipating the excitement such an "experiment" will afford her as benefactress—a thrill she too has not felt since working on the Underground Railroad (307). In behaving thus, the Bodwins appropriatively anti-witness the people they assist in order to enliven their own lives. In doing so, they negatively a-witness the fact that, since racial injustice does not end with Emancipation, they still have much to accomplish as civil rights activists. They also ignorantly a-witness their own racism in treating those they assist as instruments for amusement instead of autonomous human beings.

As if to emphasize this point, when Denver seeks help from the Bodwins, she discovers in their house a cast-iron bank, fashioned to resemble "a black-boy's mouth full of money" (300). The representation of blackness captured in the Bodwins' collectible is grotesque: The bank's head is "thrown back farther than a head could go"; its eyes "bulge like moons . . . above the gaping red mouth" that overflows with coins. "Painted across the pedestal" on which the bank-boy kneels are "the words 'At Yo Service'" (300). This figurine recalls the racist vision of the obsequious slave, ready—or "at yo service"—to offer self-effacing entertainment to whites. Moreover, the bank objectifies the black body as decorative, as a toy to be played with (or co-opted) by those with white privilege. The bank symbolizes the unexamined racism and co-optive anti-witnessing even abolitionists can demonstrate. The Bodwins are for the most part "good" white people who wish to assist their African American neighbors, but they too succumb to co-optive anti-witnessing. In doing so, they remind readers to check the tendency to anti-witness and to work instead to reposition ourselves as secondary witnesses.

Beloved does not confine its examples of co-optive anti-witnessing to white characters but speaks instead to the way all persons, independent of race, anti-witness. The African American exemplar of co-optive anti-witnessing is the mysterious figure of Beloved[3] who, in attempting to bond with Sethe, nearly destroys the object of her desire. As soon as Beloved appears on Sethe's doorstep, she demonstrates a fierce attachment to the woman she claims as mother. Beloved confides to Denver that Sethe is "the one I have to have" (89). The word "have" in this sentence is possessive, indicating that Beloved feels she must "gain ownership" of Sethe (*OED* sense 1), but it also evokes Beloved's role as ghostly co-optive anti-witness, as a "spirit, especially an evil one" who "occup[ies] and ha[s] power over" another in order to "control or dominate" her (sense 4). Beloved does not merely wish to keep company with Sethe but to "have," possess, or appropriate her. When the revenant repeats "I want to be the two of us" (253), she reveals her drive not to dual-witness with Sethe but to absorb her mother figure into herself, to embody both women ("the two of us") in her person. Denver observes that "Beloved ate up [Sethe's] life, took it, swelled up with it, grew taller on it . . . The bigger Beloved got, the smaller Sethe became" (294). If the women dual-witnessed, each would be strengthened by their communication. Instead, Beloved co-optively anti-witnesses Sethe to Sethe's peril. The inverted relationship existing between the women's bodies supports this theory: Beloved's body swells as she devours Sethe's life narrative. Sethe begins to diminish.

In view of her possessive tendencies, some critics read Beloved as a succubus, the female demon of African American folklore who sexually assaults or "rides" male victims (Puckett 568). Beloved treats Paul D in this manner when she appears to him nightly, demanding that he "touch her on the inside part" (137). As Pamela Barnett notes, what distinguishes Beloved from other succubae is that she preys not only on men but also on a woman, co-optively pursuing Sethe and depleting the woman of vitality, much as she depletes Paul D of semen (Barnett 420). The narrator recounts: "Sethe was licked, tasted, eaten by Beloved's eyes. Like a familiar, she hovered" (68). When Sethe wakes at night to discover Beloved suspended above her, presumably to "ride" her, Sethe perceives in Beloved's eyes a "bottomless" look, "loaded . . . with desire" (69). Her daughter-succubus may wish to connect with her mother-figure, but she consumes her instead. Barnett suggests that, like the nephews who "stole [Sethe's] milk" (Morrison 81), Beloved also "sucks Sethe dry" (Barnett 422). This parallel emphasizes the violence both co-optive and aggressive anti-witnessing can wreak. One form of anti-witnessing may be less malevolent than the other, but they both inflict damage. Finally, if, as critics such as Krumholz argue, Beloved personifies slavery as a whole—a traumatic past that all Americans must collectively witness (395)—then her role as succubus reveals that, when we a-witness the past (as Sethe and Paul D do), it returns to possess us.

Beloved also demonstrates how respondents can a-witness by refusing to engage another's life narrative. The Garners, for example, decline to witness the traumas their slaves suffer (and their own responsibility, as slave owners, in creating that suffering). Instead, they a-witness their victimization of human property. When Mrs. Garner hires schoolteacher to manage her plantation, she elects to ignore his violent treatment of her slaves, thereby facilitating Sethe's assault and authorizing schoolteacher's continued abuse (44). Moreover, Mrs. Garner does not restrict her a-witnessing to the traumas her slaves suffer but also a-witnesses their desires and personhood. When

Sethe informs Mrs. Garner that she wants to marry another slave, Halle, for instance, the mistress supports the coupling, anticipating that its offspring will add to her estate (31). In granting consent, however, Mrs. Garner negatively a-witnesses Sethe and Halle's parental rights to their own children, since she considers their future progeny to be her property. She also dismisses Sethe's request for a wedding ceremony (31), not only ignorantly a-witnessing Sethe's desire for her marriage to be witnessed communally but also negatively a-witnessing the couple's right to create a family unit that (from her own Christian standpoint) "God has joined together" and thus no one (not even white slave owners) can "put asunder" (Mark 10:9) via the division and selling of slaves. In this scene, Mrs. Garner a-witnesses both the legitimacy of Sethe and Halle's commitment to one another and their personhood, implying that, while black slaves may mate with the permission of their masters, only (white) humans can marry.

Instances such as these (when Sethe's humanity is a-witnessed) seem to affect the slave woman more than any other mode of anti-witnessing. While she suffers persistent anti-witnessing at Sweet Home, Sethe runs away only when schoolteacher a-witnesses her personhood. As soon as he arrives at Sweet Home, schoolteacher a-witnesses the humanity of the Garners' slaves, treating them like farm stock (and worse) instead of human beings. Schoolteacher places a bit in Paul D's mouth to remind him that his "manhood" is not inherent but depends upon the will of the white overseer (82). He names a rooster "Mister" but denies this same title to his male slaves (86). In each act, the humanity of Sweet Home's slaves is ignored and negated. When schoolteacher instructs his nephews to categorize Sethe's "human" verses "animal characteristics" (228)—implying that she is not a human but an animal hybrid—Sethe can no longer tolerate his a-witnessing. She escapes instead, and when schoolteacher returns to collect Sethe, the indignities she has suffered from his anti-witnessing induce her to try to kill her children and herself rather than be treated as parahuman once more. This "rough response" (201) exposes the violence a-witnessing wreaks, prompting Sethe to enact further violence against her Beloved and herself. Through these and other examples, *Beloved* illuminates how slavery—in fostering a system in which those with power legally own those without—a-witnesses the personhood of the enslaved.

To combat the damage anti-witnessing inflicts, *Beloved* underscores the importance of dual-witnessing. The novel does not suggest that this process is undemanding but accentuates how difficult (and yet necessary) secondary witnessing is. When Paul D and Sethe discuss the trauma of her nursing, for example, Paul D reveals that Halle observed—and was traumatized secondarily by—the assault on Sethe (81). Sethe is horrified to learn that her husband could watch two men violate her without interceding, but Paul D counters that "whatever [Halle] saw . . . broke him like a twig . . . Last time I saw him he was sitting by the churn. He had butter all over his face" (83). Unable to help Sethe or to process what he has seen, Halle shatters. The butter he smears on his face evokes the milk the nephews have drained from his wife's breasts, and his inability to witness Sethe's victimization secondarily (other than to weep butter tears for her stolen milk) reveals the contagion of trauma and the difficulty of dual-witnessing. Through such scenes, Morrison acknowledges the potentially drastic consequences of dual-witnessing but prompts readers to witness anyway. Thus, when Paul D tells Sethe about Halle's nervous collapse, she empathizes but still clamors: "He saw them boys do that to me and let them keep on breathing air? He saw? He saw? He saw?'" (81). Sethe's outrage at Halle's vicarious traumatization underscores the responsibility bystanders have to witness others secondarily, ever mindful but irrespective of personal cost.

In Sethe's case, readers are asked to dual-witness among other calamities a mother who murders her daughter to save her from anticipated traumas worse than death. With Halle, we may find that we cannot. However much we may recoil against the novel's examples of anti-witnessing, we may also find ourselves unable to witness secondarily the traumas to which *Beloved* testifies.[4] To help us, the novel offers readers the prototype of those secondary witnesses who struggle to confront others' tribulations but who, unlike Halle, are not destroyed in the process. These exemplars of dual-witnessing traverse both racial and gendered differences, affirming that one can witness across and through divergent identity constructs. Of distinct significance is the interracial female dual-witnessing that occurs between black and white female witnesses, when their shared occupation of the female sphere enables them to pass over the racial barriers between them, and the intergendered African American witnessing that develops between male and female African American witnesses, who transcend gender disparities to connect through a shared experience of race and racism.

Interracial female dual-witnessing enables the white runaway, Amy Denver, to help the black escaped slave, Sethe, give birth to Denver and find her way to freedom. As the women search for a shelter in which a battered Sethe can deliver her baby, Amy witnesses secondarily Sethe's physical and narrative needs, taking cues from the primary witness as to where, when, and at what rate they can advance—both along their journey and through their conversation. As Sethe crawls, Amy walks beside her, and when Sethe believes she can no longer continue, Amy offers Sethe the strength to do so.

"It was [Amy's] voice," Sethe remembers, "that urged her along and made her think that maybe she wasn't, after all, just a crawling graveyard" (42). By keeping engaged (or dual-witnessing) with Sethe, Amy offers her partner the strength to survive. When Sethe can crawl no longer, Amy massages her torn feet and broken legs (42), emphasizing not only the psychological but the physical energy required to dual-witness. Amy does not glamorize this process but acknowledges how difficult witnessing can be. "It's gonna hurt, now," she warns Sethe: "Anything dead coming back to life hurts" (42). In keeping pace with Sethe, Amy engages Sethe's life narrative without condemning, co-opting, ignoring, or negating it. In doing so, she transcends racial boundaries to witnesses another woman secondarily, saving not only Sethe's life but Denver's as well. Sethe names Denver after Amy to honor the white woman's role in her delivery.

As secondary witness, Amy offers Sethe the language and opportunity to witness trauma primarily. When Amy first views Sethe's scarred back, she traces the woman's wounds with her fingers (representing another instance of physical secondary witnessing) and declares: "It's a . . . chockecherry tree. See, here's the trunk—it's red and split wide open, full of sap, and this here's the parting for the branches . . . Leaves, too, look like, and dern if these ain't blossoms. Tiny little cherry blossoms, just as white. Your back got a whole tree on it. In bloom" (93). Amy does not simply transform the appalling sight of Sethe's flayed back into something beautiful (the chokecherry tree) but also both vocally and tactically witnesses Sethe's trauma. As a result, as Lucille Fultz suggests, Sethe "has an opportunity" to witness primarily—through Amy's secondary witnessing—"how badly she has been beaten" (33). Sethe later confides to Paul D, "I got a tree on my back . . . I've never seen it and never will. But that's what [Amy] said it looked like" (18). Through Sethe's depiction of her physical trauma, we realize Amy has offered her the language to speak the unspeakable, helping to convert a story of pain into one of survival.

One reason Amy and Sethe may dual-witness effectively is that their lives and circumstances have been similar, offering the women a mutual foundation on which to build reciprocity. Like Sethe, Amy has escaped the abusive master of a Kentuckian plantation where she was indentured for sixteen years (38). Although they have not fled the same form of subjugation, the women share common ground as fugitive bondswomen, each seeking freedom in the North: Amy is running to Boston, Sethe to Cincinnati. In light of their common histories and future goals, the novel pairs Amy and Sethe together as "two throw-away people, two lawless outlaws—a slave and a barefoot white woman with unpinned hair" (100). This partnership helps the women traverse difference to align through shared experience. Furthermore, as Nicole

Coonradt recognizes, if one considers the etymology of her name, Amy too is "beloved," as the French name Aimée derives from the Latin *amatus* (loved) and literally means "beloved" (170). By assigning the white runaway the same name as Sethe's black murdered daughter, Morrison unites Amy to Sethe and her female lineage, implicitly supporting a reading of interracial female dual-witnessing that is modeled through their interaction. By linking Amy to the character Beloved, Morrison also associates the white runaway with the institution of slavery itself (which Beloved embodies) and to the haunting traumas slavery effects. The novel thus suggests that we not only ought to dual-witness with one another (as Amy and Sethe do) but also ought to witness secondarily and communally the enduring aftermath of American slavery, which Beloved personifies and with which Amy (at least in name) is bound.

Part of what makes Amy a successful secondary witness is that she does not empathically anti-witness Sethe's experience. She does not imagine that, because the women share parallel histories, their suffering is equivalent. Instead, Amy acknowledges the racially charged disparities between the bondswomen's narratives. When she witnesses Sethe's flayed and festering back, Amy affirms: "I had me some whippings but . . . nothing like this . . . Whoever planted that tree beat [my master] . . . by a mile. Glad I ain't you" (94). Here, Amy embraces the spirit of Audre Lorde's message in "Age, Race, Class, and Sex" that, while women are uniformly oppressed by the patriarchy, those occupying intersecting positions of marginalization (e.g., women of color) face compounded subjugation. "Some problems [black and white women] share as women," Lorde writes, "some we do not . . . Certainly there are very real differences between us . . . But it is not those differences . . . that . . . separat[e] us . . . [but] our refusal to recognize those differences" (288). In dual-witnessing with Sethe, Amy does not gloss over racial difference but recognizes that whatever she has borne as a doubly marginalized white female servant does not compare to what Sethe has faced as a triply marginalized African American female slave.

Critics such as Nicole Coonradt and Deanna Barker equate African American slavery with Anglo servitude, since, in antebellum America, white indentured servants could be treated as "harshly" and "brutally" as slaves, and "the courts enforced the laws that made it so" (Barker 2). Furthermore, the Thirteenth Amendment to the Constitution of the United States abolishes slavery and indentured servitude in the same clause, indicating that the nineteenth-century federal legislature considered both forms of labor to be "similar ills" (Coonradt 180). Coonradt concludes: "[T]he difference between 'slavery' and 'indentured servitude'" was "primarily a semantic one" (177).

Amy takes a different stance: however much she has suffered as a white indentured servant, by virtue of her white privilege and Sethe's blackness (as well as the sociopolitical distinctions drawn between slavery and servitude), the African American slave woman has suffered more. Amy's appreciation of both her similarities to and differences from Sethe models the heteropathic identification that dual-witnessing demands and may account for why the women can transcend difference to work through trauma together.

Alongside interracial dual-witnessing, *Beloved* models intergendered dual-witnessing, emphasizing how individuals can overcome difference to witness collectively. Consider, for example, the relationship between Sethe and Paul D. Mary Paniccia Carden observes that, while critics note the "significant textual space and energy" *Beloved* devotes to Sethe and Paul D's partnership, many "relegate the romance strand of the novel to the status of subplot" (402). This approach is limiting for two reasons. First, the bond Sethe and Paul D share is not ancillary but central to the text, symbolizing the ideal of sustained (and intergendered) dual-witnessing. Second, the rapport that develops between the two ex-slaves is not significant because it models heteronormativity but because it celebrates the capacity to transcend difference in order to dual-witness. When Sethe bares her back to Paul D to witness bodily the trauma she cannot yet articulate, Paul D exhibits potential as a secondary witness. When he sees "the sculpture" Sethe's "back [has] become," he touches "every ridge and leaf of it with his mouth" (21). Like Sethe, Paul D lacks the language to address her suffering. In fact, the sight of Sethe's wounded back is so appalling that, when he first glimpses it, all he can think to say is: "Aw, Lord, girl" (21). Still, Paul D does not allow his secondary constriction to impede the couple's dual-witnessing. Like Amy before him, he traces every inch of Sethe's body in order to witness secondarily her enfleshed narrative.

Shortly after Paul D makes this gesture, he promises to witness Sethe secondarily, assuring: "Sethe, I'm here with you. . . . Jump, if you want to . . . I'll catch you 'fore you fall" (55). However well intentioned, Paul D's pledge is presumptuous. He assumes that she has not yet fallen (i.e., that he has arrived in time to save her from her trauma), that he knows how far she can and will fall, and that he has the psychological wherewithal to catch her before she does. Quickly, Paul D realizes that dual-witnessing will prove more difficult than anticipated. Although he feels equipped to witness secondarily the traumas of slavery that he has also suffered (e.g., physical and sexual assault), he finds himself powerless to engage those catastrophes that defy the limits of his imagination (e.g., mothers who murder their children). Thus, when Stamp Paid, an eye-witness to Sethe's "Misery" (201), presents Paul D with a newspaper clipping that reports Sethe's crime, Paul D looks at the article's accompanying picture of Sethe and declares by way of dismissal, "That ain't her mouth" (185). In speaking thus, Paul D negatively a-witnesses the woman he has sworn to witness secondarily. Furthermore, he denies Sethe's mouth in particular, not only a-witnessing Sethe's traumatic history but her vehicle of witnessing itself.

When Sethe, confronted by Paul D, attempts to explain why she killed her baby, Paul D a-witnesses her experience. As Sethe speaks, Paul D "[catches] only pieces of what she said"; her narrative makes him "dizzy" (189). Paul D reflects: "At first he thought it was her spinning . . . the way she was circling the subject. . . . Then he thought, No, it's the sound of her voice; it's too near" (189). Critics such as Bouson have noted that, in circling physically around the room and verbally around her subject, Sethe acts and speaks as a trauma victim, suffering from hyperarousal (*Quiet* 145). In recalling the murder of her child, Sethe becomes hyperactive and hypersensitive. She startles easily, moves erratically, and speaks frantically (189). Her attempt to witness is impeded by her trauma, which disrupts both her psyche and her speech. Consequently, Paul D has difficulty following her narrative. Paul D admits, however, that Sethe's narrative style does not impede his ability to listen as much as his own need to distance himself from the "nearness" of her story. That is, despite Sethe's hyperaroused circling, Paul D could still witness her tale secondarily if he chose to, but he does not. Sethe's narrative proves too much to bear, and Paul D a-witnesses both speaker and past rather than risk engaging the unthinkable.

When Sethe insists that Paul D acknowledge her "rough response to the Fugitive Bill" (201), he shifts from a-witnessing to aggressively anti-witness-ing.[5] When she maintains that killing her child was the only choice available to her, Paul D rebukes: "What you did was wrong, Sethe . . . You got two feet . . . not four" (194), implying that, in murdering her daughter, Sethe acted more like a quadrupedal animal than a bipedal human. In demeaning Sethe thus, Paul D aligns himself with those victimizers like schoolteacher who also negated her personhood. To Sethe, this reaction marks the ultimate betrayal. Paul D has not only refused to witness her secondarily (as he once promised to do) but also aggressively anti-witnessed her choices (by blaming her for the decisions she has made), ignorantly a-witnessed her trauma (in refusing to engage her past), and, alongside her other assailants, negatively a-witnessed her humanity (by suggesting only a beast could kill its offspring). As a result, Morrison writes, "a forest sprang up between them" (194). Since forests are comprised of innumerable trees, and *Beloved* has already established the tree as a symbol of Sethe's trauma, the novel suggests that the myriad trau-mas Sethe and Paul D have individually endured now collectively "spring up" between them, making it even more difficult for the pair to traverse difference to witness together.[6] The metaphoric forest also exemplifies the comprehensive destruction anti-witnessing effects. By responding aggressively and negatively to Sethe, Paul D compounds her trauma. The tree on her back multiplies into a forest that divides, impeding the couple's ability to dual-witness and to heal.

Sethe and Paul D's relationship cannot resolve until Paul D decides to witness Sethe secondarily. Deborah McDowell recognizes that, if the couple is to survive, "the lovers [must] engage in a mutual unburdening of the past" ("The Self and the Other" 82): They must learn to dual-witness. Although readers are not told precisely how Paul D comes to witness Sethe secondarily, we do learn that he eventually chooses to do so, breaching the figurative forest that divides them.[7] When Paul D first promises to witness Sethe secondarily, he does so without considering the scope and substance of the project he swears to uphold. Now, he has a better sense of what dual-witnessing requires, and their communication shifts. When Paul D pledges anew to "take care of" Sethe by witnessing her secondarily, he adds the phrase "starting now" (320), acknowledging that, while he made this guarantee before, he has not fulfilled it. Paul D then prepares to wash Sethe's feet (a symbolic act of secondary witnessing) but stops to ask: "Is it all right, Sethe, if I heat up some water?" (272). This inquiry reveals that Paul D no longer assumes he knows what is best for Sethe or even that he is best suited to help her. Instead, like Amy before him, he follows Sethe's lead, demonstrating that he would like to help her without presuming to do so—or how. To Paul D's offer, Sethe retorts: "And count my feet?" (320). Her question recalls Paul D's previous anti-witnessing and warns him not to betray her again. When Paul D humbly responds, "Rub your feet'" (320) and, with Sethe's consent, begins to bathe her, Sethe and readers alike are assured of his renewed commitment to Sethe as a person and to dual-witnessing as a process.[8]

Because of his willingness to witness her secondarily—or, as Paul D pledges, "to put his story next to hers" (322)—Sethe accepts Paul D as her partner. Thus, when he washes her feet, she "opens her eyes, knowing the danger of looking at him" and then decidedly "looks at him" anyway (320), recommitting to Paul D as he has to her. Instead of remaining strictly a primary witness and asking him to witness her secondarily, Sethe enters into a mutual relationship in which both parties witness primarily to—and secondarily for—one another. In order to maintain this reciprocity, Sethe recognizes that each must confront the unbearable in oneself and the other. Sethe commits to this process by fixing her gaze on Paul D and refusing to look away as he equally engages the darkest realities of her history. Paul D realizes what it means to have Sethe as a partner with whom to dual-witness. "She is a friend of my mind," he reflects. "She gather me . . . The pieces I am, she gather them and give them back to me in all the right order" (320). This description captures the spirit of dual-witnessing in which each person enters into the other's consciousness and then helps assemble the shattered pieces of the other's life into a mosaic narrative. T. S. Eliot concludes his *Waste Land*: "These fragments I have shored against my ruins" (146), affirming his intent to piece together a self and history from shattered fragments. In Morrison's model, the subject is not left to gather oneself alone but is invited to do so with the support of one's partner. By *Beloved*'s end, Sethe and Paul D exemplify this shared vision.

Beloved does not confine Sethe's narrative journey to a binary mode of dual-witnessing but extends the mutuality she shares with Amy and Paul D to the larger community, inviting her neighbors and readers to join her in communal witnessing. To model this collective spirit, Morrison draws on the African American tradition of call and response, defined by sociolinguist Geneva Smitherman as a "spontaneous verbal and non-verbal interaction between speaker and listener in which all of the statements ('calls') are punctuated by expressions ('responses') from the listener" (104). The ritual of call and response closely parallels that of dual- and communal witnessing. Both rites represent what Smitherman identifies as a "collaborative improvisation," characterizing a "shared experience" that unites listener and speaker—that is, caller and respondent or primary and secondary witness (Smitherman 119, 104). When a caller calls, respondents (or secondary witnesses) may agree with a speaker (or primary witness), urge her on, complete her statement, or emphatically affirm what she has witnessed (Smitherman 104). The group's response, Smitherman explains, assures the caller that her audience "approves of what she is saying and/or how she is saying it; it is immediate validation" (108). That is to say, in witnessing primarily, the caller's testimony is reaffirmed; her life narrative is engaged by her secondary witnesses, so that speaker and listeners may witness together what has become shared testimony. In linking dual- and communal witnessing to call and response, Morrison reaffirms the testimonial nature inherent to African American literature that at once embodies and promotes interracial and intergendered and readerly-speakerly witnessing—or call and response—out of and through the fraught histories of race and gender relations in America. In this way, as Bouson attests, *Beloved* upholds not only the "psychic cost of slavery" but also its "therapeutic alternative"—"the co-operative self healing"—or communal witnessing—of a "community of survivors" ("Approaches" 39).

In *Beloved,* the correlation between witnessing and call-and-response is evinced in Baby Suggs's preaching. Before she loses faith following Sethe's Misery, Baby Suggs, holy serves her community as preacher, leading prayer services for her neighbors at a place called the Clearing. During these liturgies, the holy woman does not "deliver sermons or preach" but "call[s]" instead to her congregants, "and the hearing hear" (208). Baby Suggs does not lecture her flock but sways communicants—through call and response (i.e., the "call" that the "hearing hear")—to witness communally the incidents of their collective life narratives. In making the call, Baby Suggs does not restrict communal witnessing to the use of the spoken word alone but invites those present to express, through laughter, dance, and tears, the unspeakable joys and pains they have experienced (185). Morrison writes: "It started that way: laughing children, dancing men, crying women, and then it got mixed up. Women stopped crying and danced; men sat down and cried; children danced, women laughed, children cried until, all and each lay about the Clearing damp and gasping for breath" (185). In her analysis of call and response, Michèle Foster notes that calls and responses are not limited to verbal communication but can also be expressed "musically, . . . non-verbally, or through dance." Baby Suggs embraces this claim by inviting children, men, and women to laugh, dance, and cry together until they connect through intersecting—or "mixed up"—forms of intergendered, intergenerational communal witnessing (185).

Although healing, the witnessing Baby Suggs leads in the Clearing leaves her communicants "exhausted and riven" (185), and they find themselves unable to sustain the practice. Although they initially answer the preacher's call to unite as a group, when they return to their individual homes, they divide, breeding a contempt for Sethe in particular that triggers collective anti-witnessing. Hence, when Baby Suggs hosts a party to celebrate Sethe's escape from slavery, the festivities only alienate the neighbors from the preacher's family and from one another. The narrator explains: "It made them angry. . . . Too much, they thought. Where does she get it all, Baby Suggs, holy? Why is she and hers always the center of things?" (161). Those gathered judge the feast's excess as indicative of Baby Suggs' and Sethe's pride. In counting the family's blessings, they do not acknowledge the eight children Baby Suggs lost to slavery (6)[9] or the assault emblazoned on Sethe's back. Instead, "the scent of their disapproval [lies] heavy in the air," allowing them to a-witness or "not [to] pay attention" to the traumas the family has suffered (162). The neighbors are so offended by Baby Suggs' presumed self-importance that they do not warn her daughter-in-law when schoolteacher appears to return Sethe to slavery (184). As a result of such a-witnessing, the community loses the benefit Baby Suggs' call to witness offered them, and any chance of neighborhood unity subsides: Sethe murders her daughter, Baby Suggs loses faith (3), Denver endures a life of isolation, and the community collapses, due largely to an unspoken decision to anti-witness Sethe. This sequence underscores, first, the lasting effects of communal anti-witnessing and, second, the community's ensuing need to witness together if its members hope to recover from the Misery in which they too share and for which—in failing to forewarn Sethe—they also bear responsibility.

Thus, although Baby Suggs, holy has long since passed away, Sethe's neighbors still need to answer her call to witness communally in order to heal collectively. A chance benefit of Beloved's possession of Sethe is that the ghost-woman's co-optive anti-witnessing prompts Denver to break her isolation to seek help from her community. Denver's willingness to reach out to those who have anti-witnessed her family inspires her neighbors, finally, to witness Sethe communally. A group of townswomen[10] join together, return to Sethe's house, and sing, utilizing music (as Baby Suggs has taught them) to witness Misery. Morrison writes, "the voices of women searched for the right combination, the key, the code, the sound . . . [to break] the back of words" (308). After years of anti-witnessing Sethe, those who would now minister to her are unsure how to do so. When they begin, they do not harmonize as they did in the Clearing but struggle to locate the "right combination" of notes to witness the un-witnessable (308). The solution to their discordance is to work together in concert to "build voice upon voice," until they hymn concordantly, now tuned into one another (308). Only when they sing in tune do they witness communally, enabling Sethe and themselves to heal. "For Sethe," Morrison writes, "it was as though the Clearing had come to her . . . a wave of sound . . . broke over [her] . . . and she trembled like the baptized in its wash" (308). Through the townswomen's communal witnessing, Sethe is renewed and reconciled to her community—and they to her.

When her neighbors witness her communally, Sethe begins to heal. The sound of their singing coaxes her out of the house in time to glimpse Mr. Bodwin approaching her yard. Confusing the white man for schoolteacher, Sethe mistakenly believes that Mr. Bodwin plans to return her to slavery, and she begins to relive her trauma (306). Here, Morrison exhibits the power of primary and communal witnessing. Whereas before the neighbors a-witnessed schoolteacher's arrival and anti-witnessed Sethe's "rough response," now they attend to her. Strengthened by this support, Sethe's reaction to danger shifts. Instead of aggressively anti-witnessing those she loves (by attempting to kill them), she strikes out against her perceived enemy, rushing to attack Bodwin-as-schoolteacher with an ice pick (306). In doing so, Sethe witnesses primarily by performing her earlier trauma but now with a revised conclusion and transformative results. Moved by this example, the towns-women respond communally, gathering about Sethe to prevent her from hurting Mr. Bodwin (306). Although the neighbors thwart Sethe's efforts, they do not anti-witness her but keep her from compounding trauma by wounding a man she has confused with her aggressor. In doing so, the towns-women also revisit the past with an improved outcome: They work together to prevent Sethe from harming the innocent (in this case, Mr. Bodwin; in the past, Sethe's daughter). In this way, the individual and community witness mutually, opening the door to collective growth. As a result of such com-munal action, the co-optive Beloved loses her hold over Sethe and vanishes. Krumholz notes that the "reconstruction" of the initial "scene of the trauma completes the psychological cleansing of the ritual and exorcises Beloved from Sethe's life" (403). Through witnessing collectively, the community surmounts shared trauma.

Such scenes model and facilitate readerly communal witnessing, particu-larly of the haunting traumas stemming from institutionalized slavery, which Beloved embodies and *Beloved* evinces. To impel readers to answer the call to witness, *Beloved*'s final chapter offers the recurring refrain: "It was not a story to pass on" (323, 324). This final exhortation is elusive in that it seems to suggest that the story *Beloved* imparts (or "passes on") is too terrible to have been written or witnessed. The admonition, however, also submits its opposite: that author, speakers, and readers alike must witness this extraor-dinary story so we do not collectively transmit (or "pass on") slavery's racist legacy to future generations. Morrison's axiom also warns that *Beloved*'s is not a story to a-witness— "not a story to [take a] pass on"—as the truths it imparts belong to our shared history and must be witnessed secondarily and communally if they are to be overcome. Finally, the injunction reminds us that *Beloved*'s is not a narrative that readily dies (or "passes on") but, rather, one that bedevils until confronted through sustained dual-and communal witnessing.[11] Through repeating this elliptical phrase, *Beloved* invites read-ers, first, like Denver, to move out into the community to witness *Beloved*'s message and, then, like those who exorcize Beloved, to witness collectively the truths of our national heritage, so that, as readers and citizens, we do not "pass on" the evils of American slavery but prevail over them.

Morrison's call to witness is not easily answered. The receptive process proves so demanding that even the townswomen who expel Beloved do not continue to witness collectively after she disappears. In the coda to the novel, the narrator recalls of Beloved:

Everybody knew what she was called, but nobody anywhere knew her name. Disremembered and unaccounted for, she cannot be lost because no one is looking for her ... Although she has claim, she is not claimed. ... Those that saw her that day on the porch quickly and deliberately forgot her. It took longer for those who had spoken to her, lived with her ... to forget [but] ... in the end, they forgot her too. Remembering seemed unwise. (323)

This passage underscores the resistance *Beloved*'s characters proffer to dual- and communal witnessing. Even after working to witness together, the community cannot sustain the practice. Once Beloved "passes on," the towns-women (including Sethe and Denver) return to anti-witnessing. Exhausted from their concerted efforts, they "deliberately forg[e]t" why they united in the first place (323). The same could be written of those Americans who anti-witness the racial trauma imbedded in our nation's literature and culture. In fact, the "they" who a-witness Beloved includes in its scope not only those in Sethe's community but "everybody" else outside it—all persons, fictive and factual, who know what slavery "is called" (in that we know it existed) but do not know its "name" (as we do not witness its history or heritage). Moreover, *Beloved* submits that such nationwide anti-witnessing represents a "deliberate" choice not to witness a past that seems, like Sethe's, too terrible to endure. The use of the word "disremembered" underscores the assertion that the decision to anti-witness is resolute. Those who a-witness America's racial legacy, Morrison suggests, do not inadvertently "not remember" but decidedly "*dis*remember." We actively forget when remembering seems painful and thus "unwise" (323).

And yet remembering (through witnessing) is precisely what *Beloved* asks us to do: to witness continually and, when we do not succeed, to recommit until the practice becomes routine. This ideal may account for why the novel places such emphasis on the concept of "rememory": the sense that the unprocessed past intrudes upon the present or, in Sethe's words, "comes back whether we want it or not" (14). Sethe is haunted by the rememory of Beloved. Readers are similarly beset by what Beloved embodies: the enduring hold of slavery on our national consciousness. But "rememory" has another potential valence: the prospect that remembering (or witnessing) does not represent a one-step process but a generative effort to rewitness through "rememory." The call not only to witness but to rewitness (or to witness repeatedly) may account for why the practice proves so difficult. Inherent in its challenge is the opportunity to choose each time to witness anew, even when one has already failed to do so. Toward the end of the novel, Stamp Paid counsels Paul D: "You got to choose" (273). Like Morrison's "they" in the passage above, the "you" of Stamp's message includes in its breadth the novel's readership. Stamp Paid reminds Paul D and all readers that, while *Beloved* can witness the traumas of slavery and of anti-witnessing, how readers respond to these traumas and negative responses is ultimately up to us. The agency to (anti-) witness is both daunting and liberating. Resurrecting the past is a painful process, and *Beloved* is an emotionally painful book to read, yet, by choosing to engage the novel in a conscientious way, in deciding to dual-witness on every page, we can begin to work through our own American Misery.

Salvage the Bones and *Sing, Unburied, Sing*: Witnessing Contemporary Traumas

While *Beloved* testifies to the realities of American slavery (and asks readers to witness them secondarily), Jesmyn Ward's novels accentuate the impor-tance of dual-witnessing in and across any era. Like Morrison, Ward treats American slavery as a national trauma that must be witnessed. Her books also encourage readers to witness other racially charged traumas, such as the devastation of Hurricane Katrina (2005) and the incarceration of African Americans as a contemporary form of slavery. Like Morrison, Ward uses ghosts in her fiction to symbolize the haunting of the past and the need for racial traumas to be witnessed. Unlike Morrison's Beloved, however, Ward's ghosts do not need to be exorcized for communities to heal. Instead, Ward emphasizes that everyone has a need and right to witness and be witnessed, though some—like Morrison's Beloved or Ward's Richie in the novel *Sing, Unburied, Sing* (2017)—die before they have the chance.[12] Too often, Ward underscores, black lives are cut short before they can witness. To redress this wrong, Ward's novels resurrect those who have been anti-witnessed before and after death to help them fictively work through their curtailed testimonies. In doing so, Ward impels readers to confront America's ghosts in order to witness secondarily (or sing back to, as the title to *Sing, Unburied, Sing*, suggests) their traumatic histories.

Like Morrison' *Beloved*, Ward's novels explore how the legacy of slavery affects America today. On an episode of *Late Night with Seth Meyers,* Ward explains that "one of the ideas" she returns to in each of her books is that America's racism cannot be relegated to the past but continues to pollute the present. In an article for *The Atlantic,* Ward asserts that "racism is built into the very bones" of America's landscape. One-hundred-fifty years after slavery, the bigoted conviction that black people are subordinate to white people persists. This lie of black inferiority, Ward writes, planted "at the beginning" of slaves' "subjugation" has "strangled" African Americans "for hundreds of years" (*Atlantic*). She cites nineteenth-century instances when "minor offenses committed by black people led to imprisonment for crimes such as vagrancy and loitering and petty thievery, especially of food, and black men and women were essentially re-enslaved," alongside twenty-first century affronts, such as when Mississippi waited until 2013 to ratify the Thirteenth Amendment, banning slavery, or when, in 2017, Biloxi Mississippi, renamed Martin Luther King Jr. Day, "Great Americans Day" (*Atlantic*). In *Sing, Unburied, Sing*, Richie, makes a similar point. Whenever he begins to hope that America "done changed" and racial oppression has abated, he wakes to discover that "it ain't changed none" (171): antiblack violence endures.

Evidence of contemporary racism can be found in America's inadequate response to the natural disaster and national trauma of Hurricane Katrina, a category 5 storm that, in August 2005, flooded the Gulf Coast of the United States. Katrina was the most destructive storm to hit the United States in history, causing $260 million in damages and destroying over 300,000 homes (Amadeo). During the storm, 1836 people died, most of them poor and black. Rotting corpses floated for weeks through lingering floodwaters (O'Neill). A total of 770,000 residents were displaced, and 700 remain unaccounted for (Amadeo). In *Salvage the Bones* (2011), Ward depicts a post-Katrina landscape as a war zone: "Look like somebody dropped a bomb," a boy named Randall observes. "Like war" (257). Disaster expert Lee Clark describes the effects of the hurricane as so catastrophic as to belie experience and belief, phrasing that evokes theorists' understanding of trauma as existing "outside" or "beyond experience," a shattering "intrusion" into the psyche that "cannot easily be absorbed" and must thus be witnessed in order to be worked through (Eyerman *America* 40).[13] Moreover, Katrina's trauma did not cease when the storm passed. Instead, Ron Eyerman reports, families and communities were torn apart, "left devastated and abandoned, without "proper provision" (*America* 7). "There can be no doubt," Eyerman writes, "as to the individual and collective trauma" Katrina wrought (*America* 7).

Those most negatively impacted by the storm were impoverished African Americans, leading cultural critics to conclude that lives were devastated not only by natural disaster but also by systemic racism and classism, which permitted wealthy white governmental officials to a-witness the trauma of impoverished black communities (Eyerman *America* ii). The Federal Emergency Management Agency (FEMA) "hesitated to take action," Eyerman explains, as poor black people died on "flooded streets" or "trapped in attics" and "stranded on rooftops and highway overpasses" (*America* 3). John Valery White attributes FEMA's failure to act to "race and class," maintaining that the agency's response would not have been as slow or deficient if the storm had hit wealthy, white New England instead of impoverished, black New Orleans (42–43). Today, Eyerman writes, the name "Katrina" evokes not only a "powerful hurricane" but the failure of a wealthy white majority to care about—or bear witness to—the trauma of an impoverished black minority (*America* 14).

Combatting this racist and classist a-witnessing, *Salvage the Bones* witnesses secondarily by proxy the brutality of the storm, which left "half drowned" impoverished African Americans to hunt the "wreckage" (or bones) of obliterated city parishes for "something to eat, something to save" or something to salvage (250). In the aftermath of Katrina, Ward writes, "people stand in clusters at what used to be intersections, the street signs vanished, all they own in a plastic bag at their feet, waiting for someone to pick them up. No one is coming" (*Salvage* 250). Ward's novel highlights the humanity of Katrina's impoverished, black victims—people who cannot be ignored or negated but whose lives and traumas deserve to be witnessed. Ward also writes in present tense, which may emphasize that Katrina's trauma is ongoing: Americans still reel from its aftermath. Sentences such as "No one is coming" (250) accentuate that survivors, who deserve to be witnessed are instead a-witnessed: no one is coming (except perhaps Ward and her readers) to engage their trauma and help them survive.

Katrina's impoverished, black survivors were not only a-witnessed but also aggressively anti-witnessed by police and the media, who first ignored their trauma and then blamed them for it. Due largely to America's racist history of criminalizing black skin—from the slave codes through Jim Crow laws—black survivors were prevented from escaping New Orleans to safety. Katheryn Russell-Brown reports that hundreds of African Americans, attempting to "flee the floodwaters" were "blocked" by armed police officers from "walking across a public bridge to safety" (115). Had these black survivors been permitted to cross, Russell-Brown explains, they would have had to pass through a white suburban neighborhood. White police officers, fearful that black refugees would disturb the comfort and safety of wealthy white suburbanites, physically blocked their retreat. Only white survivors were permitted across (Russell-Brown 116). This criminalization of black personhood compounded survivors' trauma, leaving many African Americans to suffer further and die. The media aggressively anti-witnessed black survivors by arguing that they should have evacuated earlier (though many did not have cars, buses never came to save them, and they were prevented from crossing bridges). Impoverished African Americans, trapped in a flooded New Orleans, were then accused of "looting" to survive (Troutt 5). In newspapers, images of white survivors were captioned: "Residents wade through chest-deep water after finding bread and soda from a local grocery store" (qtd. in Khan-Cullors and Bandele 145). In the same papers, an image of a black boy was captioned: "A young man walks through chest-deep flood water after looting a grocery store" (qtd. in Khan-Cullors and Bandele 145). These captions are racially suggestive: White people are residents, innocent American survivor-heroes. Black boys are turned into men, criminalized, and othered. Black men loot; white residents find. White trauma is witnessed, black trauma—aggressively anti-witnessed.

Ward explains that she treats Katrina in her novels because, as a resident of Mississippi, she "lived through it" (qtd. in Hoover.) The storm was "terrifying," she recounts. She "needed to write about that" (qtd. in Hoover). Ward is also "dissatisfied with the way" Katrina has been covered by the media as well as with how the storm has "receded from public consciousness" (qtd. in Hoover.) She remains "angry" at those who "blamed survivors" for their trauma when the hurricane struck (qtd. in Hoover). Ward writes about Katrina to witness primarily (to work through her own terror) as well as to witness second-arily by proxy for those who have been a-witnessed (their experiences have "receded from public consciousness") and aggressively anti-witnessed (they have been "blamed" for attempting to survive).

Of all her works, *Salvage* testifies most clearly to Katrina's trauma. In the novel, a poor black family boards their home to protect it from the storm, but their efforts are in vain. Katrina consumes them. *Salvage*'s fifteen-year-old Afra-American narrator, Esch, describes the hurricane as a predator: The storm is "coming for us," she observes (227). "The water is lapping the backs of my knees" (228). "The water is tonguing its way up my thighs" (228). Her depiction is both lyrical and terrifying. Katrina is not cold or removed but animal—horror brought to life. When the family seeks safety in their attic, the hurricane pursues them. "Water's in the attic," Esch testifies (229). They have nowhere left to hide or climb, while the storm "screams": "*I have been waiting for you*" (230). Katrina is not an enemy Esch's family can withstand. Nor is their trauma one readers can easily a-witness. Such scenes suggest that, whether one has personally survived Katrina (as Ward has) or only read about it in *Salvage,* one cannot avoid its destructive path. Neither can one aggressively anti-witness Esch's family members for the choices they have made. They try to protect themselves. Katrina devours them anyway. Such passages draw the reader into their current. One learns with Esch that to witness trauma is to risk devastation.

In engaging the storm's threat: "*I have been waiting for you*" (230), Esch—and the reader through her—witnesses Katrina in a way America's government, police force, and media have not. Esch faces the storm as it threatens to destroy her. In such scenes, Ward suggests that one must witness calamity, even at the risk of being demolished. Esch does all she can to survive: "I kick my legs and palm water," she narrates, "but I can barely keep my head above it" (235). She describes the hurricane as a "fanged pink open mouth that is swallowing her" (235). "The water swallows," she testifies, "and I scream. My head goes under and I am tasting it, fresh and cold and salt somehow, the way tears taste in the rain . . . I kick extra hard, like I am running a race, and my head bobs above the water but the hand of the hurricane pushes it down, down again" (235). No matter how hard Esch tries, she cannot escape. Neither can *Salvage*'s readers. The hurricane, though fictively portrayed, represents an actual catastrophe that calls to be witnessed. When we read Esch's first-person account, we hear her story in our voice. We figuratively kick and struggle and drown with her. We confront, through fiction, real terror. In doing so, we help redress the anti-witnessing that met the survivors of Hurricane Katrina.

Sometimes, even when we bear witness, trauma still overpowers. Ward's novel is not a fairytale in which the hero-protagonist battles monsters and survives, triumphant, but a trauma narrative that impels readerly witnessing, while promising little relief. Trauma compounds when reader-respondents anti-witness, but that does not mean that those who dual-witness will escape unharmed. As she drowns, Esch prays: "*Who will deliver me?*" (235). Her words recall the lyrics of the spiritual, "Didn't My Lord Deliver Daniel,"[14] as well as God's promise in Exodus 6:6 to deliver the Jews from bondage.[15] In signifyin(g) on biblical descriptions of slaves seeking deliverance, Ward links Esch's suffering to that of Jewish and African American bondspeople. Katrina, *Salvage* submits, is not an isolated incident but one in a continuum of injustices that have plagued people of color from biblical times to the present. In the spiritual, the speaker prays that, as God delivered Daniel from the lion's den (Daniel 6:16–23), God will not forsake the enslaved. In Exodus 6:6, God promises to extend "an outstretched arm" to deliver the Jews from their "burdens." For Esch, deliverance comes not from God but from her brother, Skeetah: "I feel," she narrates, "a human hand, pulling me back" and "push[ing] me up and out of the water" (235). Here, Ward may suggest that help comes not from divine intervention but from human interaction, from dual-witnessing. When Skeetah holds his sister's head above the floodwaters, "barely keeping" her and himself "afloat" (235), Ward underscores the concurrent necessity and difficulty of dual-witnessing. Engaging trauma (or extending one's hand to meet another) helps humans survive, but doing so can be challenging. When secondary witnesses lend an ear (or extend an arm), they risk drowning too. Esch's family escapes their flooded house through a broken window, but they are cut to pieces in the process (239).

They survive by witnessing with one another—by holding onto one another and pulling each other through—but their experience is not pain-free. They outlast Katrina but bear its scars. Those who witness, *Salvage* suggests, do not survive unscathed. If, however, we hope to prevail, we must shoulder the storm with and for one another. We must witness secondarily and communally to salvage each other's bones (and life narratives) from those catastrophes that threaten to shatter us all.

In addition to Katrina, Ward witnesses secondarily by proxy other cultural traumas that affect African Americans in particular, such as the trauma of mass incarceration, which functions as a contemporary form of slavery. Ward's *Sing, Unburied, Sing* details the trauma black men and boys endured in the 1940s at Mississippi's Parchman penitentiary. On *Late Night with Seth Meyers,* Ward explains that the Parchman prison in *Sing* is based on the "actual" Parchman prison in Mississippi, which "basically" functioned as a slave "plantation." "The legacy of slavery," Ward attests, manifests at Parchman, where prisoners were "enslaved" long after Emancipation. The incarcerated were "whipped," "made to work in the fields," and "rented out to industrial barons" (*Late Night*). In *Sing,* Pop, who served time at Parchman, makes a similar point: prison is the new slavery. "*When I first got to Parchman,*" he tells his grandson, Jojo, "*I worked in the fields*" like a slave (22). Pop tells Jojo that "poor and starving" African Americans were sent to Parchman simply for "*stealing food*" (21). Pop argues that poor blacks are criminalized in America, whether they steal food to stay alive in the 1940s or "loot" grocery stores to survive Katrina in the 2000s. Pop contrasts these black prisoners with Parchman's white guards, "*trusty shooters*" who "*like to kill*" (22). He notes that "*the sergeant*" at Parchman "*come from a long line*" of antebellum "*overseers*" (22). African Americans, Ward suggests, are sent to prison for stealing to support themselves. White criminals who commit infractions "*worse than getting into a fight at a juke joint*" (22) become "*inmate guards*" (22). The slave-era mentality does not cede when slavery is abolished but transfers from one institution (slavery) to another (prison). Whether treating the traumas of Katrina or mass incarceration, Ward's novels witness the violence done to African Americans by racist structures and those who uphold them.

Ward also writes her novels from the perspective of those most marginalized: poor black children, such as Esch in *Salvage* and Richie in *Sing.* Ward explains that, in the 1940s, "black children as young as twelve," were "charged with petty crimes, like vagrancy or theft or loitering," then sent to Parchman, where "they were basically re-enslaved" (qtd. in Brown). *Sing* makes this point through the character of Richie, a twelve-year-old black boy who is incarcerated for stealing food to feed his nine siblings (24). When Richie accidentally breaks his hoe while farming, the white sergeant beats him:

> *After supper, sergeant tied him to some posts set at the edge of the camp. . . . and the boy laid there spread-eagle on the ground in the dirt with his hands and legs tied to them posts. When that whip cracked in the air and came down on his back, he sounded like a puppy. Yelped so loud. And that's what he kept doing, over and over. Just yelping for every one of those lashes . . . When they untied him, his back was full of blood, . . . laid open like filleted fish . . . Sergeant gave him a day to heal, but when they sent him back out in the field, . . . [H]is back wasn't anywhere near healed.* (120–21)

This scene evokes Vyry's whipping in Margaret Walker's *Jubilee* but describes not the flaying of a nineteenth-century bondswoman but of a twentieth-century boy, supposedly born free. In linking the abuse of antebellum slaves to postbellum prisoners, *Sing* reminds readers that the Thirteenth Amendment to the United States Constitution abolished slavery "except as a punishment for a crime" (sec. 1) and that slavery has been perpetuated since Emancipation through the mass incarceration of African Americans. Like Vyry's breast, Richie's back does not heal, symbolizing America's inability to recover from the racism inherent in the institutions of slavery and prison.

After the sergeant beats Richie, Richie tells Pop: "*I can't hardly breathe*" (126). His words recall those of Eric Garner, an unarmed African American man, who, in 2014, repeated eleven times "I can't breathe," as Daniel Pantaleo, a white police officer, choked him to death (Garner Video).[16] When Richie, after being whipped like a slave, repeats Garner's words, *Sing* links the past (slavery) to the present (the criminalization of blackness that empowers white police officers to kill African Americans without consequence). The novel reinforces this point when a white police officer points a gun at Jojo, another unarmed black boy. Jojo's mother, Leonie, narrates: "The officer draws his gun on him, points it at his face, Jojo ain't nothing but a fat-kneed, bow-legged toddler. I should scream but I can't" (163). In this passage, Ward asks readers to witness what a racist white police officer and a constricted black mother cannot: that Jojo is not a criminal but an innocent child, a boy even his mother cannot protect due to the persistent a-witnessing of his innocence and aggressive anti-witnessing of his personhood.

To combat such anti-witnessing, Ward—in the tradition of Hurston, Walker, and Morrison—witnesses secondarily by proxy the lived experiences of African Americans, asserting through her work that black lives matter and are worthy of both literary representation and readerly engagement. Ward explains that she writes about "the experiences" of "poor," "black" Americans "so that the culture that [has] marginalized" them "for so long" will recognize that their "stories" are also "universal," their "lives" also "fraught and lovely and important" (qtd. in French). Witnessing black lives secondarily by proxy does not mean that Ward lionizes them. Her black characters beat and neglect their children. They rape and murder and steal. Many abuse drugs and one another. But they also love and save and fight for each other. Ward does not need to glorify her characters to witness their lives secondarily by proxy. She writes with what she calls a "narrative ruthlessness," refusing to "dull the edges" of her characters' stories in an attempt to "spare" either them or her readership (qtd. in Hoover). "Life," she asserts "does not spare us" (qtd. in Hoover). Instead, Ward's work "celebrates" African Americans' "fight to survive" and "thrive" in the face of race-related trauma and anti-witnessing (qtd. in Thorpe). Novels such as *Salvage* and *Sing* bear witness to an oppressed people's strength in struggle. They compel readers to do the same.

For those who wrestle to witness secondarily, Ward offers models such as *Sing*'s Jojo, a thirteen-year-old biracial boy[17] who possesses the unique ability to dual-witness with those he encounters. When Pop tells him stories, Jojo witnesses them secondarily, connecting to his grandfather both psychically and physically: "Hearing him," Jojo explains, "makes me feel like his voice is a hand he's reached out to me" (17). The boy does not anti-witness his grandfather's outstretched arm or voice. Like Esch and Skeetah in *Salvage*, Jojo meets Pop's narrative with secondary witnessing. When his grandfather has trouble witnessing primarily, Jojo draws his story out. "Will you tell me again?" he prompts. "What happened, Pop?" (68). Strengthened by Jojo's interest, Pop finds the words to witness (68).

When language eludes his grandfather, Jojo helps him witness without words: "I stepped in to Pop and hugged him" (61). Sensing that his grandfather needs to witness but lacks the vocabulary to do so, Jojo pats him "on his back," then "let[s] him go" (61). "It seemed important to do it then," Jojo narrates, to fold my arms around him and touch my chest to his" (61). Here, Jojo connects to Pop physically rather than linguistically. As a secondary witness, he acknowledges his grandfather's pain by hugging him, then "let[s] him go" so he can continue to witness primarily. When Pop searches for words, Jojo does not a-witness his narrative. Nor does he aggressively anti-witness his grandfather for his inability to speak trauma. Instead, he makes contact, giving Pop the courage to continue without saying a word. In doing so, Jojo also does not anti-witness co-optively. He does not cling too long to Pop or override his grandfather's narrative with tales of his own. He embraces the primary witness, then releases him, and Pop responds in kind: "He put his hands on my shoulders," Jojo remembers, "and squeezed" (61). Witnessed secondarily by his grandson, Pop finds the strength to continue his narra-tive—first physically and then, once again, with words.

Jojo often witnesses secondarily without words. Although Ward is an expert storyteller, her novels decenter logocentrism, suggesting that dual-witnessing can exist in many forms, including those that transcend language. One does not need to speak or write in order to witness, Ward suggests. "Bodies" themselves can "tell stories" (*Salvage* 83). Ward emphasizes this point when Jojo dual-witnesses verbally and physically with his sister, Kayla. At three-years-old, Kayla's lexicon is limited, but, when she cannot converse, she can still dual-witness. Sometimes dual-witnessing takes the form of an extended embrace: Jojo "holds" Kayla, as if "he could curl around her," join "his skeleton and flesh" to hers in order to witness secondarily her person-hood and pain (133). Jojo also witnesses verbally with his sister. To work through their shared trauma (the imprisonment of their father, the drug addiction of their mother, the abuse and neglect they face from both par-ents, and the racism and classism they encounter as impoverished children of color), they speak and sing and listen to each other (180). We "sing in a whisper" (180), Jojo relates: "I listen. Then Kayla stops singing and she listens too" (180). They use the tools available to them to dual-witness. They model for readers how to do the same.

Jojo's ability to dual-witness extends beyond humans. When the pigs "snuf-fle," goats "eat," and chickens "scratch," he can "almost hear them talk[ing]" to him (14). Jojo can "communicate" with animals (15), but he does not co-opt their testimony. He does not assert that he can understand them fully but maintains that he can "almost," not certainly, "hear" them (14). In sensing the animals' testimony without presuming to comprehend it precisely, Jojo dual-witnesses. When he and Pop slaughter a goat for his birthday, Jojo wit-nesses the goat secondarily. "I don't look away, don't blink" (2), he narrates, underscoring the importance of dual-witnessing even as one risks harming a primary witness in the process. Although Pop, not Jojo, kills the goat, Jojo does not a-witness the role he plays in the animal's death but witnesses sec-ondarily its sense of betrayal at being slaughtered. He intuits that the animal holds Jojo responsible for its death, "like I was the one bleeding it out, turning its face red with blood" (2). He does not defend himself from this accusa-tion but takes responsibility for his aggressive stance toward the animal and bears witness to its death, including its smell: "It's the smell of death, the rot coming from . . . something hot with blood and life" (6). Whether or not he holds the knife, Jojo knows he contributes to the animal's pain. In fact, Pop kills the goat for Jojo: "the smoke and barbecue to celebrate my birthday" (8).

The words "smoke" and "barbeque" recall those used to describe lynchings, when white mobs hanged and burned black bodies (Litwack 10). The scene reminds readers not only to acknowledge the potential harm we can inflict on primary witnesses (as Jojo does when he helps slaughter the goat) but also to witness secondarily America's history of racial violence. Jojo, as aggressor, bystander, and witness, shows us how.

Jojo witnesses not only with humans and other animals but also with ghosts. Morrison's *Beloved* suggests that readers need to confront the ghosts of our past in order to exorcise them. Ward's works propose that everyone who has suffered trauma deserves to witness primarily, but some die before they have the chance. On *NPR's All Things Considered,* Ward explains that she includes ghosts in her novels to try to combat the "suffering" and "erasure" trauma victims face by offering her characters the ability to witness even after death (qtd. in Block). In doing so, Ward hopes to use her novels to help "right" social "wrongs" (qtd. in Block). *Sing, Unburied, Sing* is replete with ghosts, from Given, an African American high-school senior who is murdered by a white teenager, to Richie, who needs to witness what happened when he escaped from Parchman prison. Ward writes such ghosts into her novels to empower them to witness primarily and to prompt readers to engage their narratives secondarily, so that, if only "in a fictional way" (qtd. in Block), even the dead have the opportunity to heal.

Richie is the clearest example of a ghost who feels compelled to witness in order to prevail over trauma. Of Richie, Ward writes: "This person has to speak. This person has to have agency, the kind of agency that he didn't have when he was alive" (qtd. in Block). Richie struggles to witness because he cannot remember the details of his attempted escape. He thus asks Jojo to help him work through his traumatic past so he can lay it to rest. "I've got to know" what happened, he pleads (181). Only by witnessing his story can he stop haunting the site of his trauma (Parchman) and find peace or, as he puts it, "get home" (182).

Richie knows he needs a secondary witness to accomplish this feat because one has helped him before. When Richie was whipped by the prison guards, Jojo's grandfather, Pop (whom Richie knows as River), watched over him. River could not stop Richie's torture. He lacked the power and privilege to do so. But River's physical presence and refusal to leave helped Richie feel witnessed secondarily. By standing over Richie, River empowered him to survive. "I could feel him there," Richie tells Jojo (135). "[I] knew that he would carry me after they let me loose" (135). Here, Richie articulates an essential function of the secondary witness: to carry the primary witness through his trauma. As River cannot stop Richie's torment, even the most engaged respondent cannot end another's pain. One can, however, help bear the primary witness's suffering. One can carry the other, as River does Richie, or as the reader holds Ward's novel in one's hands.

Richie, cognizant of the power of dual-witnessing, searches unsuccessfully for River when he resurrects as a ghost (136). He does not find a secondary witness until, years later, he encounters River's grandson, Jojo. When he meets Jojo, Richie asks him if he knows his name. "*Richie*," Jojo mouths (171). Jojo intuits the ghost's identity from stories Pop (River) has told him. In answering Richie's question correctly and naming the ghost before him, Jojo signifies to Richie that he can dual-witness. He recognizes Richie and witnesses his identity back to him. Richie then begins to witness primarily. He tells Jojo about Parchman, where white guards beat and otherwise "violate" black boys (180). When Richie can no longer sustain the abuse, he escapes. "Did Riv tell you that?" he asks Jojo (181). In asking whether River (Pop) told Jojo about him, Richie attempts, first, to see if Jojo is paying attention and, second, to gauge how much his trauma mattered to River. Did River, Richie's original secondary witness, care enough to witness his trauma secondarily by proxy to Jojo? When Jojo nods, confirming that Pop (River) told him the story, he communicates to Richie that not only is he following Richie's narrative, River was too. Pop laid the foundation for dual-witnessing between ghost and boy by sharing with Jojo some of the traumas Richie endured. When Richie receives this confirmation, he witnesses a hard truth: "I guess I didn't make it" (181). He died before he could escape Parchman and work through what he suffered there. He then admits: "But I don't know how. I need to know how" (181). Richie has resurrected as a ghost to witness catastrophes he cannot access. To fill in the blanks of his memory, he will need a secondary witness: Jojo and, through him, the reader.

To heal, Richie must witness not only the trauma he endured at Parchman but also what he perceives as River's abandonment of him. While he did not expect River to save him from the whipping, he also did not anticipate that his secondary witness would let him die before he could work through his trauma. When Richie realizes he has died and River has not, he feels discarded and a-witnessed. When he meets Pop (River) in the present, he grieves: "I need to know why you left me" (222). Here, *Sing* suggests that it is not always enough for a survivor to witness trauma primarily. To prevail, one must also work through the anti-witnessing one has suffered—especially by those one loves the most. As secondary witness, then, Jojo must do more than help Richie remember his past. He must also help him work through Pop (River)'s abandonment.

Jojo must also help Pop reconcile his own feelings of guilt over Richie's death. Jojo must help Richie and Pop dual-witness with each other, if either is to overcome his past. Dual-witnessing is always challenging, but Richie's and Pop's is complicated by the fact that Pop cannot see or hear Richie as a ghost. He thus cannot witness Richie secondarily. Pop's inability to recognize Richie as a ghost compounds Richie's sense that he has been a-witnessed. Both Richie and Pop thus rely on Jojo to help them work through their overlapping traumas. When Pop cannot hear Richie, Richie tells Jojo: "You've got to ask him about me" (229). When Jojo responds: "What if Pop don't want to tell that story? What if it something he don't want to say?" (230), Richie answers: "Don't matter what he want. It matter what I need" (230). Dual-witnessing, Richie recognizes, is hard but necessary work. One may not want to confront trauma, but that is what *Sing* demands of its characters and readers alike: to witness the unwitnessable, which can begin by acknowledging (as Jojo does with the goat and Pop will with Richie) how one has contributed to another's trauma.

To facilitate Richie and Pop's dual-witnessing, Jojo adopts the position of secondary witness to—and secondary witness by proxy for—Richie. He draws his grandfather out, prompting him to witness Richie's trauma both secondarily and secondarily by proxy. "Pop," Jojo queries, "You never told me the end to that story" (250). "What story?" Pop asks. Pop knows what Jojo is talking about. He has tried several times to tell Jojo the story of Richie's death, but he cannot bring himself to finish it. He stalls here, but he also attempts to discern how invested Jojo is. At one point, he "looks at" Jojo to "figure out how tall" he is (250). He tries to determine whether or not the boy is ready to engage another's trauma. Jojo silently assures him that he is: "I look at him and raise my eyebrows. Tell him without saying it: *I can hear this. I can listen*" (250). Pop cannot risk witnessing primarily and secondarily by proxy if Jojo is not ready to witness secondarily. Jojo's response is also a challenge to Ward's readers: Can we respond: "*I can hear this. I can listen?*" Whether or not we can, Jojo and Pop proceed. Jojo reminds Pop that he was telling a story about Richie: "You said he was sick. He'd just got whipped and he was hot and throwing up. You said he wanted to go home" (250). When Jojo confirms that he can witness Richie's trauma, the ghost remembers: "That's what I said" (250). Although Pop does not hear this confirmation, he "nods" (250). He tells Jojo: "He tried to escape. Well, naw, he ain't try. He did it" (250). This scene underscores how witnessing takes place through careful collaboration. Only when Jojo presses his grandfather to impart repressed stories can Pop articulate what happened to Richie; only when Pop checks in with Jojo can he ensure the boy is ready to witness; and only when Pop and Jojo witness Richie's story together can Richie fill in the missing pieces of his own history to witness his trauma and find his way home.

Together, ghost, boy, and grandfather establish intersecting roles to witness together: Richie is a primary witness. Jojo is a secondary witness to Richie and Pop as well as secondary witness by proxy for Richie. Pop is a primary witness to his trauma (the death of Richie) as well as a secondary witness by proxy for Richie. Only when *Sing*'s characters adopt these interconnected roles and witness communally do readers learn the full story: a convict named Blue raped a woman at Parchman. When Richie discovered the crime, Blue threatened to kill him if he did not escape with him, so Blue and Richie ran away together (250–51). Even with the support of Jojo and Richie, Pop cannot bear to witness the next part of the story, so Jojo asks: "You went after them?" (251). "Yes," Pop admits (251). A main source of Pop's trauma is that after Richie escaped, he tracked him with dogs (as fugitive slaves were tracked by slavecatchers) in order to return him to prison. Here, River (Pop) functions for Richie as schoolteacher does for Sethe. He tracks a fugitive slave with the intent to return him to slavery. When Pop witnesses this truth in the present, he "squeezes" a hammer he is holding "so hard his knuckles whiten" (251). This passage reveals how difficult witnessing is for Pop. He is disturbed and ashamed that he tracked Richie instead of allowing him to escape. He holds himself responsible for how Richie died. He needs to acknowledge his part in Richie's death to heal from its pain, but he cannot forgive himself for destroying the boy. Literally, Pop's knuckles whiten because he grips the hammer too tightly. Figuratively, his hands become white to signify how he has participated in (and thereby helped advance) white supremacy. In tracking Richie, River became the hands of white authority. When he admits this truth, Richie echoes: "Yes" (251). When Pop accepts his guilt, Richie can witness more of his trauma, including his friend's betrayal of him.

Supported by Jojo, Pop testifies: Blue was discovered before Richie was. Rather than return the convict to Parchman, a white mob lynched him. They cut "pieces of him off" him, while Blue was still alive: "Fingers. Toes. Ears. Nose. And then they started skinning him" (254). When Pop describes Blue's torture, he implicitly asks Jojo, Richie, and *Sing*'s readers to join him in witnessing the magnitude of the scene's racial violence. Blue is a rapist who elicits little empathy in the text, but the manner of his death—and the depiction of a white mob's total disregard for a black man's humanity—is still difficult to stomach. Ward, however, refuses to spare us. When Pop hesitates to continue, Jojo, as secondary witness, impels him: "What happen?" (254). Sustained by his grandson, Pop continues: Though Richie is innocent of Blue's crimes, River knows the mob will lynch him when they find him. "They was going to . . . cut him piece from piece," Pop shudders, "till he was just some bloody, soft, screaming thing, and then they was going to string him up from a tree" (255). Pop struggles to articulate the depth of his trauma, but strengthened by Jojo, testifies: "He wasn't nothing but a boy, Jojo. They kill animals better than that" (255). Jojo nods. He knows how animals are killed. He helped slaughter the goat. Richie, like Blue, will not be slaughtered but butchered alive. Again, Ward writes this scene in present tense. Although Blue's murder took place years before, it haunts Pop in the present. Only through witnessing with Jojo can he work through his history.

With Jojo's help, Pop finds the strength to witness. He killed Richie to save him from the mob.[18] "I said: *It's going to be all right, Richie. He said: You going to help me? Riv?*" (255). River does help Richie but not in the way the boy expects. Like Morrison's Sethe, River decides on behalf of another that death is preferable to slavery (or, in this instance, lynching). Pop testifies: "I . . . held out my hands to him . . . Moved slow. . . . Said: *We gone get you out of this.* . . . Touched his arm: he was burning up . . . I squatted down next to him . . . and I looked at him . . . And then I took the shank I kept in my boot and I punched it one time into his neck. In the big vein in the right side. Held him till the blood stopped spurting" (255). River's killing of Richie is an act of mercy. He fatally stabs the boy in as painless and loving a way as possible. As he kills Richie, River witnesses his trauma secondarily. He comforts the boy, engaging his pain (Richie is feverish, burning up). He refuses to a-witness what he has done but maintains eye contact. He holds Richie until he dies. In doing so, River serves as both aggressor and secondary witness to Richie, as Jojo once did to the goat. Pop, however, never recovers from the trauma he inflicted on the boy. "I washed my hands every day," he tells Jojo, but "that damn blood ain't never come out" (256). Pop cannot forgive himself for killing Richie, even if doing so spared his friend further violence. Richie returns as a ghost to witness unsung traumas, but, just as Sethe needs to witness the murder of Beloved to heal from it, Pop also needs to witness the role he played in Richie's death if he is to recover from it.

When Pop witnesses his central trauma, that he killed the boy he loved, Richie howls. At first Jojo thinks Richie is "singing" or witnessing, but then he realizes the sound the ghost emits is not one of peace and fulfillment but a "whine that rises to a yell that rises to a scream" (256). Richie is not comforted to know the truth of his death. The "look on his face" is not reconciliation with the past but "horror" at its trauma (256). Richie's reaction reminds readers that trauma is not always resolved in a single witnessing session but is overcome, in time, through a series of sometimes devastating conversations. Esch and her family do not prevail over Katrina when they first confront the hurricane. They witness with the storm and one another and still risk everything, including death, to survive. Richie does not find peace when he learns about his escape from Parchman. Confronting trauma may be the best way to heal from it, but that does not mean one will avoid injury in the process. When they encounter trauma, Esch's family is cut to pieces; Richie is psychically shattered.

To avoid succumbing to the pain of their narratives, Ward's characters must sustain witnessing. For the moment, Richie cannot. He tells Jojo that he initially believed that, when he heard his story, he would "cross the waters," find peace, and arrive "home" (281), but, even with Jojo's support, Richie cannot bear to witness what he has discovered. Though he returned as a ghost to uncover the past, he did not predict the magnitude of the trauma he would encounter or how arduous dual-witnessing would feel. He is now stuck, unable to witness unbearable pain. Note too that this scene does not mark the end of Ward's novel. Two additional chapters remain, reminding readers that the book does not close on one's narrative when one first acknowledges trauma. Readers must continue to engage history's horrors if we hope to surmount them.

Witnessing may also require more than two participants (or three, in Richie, Jojo, and Pop's case). Richie will require an entire community to help him process trauma. Communal witnessing is modeled in the novel's final scene, when Jojo discovers growing in his backyard a tree "full with ghosts" (282). As with Sethe's back in *Beloved,* the tree evokes one's family tree (and Richie's sense of betrayal by River, whom he considered family); the cross on which Jesus was crucified (and the violence and oppression innocents face); and the trees on which African Americans, such as Blue (and nearly Richie), have been lynched. The placement of the tree suggests that Americans cannot escape racial trauma. It is growing in our backyards. Jojo recognizes among the tree's branches "black and brown" ghosts, "women and men and boys and girls. Some of them near to babies" (282). He can "see" or witness trauma in their "great black eyes"[19] (282). As he has before, Jojo begins to dual-witnesses silently. He recognizes the ghosts' trauma and responds wordlessly. Sensing his acknowledgment of their pain, the ghosts also witness nonverbally, testifying "with their eyes" to the manifold traumas African Americans have suffered:

> *He raped me and suffocated me until I died I put my hands up and he shot me eight times she locked me in the shed and starved me to death while I listened to my babies playing with her in the yard they came in my cell in the middle of the night and they hung me they found I could read and they dragged me out to the barn and gouged my eyes before they beat me still I was sick and he said*

I was an abomination and Jesus say suffer the little children so let her go and
he put me under the water and I couldn't breathe. (282–83)

The ghosts witness simultaneously. They speak as trauma victims often do: in fragmented and unpunctuated prose, language that must be pieced together and worked through. This multivoiced, stream-of-consciousness testimony, written in the present tense, reminds readers that racial trauma in America cannot be relegated to the past but extends into the present. If readers run out of breath as they read out loud the ghosts' litany, they join those debilitated by violence, like Richie, Esch, and Eric Garner, who "cannot breathe." To transform a cacophony of pain into communal witnessing, the ghosts must sing their agony together. They must meet Baby Suggs, holy in the Clearing. They must call and respond to—and witness with—one another, not once but many times, until they hurt and haunt no more.

Confronted with the ghosts' collective witnessing, Jojo falters. He has exerted tremendous energy to help Pop and Richie witness—with limited success. Richie has not processed his trauma but continues to scream and wail. Pop has improved but will likely need to witness more to overcome his guilt and grief. Jojo does not know how to proceed, but his sister, Kayla, does. She "faces the tree, nose up to the air," her "head tilted back to see" or witness the ghosts more clearly (284). "Go home," she tells them. They "shudder, but they do not leave" (284). They cannot be exorcized away. They must witness. To help, Kayla "begins to sing, a song of mismatched, half-garbled words" that Jojo cannot comprehend (284). Jojo recognizes that Kayla is witnessing with the dead, but he does not understand what she is communicating. He also does not co-optively anti-witness her narrative by presuming to understand it. Instead, he describes Kayla's interaction with the ghosts as a "melody which is low but as loud as the swish and sway of the trees, that cuts their whispering but twines with it at the same time" (285). Jojo may not know what his sister and the ghosts impart to one another, but his depiction perfectly describes dual-and communal witnessing: a "melody" or conversation that "cuts" through and "twines" with trauma "at the same time" (285).

When Kayla communes with the ghosts, she releases them from their trauma. She empowers them to witness communally, to "open their mouths wider" and "sing" (285)—not the scream Richie emits when he learns how he died but a shared "melody" that enables them, in the words of Richie, "to get home" (182). As the ghosts witness with Kayla, she continues to sustain their melody, singing louder and encouraging them to do the same. Jojo observes his sister "wave her hand in the air as she sings" (285), as if she is conducting a choir. Kayla uses language, silence, and movement to witness.

Her movement reminds Jojo of how his mother rubbed their backs when they "were frightened of the world" (285). Though Jojo does not witness communally with Kayla and the ghosts, he too begins to feel peace. In this scene, Ward underscores that witnessing's form is open and fluid. Traumatic healing, like call and response, comes not only from spoken language but through song, dance, and silence. "Kayla sings, and the multitude of ghosts lean forward, nodding" (285). They witness with and for one another to find their way "*Home*" (285). Earlier in the novel, Richie tells Jojo that home is "a song. The place is the song and I'm going to be part of the song" (183). His words underscore a benefit of dual-and communal witnessing: One can feel at home with oneself and in the world when one has witnessed the traumas that prevent one from getting there.

At the end of *Beloved,* Morrison's characters sing a ghost home, but they do so to exorcise and erase her. Beloved does not join the woman's chorus; their singing helps Sethe but silences Beloved. When Morrison's ghost disappears, the community does not witness her memory but attempts to forget her. And because they do not sustain their witnessing of the trauma Beloved represents, she haunts them still: "Her footprints come and go" (324). Ward's characters, conversely, sing not to exorcise America's ghosts but to witness with them. We cannot right the past, *Sing* suggests, but we can help the dead bear witness. We cannot erase trauma, but we can engage it. We can bring one another peace by singing in concert.

Morrison's and Wards novels underscore that witnessing is challenging, requiring a degree of psychological finesse and a commitment to constant practice. While this process is demanding, if we can sustain it, these novels extend to readers the same benefit they offer their characters: the healing that proceeds from reciprocal engagement. Judylyn Ryan attests that Morrison "reveals" in her fiction "the world as it is with such clarity that readers are prompted to consider what needs doing, what must be done" (160). The same can be argued of Ward. Novels such as *Beloved, Salvage the Bones,* and *Sing, Unburied, Sing* testify to our nation's darkest realities and provoke readers to witness secondarily not only their fictive truths but those of our own country. In this capacity, Morrison and Ward build upon and also diverge from Faulkner's approach in novels such as *Absalom, Absalom!.* Instead of asking readers to witness what they sense they cannot (as Faulkner does), Morrison and Ward accomplish what their readers may have not (yet): they testify (through fiction) to the multiethnic, nonpatriarchal, enslaved, and traumatic experiences at the heart of American personhood, literature, and history and then invite us to take up their mantle and carry their work forward into the real world.

This readerly response-ability is explicated in Morrison's Nobel lecture, which takes the form of a parable. In Morrison's tale, two children, in an attempt to toy with their town's blind elder, approach the woman and tell her they hold a bird in their hands.[20] They demand to know whether the bird is living or dead. The woman responds: "I don't know whether the bird you are holding is living or dead; . . . what I do know is that it is in your hands" (199). Morrison explains that the bird symbolizes language (i.e., all that is witnessed in her novels), and the woman represents the "practiced writer" who worries about how her messages will be "put into service" or witnessed secondarily (199). When the woman tells the children that the bird's life is in their hands, Morrison expounds, "her answer can be taken to mean: If it is dead, you have either found it that way" (i.e., the text did not witness in the first place) "or you have killed it" (the reader did not respond productively) (199). "If it is alive," she continues, "you can still kill it," as the reader can always anti-witness what has been witnessed primarily. "Whether it is to stay alive," she concludes, "is your decision. Whatever the case, it is your responsibility" (199). Once the bird (or text) passes from an author to her readers, the power to dual-or anti-witness is our own. The best novels, like Morrison's and Ward's, sing to us, witnessing unburied truths, like the live bird. As engaged readers, we struggle to keep the bird alive, allowing its testimony to resonate long after we have finished reading the novel in which it witnesses. Keeping the bird alive is hard work, demanding much of author, characters, and readership. But only with such effort may we witness with the wise woman her final, Nobel words of hope: "How lovely it is, this thing we have done together" (203). Only with such effort may we sing our way home.

Conclusion
Dual-Witnessing as Revolution

In a graduate seminar entitled "The Poetics of Slavery" (University of New Hampshire, 2010), my professor showed our class the episode from the 1977 miniseries *Roots* in which Kunta Kinte, a Gambian-born American slave, is strung up and flogged repeatedly until he rejects his native name and accepts the slave name his master has given him, "Toby." After many lashings have broken his body and psyche, Kinte submits—"My name is Toby"—to which the overseer responds, "Aye, that's a good nigger," and cuts him down. Although I had seen *Roots* several times before, I found Kinte's brutal transformation from Mandinka[1] to slave and from man to "nigger" difficult to watch. Our professor had asked us to take notes, but, distressed, I instead sat still, almost constricted, anxiously waiting for the episode to end.

Most of my discomfort came from what I was watching, but my response to Kinte's whipping was compounded by my presence in an academic setting, wherein I was uncertain about the "validity" of engaging (or even acknowledging) a text's emotional versus scholarly impact. When my professor turned off the television and turned on the lights, I expected him to invite us to share our critical interpretations: whatever my classmates had written down and I had not. Instead he asked, "How did that make you feel?" The question made me even more uncomfortable. I had just watched a violent episode that seemed to have rendered me senseless, and now I was being asked to express my feelings in a classroom—a space I associated not with sentiment but with analysis. I was also aware that, if I expressed emotion in class, as a woman, I risked being perceived as less intelligent and professional than and by my male peers. How could I respond both intelligently and emotionally? *What happened to me as I watched that episode? I wondered. Why did I feel all tied up inside? Why do I still feel unable to move—or speak? Why do I feel as if I have experienced something similar to what I witnessed?*

As I considered my reaction, several of my classmates volunteered their own. "While watching this scene," a white male student asserted, "I felt nothing. I know that guy—the guy from *Star Trek* and *Reading Rainbow*[2]—is an actor paid to play a role. He isn't a slave. He isn't in pain. His name isn't 'Kunta Kinte' or 'Toby.' Why should a man doing his job make me feel anything at all?" *Because part of his job is to make you feel something, I thought. Because, as Kunta Kinte, he represents an actual, historical person,[3] and, as an American slave, he signifies a larger group of people divested of identity, agency, safety, and freedom.* I was becoming angry in addition to uncomfortable. *What is the point of studying literature, I wondered, if we can dismiss it as "not real" and thus "not effective?" Can literature testify to historical truth? If so, what happens when readers refuse to engage it?*

As I reflected, a white female student said, "The scene made me angry," *Yes, I thought,* until she continued, " . . . at Toby.[4] Why couldn't he have accepted the name his master gave him? He could have saved himself unnecessary pain. The whole time, I kept thinking, 'God, he's stupid,' and then I just got really mad." I flinched. *Have we, as Americans, and maybe even as graduate students who study African American literature, become so comfortable with racial violence that we allow someone to imagine that blaming the victim and not the victimizer is acceptable? How could someone think this?*

I was becoming increasingly upset—not only by what I had viewed on the screen but at what I was observing in the classroom. *There's something wrong with these responses, I thought.* Those contributing to the discussion had all professed an interest in writing about and teaching African American literature, and yet their commentary betrayed a certain ignorance and privilege and the inability to engage empathically a scene of psychophysical torture. *Why are they so quick to dismiss what happened? I wondered. Why do they blame the victim instead of his victimizer?* Earlier that week, I had read Patrocinio Schweickart's "Reading Ourselves: Toward a Feminist Theory of Reading," and I thought, *Just as we need a feminist theory of reading, we need a theory of reading trauma. How we respond to others' pain (even as portrayed in fiction) is important. What can readers do instead of ignore, negate, blame, and—as I feared I had done—overidentify with (and thereby potentially appropriate) other characters' life experiences?*

I did not have the vocabulary for it yet, but I had begun to think about anti-witnessing and the ways readers contribute to trauma when we respond to its literary depictions both nonempathically and overly empathically. I was repelled by the one student's a-witnessing of Kunta Kinte's torture; I was disturbed by the other student's aggressive anti-witnessing of his flogging; and I was concerned about my own empathic anti-witnessing, fearing that, instead of analyzing the film, I had overidentified with its subject matter to the point that I could add nothing to the conversation. (By declining to join the conversation, I had also a-witnessed both what happened in the film and what took place in class. By keeping silent, I had inadvertently aligned with the student who professed he felt "nothing." If I had risked speaking up, even when doing so made me uncomfortable, I could have promoted dual-witnessing instead of anti-witnessing.) *How can we respond both critically and compassionately to trauma narratives?* I pondered. *How can we engage scenes such as this one to combat rather than contribute to the suffering they portray?* I looked around the classroom. Every student in the seminar was white. *How do racial dynamics inform our reading of racial violence? How can readers transcend racial (and other forms of) difference to witness (literary) trauma?* My theories of reading trauma and (African) American literature and, ultimately, this book developed out of this event and the questions it raised.

In treating reader response to traumatic and testimonial (African) American literature, *Reading Testimony* addresses queries that arose in that graduate seminar: how does a reader respond conscientiously to literary trauma? How does one transcend differences such as race and gender[5] to engage a character's depicted experiences? How does a reader bear witness to representations of historical trauma—such as institutionalized slavery and its legacy of racist, sexist, and psychosocial violence—in (African) American literature? In answer, my scholarship invites the reader, first, to acknowledge one's tendency to anti-witness (literary) trauma; second, to recognize the specific ways one is personally inclined to anti-witness (e.g., aggressively, ignorantly, negatively, and/or co-optively); and third, to position oneself against these destructive tendencies by situating oneself at the liminal core of a Venn diagram of secondary witnessing, wherein one aligns not merely aggressively with the victimizer, passively with the bystander, or co-optively with the victim but with and against all at once.

In our graduate seminar, I could have resisted empathic anti-witnessing by divulging how *Roots* affected me emotionally. I could have avoided a-witnessing by addressing both the scene's emotional impact and my classmates' reactions to it. Voicing my discomfort could have offered the class the opportunity to witness not only Kunta Kinte's flagellation but also how we, as readers, respond to fictive depictions of cross-racial trauma. Had I shared these thoughts, we could have practiced a communal form of Venn liminality in which those students who a-witnessed and aggressively anti-witnessed the scene helped me establish critical distance between reader and text, and I encouraged them to treat with greater sensitivity the traumas *Roots* witnessed fictively. As a class, we could have held one another accountable, working together to witness collectively. That day, the opportunity to witness was lost. From the experience, however, I learned the concurrent difficulty and necessity of witnessing traumatic and racially charged texts. This early lesson informed my future scholarship.[6]

A Revolutionary Response

If the theories of dual-witnessing and Venn liminality do indeed help reader-respondents engage (literary) testimony, the questions arise: where does this critical project lead? What is the psychosocial value of witnessing secondarily, and what sort of real-world effect can it have? At its best, dual-witnessing extends out of the individual conversation between speaker-survivor and reader-listener into a larger, collaborative engagement with pervasive trauma. In this vision, dual-witnessing serves not only as an intellectual endeavor but also as a social practice, offering, as Sophia McClennen writes of human rights theory, a "bulwark against human wrongs" (11). Critics such as Harold Bloom are "skeptical" of such claims, challenging the premise that "care for others can be stimulated by engaging others' testimony" and rejecting arguments that connect the process of "reading to the public good" (22). Contra Bloom, dual-witnessing is predicated on the belief that reading and reader response can transform readers and engender empathy. "What is the point," Mark Bracher queries, if the "aim is *not* to get [reader-respondents] . . . to behave more humanely with regard to such individuals and situations . . . in their everyday lives?" (466–67). In *Can Literature Promote Justice?* (2006), Kimberly Nance maintains that a principal goal of encouraging readers to engage writers' testimony is to help "change their minds about individuals and the world, a development that may, in turn, lead to activism" (159). When dual-witnessing helps secondary witnesses respond to traumatized persons and traumatic incidents in literature and then life, it functions as more than theory. It becomes, as Judith Fetterley writes of feminism, a sociopolitical undertaking, "whose aim is not simply to interpret the world but to change it by changing the consciousness of those who read and their relation to what they read" (viii). Per human rights scholar James Dawes, "generating empathy" is the "first and most important step" in addressing human rights violations (429), and dual-witnessing is the manifestation of empathy in and through texts.

Dual-witnessing prompts reader-respondents, first, to acknowledge society's ills and, second, to work against them. Too often, Carolyn Heibrun explains, people are "rooted in [their] own vantage points" and see only what they want to see (quoted in Fetterley xviii). Reader-respondents can also be blinded by their privilege, which protects them from various social problems. White Americans, for example, may struggle to recognize systemic racism because they do not experience it personally. Men may not perceive sexism because they do not face gender-based oppression. Penelope Andrews notes that, despite "national laws prohibiting violence . . . against women," such violence remains "common because it is culturally accepted" and has been "ingrained in the norms of public and private behavior" (qtd. in Musiol 391). Dual-witnessing works against such violence. To create a more empathic and equitable society, all citizens are called to witness the traumas and oppressions that suffuse it—even when such traumas and oppressions do not appear to affect them directly. With this understanding, critics such as Gillian Whitlock, Charles Davis, and Henry Louis Gates Jr. celebrate imparted and received testimony as one of the "most powerful vehicles" to challenge "institutionalized and systemic inequalities" and human rights abuses (Whitlock 206–7; Davis and Gates xiii). As McClennen posits, the power of narrative is why organizations that "intervene in humanitarian crises" do so explicitly through "language" rather than through food, medicine, or weapons (10). "The most important act of rescue" for such groups is shared testimony, which inspires action (McClennen 10).

McKenzie emphasizes that heightened consciousness alone will not change the world. Once one commits to witnessing trauma, one is also compelled to act. "Words," Oluo upholds "matter" (229). They "help us interpret our world and can be used to change the way in which we think and act," but "understanding, on its own, will never equal action" (229). "Talk," witness, but "also act" (230). Butler explains that there is "something to be gained" from remaining exposed to trauma's "unbearability" (392). When engaging another's experience, one is "returned" to one's "responsibility" for the lives of others (392). Richard Rorty, Lynn Hunt, and Martha Nussbaum likewise assert that responding to another's trauma "promotes" not only engaged reading but "virtuous citizenship" (Jaggar 55). In witnessing Afra-American testimony, the reader-respondent acknowledges the violence done to others and is compelled to combat it. Secondary witnesses may, for example, volunteer for black women's advocacy groups or urge their elected officials to protect human rights. As Luz Angelica Kirschner attests, the engagement of black women's testimony is a "catalyst for cultural transformation and political change" (2016:361). Dual-witnessing is a revolutionary act.

In an attempt to witness women's silenced voices, Lilit Marcus read only women authors for a year. The project helped her to respond to women in both literature and life. Marcus's experience demonstrates the capacity of dual-witnessing to inspire: witnessing women secondarily can facilitate the delivery of their narratives, encourage their healing, and empower reader-respondents to act on survivors' behalf. Dual-witnessing can combat the silence and violence many black women face simply for being black women. When we engage another's testimony, even if we read in the comfort of our private living spaces, we channel the power to change the world. In *This Bridge Called My Back,* Toni Cade Bambara writes: "Now that we've begun ... to break through ... barriers and can hear each other and see each other," we can "rise up and break our chains as well" (xxix). In this light, dual-witnessing serves as more than a theory of reading or an expression of faith in the good of humanity. It acts as a "revolutionary tool" that begins with Afra-American voices and ends in the "hands of all people" (xxix). Through the duality and plurality of witnessing, "the revolution begins at home," as Moraga and Gloria Anzaldúa suggest, and from there it cries into the world (xlvi).

Glossary of Terms

A-Witnessing: When a reader disengages from the primary witness's testimony. Here, the reader aligns with the so-called "impartial bystander," ignoring or denying the speaker's narrative and adding to the speaker's trauma by increasing her feelings of worthlessness and isolation. To a-witness, a reader may (1) ignore a speaker and her testimony, silencing the primary witness by refusing to acknowledge her trauma (what I call *ignorant a-witnessing*) or (2) negate a speaker's testimony (*negative a-witnessing*), claiming that the witnessed events did not happen or could not have happened (as in the case of Holocaust deniers).

Aggressive Anti-Witnessing: When the reader aligns with the victimizer instead of the victim, thereby adding to a speaker's trauma by either (1) blaming her for her own experience (e.g., when a rape victim is censured for what she wore or how she acted before being raped) or (2) objectifying her experience and treating it sensationally (e.g., when the details of a personal trauma are salaciously consumed by a scandal-hungry public). The former I term *accusatory anti-witnessing* and the latter *voyeuristic anti-witnessing*.

Anti-Witness: The addressee who refuses to engage a primary witness's testimony

Anti-Witnessing: The failure to engage a primary witness's testimony

Co-optive Anti-Witnessing: When a reader aligns too closely with a traumatized speaker. Two kinds of co-optive anti-witnessing exist: *empathic* and *appropriative*. An *empathic anti-witness* may believe that, by virtue of having heard a victim's testimony alone, she too has become an actual victim. An *appropriative anti-witness* may use the speaker's trauma for some other purpose (e.g., when amanuenses used slave testimony to forward abolitionism).

Dual-Witnessing: When a speaker and reader(s) witness traumatic events collectively

Primary Witness: The speaker-survivor who witnesses her life-testimony

Primary Witnessing: When the speaker-survivor witnesses her life-testimony

Secondary Witness: The addressee who receives the primary witness's narrative

Secondary Witnessing: When the addressee receives the primary witness's narrative

Venn Liminality: A type of reading that represents a careful navigating of a liminal space, in which the reader realizes her indivisible roles as (1) potential victimizer of the narrative; (2) empathic bystander outside the narrative; and (3) survivor in solidarity, a reader who—though not a victim herself—witnesses alongside and with the traumatized victim. In engaging testimonial narratives with this consciousness, one may engage in dual (or even communal) witnessing, in which speaker and reader(s) alike witness trauma collaboratively.

Figure 1: Dual-Witnessing

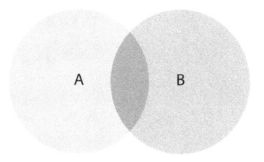

A: **Primary Witnessing:** The speaker-survivor witnesses her life-testimony.
B: **Secondary Witnessing:** The reader-listener receives her life-testimony.
Liminal Space in Center (AB): Dual-Witnessing: The speaker and reader witness together.

Figure 2: Anti-Witnessing's Relationship to Dual-Witnessing and Venn Liminality

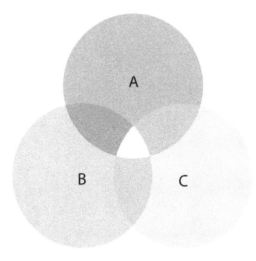

A: **Aggressive Anti-Witnessing:** The reader aligns with the victimizer instead of the victim.
B: **A-Witnessing:** The reader disengages from testimony.
C: **Co-Optive Anti-Witnessing:** The reader aligns too closely with the speaker-survivor.
Liminal Space in Center (ABC): The practice of dual-witnessing and Venn liminality.

Notes

Introduction

A section of this introduction was previously published in "'The Revolution Begins at Home': Exploring Women's Testimony as Reader and Witness" in *The International Journal of Conflict and Reconciliation,* vol. 3, no. 1, November 2017, pp. 1–43.

1. As a literary critic, I do not claim clinical expertise in the area of trauma. Instead, I place in conversation trauma theory, critical race and gender studies, and reception theory to explore how readers can respond to literary representations of catastrophe.

2. Michael Rothberg cautions that we must not overgeneralize trauma by subsuming "all forms of violence, dislocation and psychic pain" into one broad, overarching category (xiii). Every painful experience, he argues, is not automatically "traumatic." Because, however, definitions of trauma remain so open as to defy easy classification, this book treats "trauma" as any experience an author-narrator depicts as psychosocially shattering.

3. With Patricia Hill Collins, I define oppression as "any unjust system where, systematically"—and for an extended period of time—"one group denies another group access to the resources of society" (*Black Feminist Thought* 6).

4. To link literary portrayals of racism, sexism, and trauma is not to suggest that any individual or group—literary or otherwise—is somehow "traumatized" by social identity. I do maintain, however, that literature that witnesses constructs of race and gender also testifies to the status of power, privilege, and oppression; discrimination and prejudice; and exclusion and inequality that emanates from one's sociopolitical positioning, in this case as black and/ or female. I build on the work of Debra Walker King who, in *African Americans and the Culture of Pain* (2008), asserts the need to examine marginalized identity constructs, such as race/ethnicity and sex/gender, in conversation with psychic trauma studies (7–8), in order to

interrogate, first, how trauma, race, and gender (and traumas stemming from one's racial and gendered positioning) are witnessed in American literature and, second, how readers can join authors, texts, speakers, and characters in engaging such traumas and testimonies.

5. In presenting literary examples of traumatic witnessing, I do not mean to conflate factual reality (what actual victims suffer) with fictive constructs (what characters experience in a novel). My theoretical explorations engage both reality and fiction, because I maintain that fiction—and African American fiction in particular—has the power to witness traumatic realities.

6. I treat oral and written testimony as evidence of *primary witnessing* and listening and reading as examples of *secondary witnessing*. While differences exist between speaking and writing and listening and reading, with critics such as Patrocinio Schweickart, I discount these in favor of underscoring, first, the witnessing power of both oral and written testimony and, second, what Schweickart calls the "receiving function" inherent in listening and reading: the act of "understanding the utterance of another" or, in my schema, *secondary witnessing*. As Schweickart explains, treating oral and written testimony together helps us recognize listening as "an activity different from speaking" and reading as "the interaction between different subjectivities" (10). Within this framework, what Schweickart calls "communication" and I call *dual-witnessing*—whether spoken and heard or written and read—can be defined as "a linguistically mediated interaction between subjectivities in two different communicative roles: the expressive role of speaking and writing"—or *primary witnessing*—"and the receptive role of listening and reading" or *secondary witnessing* (Schweickart 11). When theorists underscore the importance of traumatic witnessing, they do not specify whether a survivor must speak or write through traumatic experience. Indeed, Sandberg assures readers that, if they do not "enjoy writing" as a means to witness, "talking . . . works just as well" (63). In an effort not to elide any style of testimony from my critical purview, my analysis thus focuses less on the specific form witnessing takes in favor of how one engages another's testimony once she has spoken or written it. African American literature works particularly well for this project because it is so speakerly, transcending the demarcations sometimes drawn between oral and written work.

7. Others refer to the secondary witness as the "adequate witness" (Gilmore *Tainted* 5), "participant-observer" (Strozier xi), "present listener" (Laub, qtd. in Caruth *Listening* 48), and "witness in the second degree" (Felman, qtd. in Caruth *Listening* 322). No one yet explains how this person facilitates traumatic witnessing.

8. The word "witness" exists as both a noun (the witness) and a verb (to witness). Similarly, the terminology I use includes both noun and verb forms. One can function as a "primary witness" (n) or secondary witness" (n). One can also "witness primarily" (v) or write through one's traumatic experience and "witness secondarily" (v) or receive another's traumatic testimony.

9. In recounting this story, Blow may also ask his readers to do what his doll could not: engage his narrative actively and witness his trauma secondarily.

10. One may consider a corpse an odd witness, as the dead do not speak or write. In this case, Till's body serves as both sign and symbol of his torture and murder, of his family's pain, and of the violence enacted on black bodies in a racist America. The pictures taken of—and articles written about—Till's body also bear witness to these psychic and cultural traumas.

11. Twitter can also be a site of communal *anti-witnessing*, when individuals and groups refuse to engage others' trauma empathically and instead celebrate their pain—an unfortunate response, which also followed Martin's death.

12. Like the word, "witness," "anti-witness" exists in both noun and verb forms. An anti-witness (n) refers to a reader-respondent who refuses to engage another's trauma. "To anti-witness" (v) is to disengage from the writer-narrator's traumatic narrative.

13. This example demonstrates how one can be anti-witnessed not only for what one has experienced (e.g., a traumatic event) but also for who one is (in this case, a black lesbian). Whether one is anti-witnessed for having suffered trauma or for embodying divergent identity constructs, anti-witnessing engenders further trauma, as the subject, already marginalized by experience and/or identity, is harmed further when others mistreat her.

14. While all traumas are different, so too are readers. Some may even be survivors themselves, adding to the complexity of secondary witnessing.

15. This readerly navigation (or Venn liminality) varies from reader to reader, text to text, and even within individual texts or passages.

16. Virginia Woolf writes in A Room of One's Own that, "When a subject is highly controversial," such as the traumas inherent in institutional slavery, "one cannot hope to tell the truth" (4). In such cases, Woolf posits, fiction "is likely to contain more truth than fact" (4). She proposes utilizing fiction or "making use of all the liberties of the novelist" to witness "highly controversial" (e.g., traumatic and testimonial) subjects (4).

17. In The Psychic Hold of Slavery (2016), Soyica Diggs Colbert explains that, although the physical conditions of nineteenth-century slavery have been abolished, the "violent conditions of being black" in America persist (14). Taylor reports that, since slavery was abolished, African Americans have enjoyed only "illusory freedom" (107–8). Following Emancipation, black Americans have faced Black Codes, convict leasing, Jim Crow laws, lynching, medical experimentation, redlining, disenfranchisement, disproportionate incarceration, police brutality, and what DeGruy calls "grossly unequal treatment in almost every aspect" of American life (107–8). DeGruy writes that 385 years of antiblack "physical, psychological, and spiritual" trauma have taken their toll on African American psychosocial life.

18. To focus on African American trauma, grounded in American slavery, is not to suggest that every black person in America feels traumatized by virtue of being black or by having ancestors who were once enslaved. Nor should "African American trauma" be read as an essentialist category that affects all black people in the same way or to the same degree. Nevertheless, this book recognizes American slavery as a national trauma and referent that demands to be witnessed primarily, secondarily, and communally.

19. Government scientists mapping human DNA in the Human Genome Project concluded that humans are 99.9 percent similar and that, in fact, only one race exists: the human race. Building on the information collected from the Human Genome Project, the Association of American Medical Colleges concludes that there are neither "black" genes, "white" genes nor, as Krista Ratcliffe adds, "brown genes, yellow genes, or red genes" (13). Although DNA variation occurs among groups of people, such variation is not, as Ratcliffe acknowledges, "synonymous with racial difference" (13). Consequently, race becomes a "fictional category possessed of all-too-realistic consequences"—a word or trope with "no scientific grounding," which nevertheless "functions with tremendous ideological force" (Ratcliffe 13).

20. Chapter 2 also analyzes literature, written by non-African Americans, that (anti-) witnesses black personhood, culture, and trauma.

21. Kenneth Warren problematizes this long view, arguing in What Was African American Literature? (2012) that what many consider "African American literature" is in fact a "historical entity" specific to the Jim Crow era "rather than the ongoing expression of a distinct people"

(8). Warren attests that since African Americans (versus Negros, African-Americans, Afro-Americans, and black Americans) identified as a distinct group exclusively during the Jim Crow era, although black authors wrote before and after Jim Crow, what they wrote was not, strictly speaking, "African American" literature (8). Warren's claims are provocative, but I join critics such as Graham, who read Warren's definition as a "narrowly circumscribed vision" ("Black Is Gold" 68). Just because black people in America have employed different identifiers over time does not mean that the genre of African American literature did not exist before the term "African American" did. Gates explains that, while black writers have "created new words and phrases"—such as "colored, Negro, Black, Afro-American, African-American and African"—to speak to "who we are and what we want," these diverse identifications intersect under the overarching umbrella of "African American literature" (*Talk That Talk* 13). Nor does African American literature necessarily end with Jim Crow. (In fact, critics such as Michelle Alexander argue that Jim Crow did not end with the civil rights movement but continues today under a different name.) Graham explains that, in refusing to categorize as "African American literature" writing by and about black Americans, before and after Jim Crow, Warren myopically privileges "one or maybe two generations" of African American literature ("Black Is Gold" 68). The "limitations" Warren "imposes," Graham writes, "fly in the face" of contemporary scholarship on the "origins and development" of African American literature and also needlessly exclude from the African American literary canon seminal authors and works that have significantly shaped the genre as a whole, from the essays of Frederick Douglass through the novels of Toni Morrison (68). In response to the critical conversation, *Reading Testimony* aligns with those who treat black writing—referred to throughout the book as "African American literature"—written and published during the nineteenth through twenty-first centuries.

22. In *Words of Fire* (1995), Beverly Guy-Sheftal explains that, while what Braxton calls "the Afra-American experience" (Braxton 10) is certainly not a "monolithic, static ideology," and while "considerable diversity" exists among how black women experience their social positioning in America, Afra-American writing is nevertheless able to witness certain predominant experiences particular to black and female persons living in the United States: (1) Afra-Americans endure a "special kind" of racist, sexist, and classist oppression and suffering that relates directly to their "dual racial and gender identity" and their "limited access to economic resources"; (2) This multiple jeopardy suggests that the "problems, concerns, and needs" of Afra-Americans are "different in many ways" from those of both white women and black men; (3) Afra-Americans must simultaneously strive to secure both black liberation and gender equality—as well as all other corresponding and compounding "isms," which "plague the human community," such as classism and heterosexism; (4) Afra-Americans' demonstrated dedication to the liberation of blacks and women is "profoundly rooted in their lived" experience (Guy-Sheftal 2).

23. Race and gender are not the only identity constructs that could be analyzed in this book, but they do represent major categories through which identity is constructed and people are positioned (and marginalized) in American society. They also surface consistently throughout African American literature.

Chapter 1

1. Morrison observes that while "no slave society in the history of the world wrote more—or more thoughtfully—about its own enslavement" than the author-narrators of African

American emancipatory narratives, nineteenth-century mores proscribed black and female writers from "dwelling too long or too carefully on the more sordid details of their experience" (qtd. in Bouson *Quiet* 132). Bouson adds that most Afra-American writers could not risk offending white readers by witnessing the extent of their traumatic histories (*Quiet* 132).

2. Although Jacobs's utilization of "Linda Brent" risks distancing both her speaker and readers from herself (as she does not claim her experiences as her own but as Brent's), the pseudonym also enables the author to publish her narrative without exposing her identity and jeopardizing her freedom. (When *Incidents* was published in 1861, the Fugitive Slave Act required all escaped slaves, upon capture, to be returned to their masters.) The decision to publish the narrative under the name "Linda" instead of "Anonymous" preserves the personal element of Jacobs's testimony, helping readers engage her narrative.

3. I am not suggesting that beating animals is unproblematic but that the location of Truth's beating exacerbates the dehumanizing effect of the violence she suffers.

4. Isabella Baumfee renamed herself Sojourner Truth in 1843.

5. Dumont promised to grant Truth her freedom a year before state emancipation, "if she would do well and be faithful" (27). After Dumont changed his mind and refused to set Truth free, she escaped.

6. On the relationship between silence, female homosexuality, and violence, consider Terry Castle's work in *The Apparitional Lesbian* with Lynda Hart's in *Fatal Women*. Since the eighteenth century, Castle attests, Western literature has "ghosted"—that is, made into apparitions, visible but not quite present—female homosexuality, so that sexual contact between women remains "elusive," "vaporous," and difficult to spot," even when it exists "in plain view" (2). Hart distills how Western literature's "invention and circulation" of female homosexuality as a "haunting secret" (vi) correlates to its treatment of female violence and aggression. The production of violent women in literature, Hart argues, relies on a "disarticulated threat of desire between women" (vii). Likewise, the "lesbian's absent presence" in literature both "permits women's aggression to enter the specular field" and "diffuses the full force of its threat" (vii).

7. In engaging *The Narrative*'s gaps, some critics presume that Truth's master, John Dumont, sexually assaulted his slave. In *Words of Fire*, editor Beverly Guy-Sheftall asserts that John Dumont raped Isabella (5). Margaret Washington speculates that the master and slave were "sexual partners" because the tension between Isabella and her mistress, Sally Dumont, is so marked that the mistress likely suspected a sexual relationship between her husband and their slave and resented Isabella for it. (Washington does not consider the possibility that Sally Dumont assaulted Isabella, and Isabella hated her for it.) Washington even suggests that Isabella "accepted John Dumont's advances," raising the ire—and inspiring the physical abuse—of Sally Dumont (Washington 72). *The Narrative*, however, presents no evidence of a sexual relationship between John Dumont and Isabella Baumfree. Moreover, to presume that a slave woman can "accept the advances" of a master's assault, as if free white masters and black bondswomen share equal status and power, is problematic. While we know that, historically, white masters raped black bondswomen, Truth's *Narrative* points most explicitly to her mistress as sexual predator. Because, however, of the elusiveness with which Gilbert narrates Truth's history, it is difficult to determine how Truth was abused and by whom.

8. Baumfree was born and raised in Ulster County, whose Huguenot settlers spoke only Dutch (Painter viii).

9. Keckley's historical "school teacher" prefigures Morrison's fictional "schoolteacher," who also whips slaves to teach them that "definitions belong to the definers—not the defined" (225).

10. Sexual abuse can also be physical. When I differentiate between physical and sexual violence, I define (for the sake of clarity) "physical abuse" as abuse that is physically violent but not explicitly sexual (though such abuse can have sexual resonances, as in the case of flagellation). I define "sexual abuse" as abuse that is explicitly sexual but may or may not also be physically violent (e.g., the nonphysical, whispered harassment of Linda Brent by Dr. Flint and the rape of Elizabeth Keckley by the "white man").

11. Neither narrative suggests that darker-skinned women or women who were considered less attractive did not also fear rape. While white men may have used black women's (light) skin color to justify raping them, historically, light- and dark-skinned bondswomen were raped in equal measure (White 123). Nor do either Keckley or I contend that light skin is actually more attractive than dark skin. Instead, Keckley implies, and I maintain, that the racist preference for light skin over dark skin was evinced by nineteenth-century (white male) Americans, exposing a white idolization that persists today.

12. This narrative technique is not unique to Keckley. White explains that nineteenth-century female slave narrators alluded to the prevalence of sexual violence in slavery by detailing the nonsexual violence they suffered as bondswomen. Whipping scenes in particular, White expounds, "carried sexual tones, due to the exposure of women's bodies during whippings" (33).

13. Keckley's publisher may have encouraged her to emphasize the erotic sense of her assault in order to attract a larger readership. If this is the case, Keckley was induced to anti-witness her own narrative, a theory that, if true, demonstrates the anti-witnessing power of her publisher. The potential also remains that Keckley's lurid depictions could attract resistant readers, whose perspectives could be transformed through exposure to slavery's depravity.

14. The shift from witnessing primarily to witnessing secondarily also offers relief from the struggle to witness traumas the narrator cannot articulate.

15. The "black envelope" Keckley provides for Mrs. Lincoln's narrative is radical, subverting social hierarchies, even as she elides her own story and anti-witnesses her employer's.

16. Keckley worked briefly for the First Lady of the Confederacy, before moving to Washington to work for Mrs. Lincoln.

17. In mocking Keckley's traumatic stutter, the parodist also (howsoever unwittingly) suggests that her rape shattered her identity not (only) into two parts but into many (six). Thus, even as the author jeers at sexual assault, he or she underscores its devastating aftermath.

18. In December 2013, this review was removed from amazon.com. Perhaps a site administrator found the praise of a racist text problematic, or the commentator rethought and rescinded his or her initial position. Whatever the case, the original posting and its subsequent removal signify the persistence of systemic racism in our contemporary era as well as the wish to deny (by deleting) this reality.

19. Masur notes that, while historians have long established that African Americans were "crucial agents in their emancipation," *Lincoln* portrays them exclusively as "faithful servants, patiently waiting for the day of Jubilee." In doing so, the film "helps perpetuate the notion" that African Americans "contributed little to their own liberation"—a historical and literary invention that ignores and negates black agency and allocates greater power to those who already monopolize social privilege.

20. Presumably, this "extraordinary woman" is Elizabeth Keckley, though, given Chiaverini's mistreatment of the dressmaker's life and history, the accolade could refer to Mrs. Lincoln or even to Chiaverini herself.

Chapter 2

A section of this chapter was previously published in "'You got tuh go there tuh know there': Reading Race, Gender, and the 'Womanshenegro' in the Novels of William Faulkner and Zora Neale Hurston" in *Faulkner and Hurston,* edited by Christopher Rieger and Andy Leiter, Southeast Missouri State University Press, 2017, pp. 111–28.

1. Even if fiction writers have individually experienced the incidents they witness through their novels, they still do not have to testify directly to their own experiences and may thus find themselves less constricted by traumatic memory and other contributing factors than those who strive to witness their own shattering experiences through nonfictional accounts.

2. Whether Faulkner or his editor selected the title for this piece is unclear. In either case, the title represents co-optive anti-witnessing.

3. Christmas's grandfather, Doc Hines, "knows" his grandson is "black," as "I know evil" (128), as if blackness itself—or the mixture of black and white—is itself evil. Gavin Stevens, representative of the law, offers an analysis of Christmas's black and white blood, in which the "stain" of "bad" and "black" blood (which eventually kills Christmas) adulterates and overcomes his purer "white blood" (448).

4. Margaret Walker writes in "Faulkner and Race": "Faulkner was, in fact, a racist—but two or three things are important to note. First of all, he knew that and knew it thirty-five or forty years before anyone much talked in such terms. Second, he knew that the whole of American society in these United States—North and South—was racist. Third, he moved beyond where many people are today to discover that, in an important way, to say that one is a racist is to say one is human and the product of his culture. Fourth, and most important, he did not conclude that this realization (that is to be racist is to be human) removed any of the guilt and responsibility from the perceiver. For Faulkner devoted a good share of his work, his ability, to the problem of coming to terms with his racism (in a social context). Learning this, and attempting to do something about it, is what [his work] is all about." (137). In other words, Faulkner recognized he was a racist and strove against racism in his fiction (much as secondary witnesses recognize and work against their propensity to anti-witness). Moreover, although Faulkner failed to combat his racist upbringing, he provoked readers to recognize racism where and when he did not and taught them to witness secondarily what he struggled to witness primarily.

5. Throughout the book, Christmas demonstrates a pattern of violence against women. As an adolescent, he beats a black woman shortly after she has been raped by four of his white friends (156). Several years later, he hits his girlfriend, Bobbie, while "calling her his whore" (199). As a young man, Christmas beats a prostitute so severely the police believe he has killed her (225). The instances of repeated brutality underscore the power through violence Christmas establishes over women.

6. Faulkner does not describe this incident as rape but writes that one of the older white boys "arranged" for the group to have sex with the "womanshenegro" (156). For this reason, some critics assume that the woman willingly participates in the encounter. More likely, however, she is raped. While *Light in August* does not inform readers how the arrangement was conducted (further evidence that the novel privileges white and male over black and female perspectives), readers do learn that, once Christmas enters the shed, the woman expresses not consent but terror, escaping as soon as she can (157). The use of the verb "arranged" suggests that the older white boy—not the "womanshenegro"—dominates the

encounter. Faulkner does not write, for instance, that the group arranged to have sex *with* the woman (denoting mutuality) but that one of the white boys (whose combined race and gender grants him power over the black woman) "arranged it," indicating control, not consent. The other boys in the group "dr[a]w straws for turns" with the woman, treating her like a prize, not a partner.

Furthermore, Faulkner describes the "womanshenegro" as "something"—not someone— "prone and abject" (156). "Something" is a word Faulkner uses to connote rape in particular (e.g., Temple's phrase "something is happening to me in *Sanctuary* [102]) and violence in general (e.g., Christmas's thought that "something is going to happen" before he kills Joanna Burden [104]). If the woman is not "someone" but "something," she embodies—according to Faulkner's lexicon—rape and violence versus personhood and agency. Moreover, the woman exhibits psychic constriction. When Christmas enters the shed, she responds with "sound[s]" that are "completely unaware." Her eyes are "black well[s]," which reflect "dead stars," demonstrating a lack of cognizance. One who is "prone," "abject," and "completely unaware" cannot consent to sex; sexual engagement with such a person becomes assault (Friedman 215).

Finally, Faulkner avoids the word "rape" in his fiction. "Rape" does not appear once in *Sanctuary*, a novel about sexual assault. If Faulkner wished to convey rape in this scene, he likely would not use that word to describe what happens. For these reasons, the scene reads as assaultive not consensual. That Christmas beats rather than penetrates the woman heightens the passage's sexual violence.

7. Other black women appear in *Light in August*, but, like the "womanshenegro," they are textually appropriated to illuminate the narratives of white (or, in Christmas's case, ambiguously raced) men. Christmas, for instance, briefly cohabitates with a dark-skinned woman in the North (225). Rather than witness this woman's experience, the novel utilizes her existence to explore Christmas's feelings about his blackness. When Christmas lies next to her, for example, he attempts to "breathe into himself . . . the dark and inscrutable thinking and being of negroes," while expelling from himself "the white thinking and being" (225–26). While Christmas is breathing and thinking, the woman beside him is inert, described as an object, "an ebony carving" (225). The novel does not illuminate her experiences but exploits her presence to help Christmas work through his racial positioning.

8. Christmas's inability to rape the woman may indicate that Faulkner does not fully understand the crime of rape (perhaps another reason he has difficulty witnessing the experiences of rape victims). Christmas's reluctance to assault his victim sexually suggests that Faulkner may consider rape to be a crime of lust (and the self-loathing, biracial Christmas would never lust after a black woman) instead of sexualized aggression.

9. Jason Compson Sr. is the patriarch of the Compson family. Jason Jr. is his son.

10. Quentin narrates "That Evening Sun" in 1913, the fiftieth anniversary of the Emancipation Proclamation.

11. Since Nancy has had sex with white men, such as Mr Stovall, Mrs. Compson may fear she will also sleep with Mr Compson. She may thus not want Mr Compson to walk Nancy home or for Nancy to stay in their house at night. In fearing that Nancy will seduce Mr Compson because she has had sex with other (white) men, Caroline perpetuates the Jezebel stereotype, which characterizes black women as lascivious for and promiscuous with white men. This stereotype was originally promoted during slavery to rationalize white men's assault of black women. White slave masters who raped black bondswomen argued that they could not be held accountable for their "sexual indiscretion" since the "Jezebels" had seduced them (White 31).

12. In Zora Neale Hurston's *Their Eyes Were Watching God* (1937), Janie's grandmother makes a similar point: black women are "de mule uh de world" (14), subjugated by white people and black men.

13. "That Evening Sun" was composed by W. C. Handy and popularized by Bessie Smith and Louis Armstrong in 1927 (Bennett 339).

14. *As I Lay Dying* (1930) has a chapter narrated by the dead matriarch, Addie (who is also strong), but she does not maintain her narration, as Rosa does, for half of the novel. None of Faulkner's other novels have sustained female narrators.

Chapter 3

The Hurston section of this chapter was previously published in "'You got tuh go there tuh know there': Reading Race, Gender, and the 'Womanshenegro' in the Novels of William Faulkner and Zora Neale Hurston" in *Faulkner and Hurston,* edited by Christopher Rieger and Andy Leiter, Southeast Missouri State University Press, 2017, pp. 111–128.

1. Trudier Harris explains that black protest fiction includes diverse methods, including witnessing "the plight of enslaved persons," "challenging the larger white community to change its attitude toward those persons," and "providing specific reference points for the nature of the complaints presented." The genre testifies to and against inequalities among black and white races and socioeconomic groups in America and—through readers engaging its texts— provokes transformation in the society that produces and preserves such inequalities.

2. Margaret Walker attributes Hurston's critical reception to the author's black woman-hood. "The problem of the black woman novelist," Walker writes, is "perhaps best illustrated in Zora," an Afra-American author of "great brilliance and talent" who nevertheless "felt the sting of racism and prejudice even among her own" ("Reflections" 46). Upon writing and publishing *Their Eyes,* Walker contends, Hurston was "criticized and belittled by her male peers" who were "not one whit smarter" or more "talented" than Hurston but who—"jealous" of her literary prowess—exercised their patriarchal authority and control to dismiss and denounce Hurston's work. In doing so, Walker concludes, Hurston's critics demonstrate how "sexual politics" thrive in African American literature and "sexual discrimination persists along with racism in white American literature" ("Reflections" 52).

3. Readers may note that, in the discourse of Janie's community, initial and final conso-nants are frequently dropped; "you" becomes "yuh," "I"— "Ah," and "himself"—"hisself." A word's final "r" is often softened to "ah," the final "th" to "f." "Us" may occur as the nominative, and verbs are commonly omitted. In addition to patterns of dialect, Janie and her neighbors speak a language rich in regionalisms (such as "zigaboos" [6] and "breath-and-britches" [13]) and folk references (e.g., picking in the jook joint [131], playing the dozens [78], and consult-ing root doctors [84]).

4. The incorporation of AAVE into the narrator's voice suggests that *Their Eyes* is a double-voiced text in which one voice does not dominate but converses equally with the other, modeling dual-witnessing between Hurston's narrator and protagonist.

5. *Gone with the Wind* anti-witnesses black personhood through characters such as Mammy, Prissy, Big Sam, and Pork, all of whom exemplify the racist stereotypes their names denote. Mammy is the archetypal "mammy"; Prissy is silly, squeamish, squeaky-voiced, and the novel's comic relief (as if the plight of Afra-American bondswomen is

somehow humorous); Big Sam is the protector of white womanhood (explicitly, Scarlett O'Hara) who risks his life repeatedly, even when freed, to save a thankless mistress. Like Sam (but without his stature), Pork, named for a cheap, unclean meat, remains loyal to the O'Haras following Emancipation.

6. The Civil War epic is written exclusively from a white Southern perspective. The end of slavery and Northern victory are depicted as coinciding tragedies (of both the novel and the nation), and those white Southerners, such as Scarlett O'Hara, who withstand the war and prevail over it are celebrated as victors. Black characters are either ignored, degraded, or vilified. Those African Americans who are commended are those, such as Mammy and Big Sam, who remain loyal to their former masters even after they have been granted legal freedom.

7. The house covered in molasses and feathers evokes *Jubilee's* later depiction of an Afra-American woman who, during Reconstruction, is tarred, feathered, and murdered by the Ku Klux Klan (365–67). While this victim of racist and sexist violence suffers more than the white owners of the destroyed plantation, the two images signify on one another to demonstrate how intersecting forms of oppression collaborate in America to create a "mess" that must be witnessed to be rectified.

8. The distinction between (1) Vyry's understanding of marriage as dual-witnessing and Innis' conception of family as communal witnessing and (2) heteronormative definitions of marriage and family is reinforced by the fact that the members of the novel's more traditional marriages and families often anti-witness one another, instead of witnessing each other secondarily and communally. Randall Ware initially abandons rather than witnesses his wife, and Vyry's biological father does not witness (or even ever recognize) his multiracial daughter. Similarly, in *Their Eyes,* Janie and Pheoby foster more of a marriage and a family than do Janie and any of her (ex)husbands or even Janie and Nanny, who, despite her best intentions, persists in anti-witnessing her granddaughter. Accordingly, both novels suggest that "marriage" and "family" do not always represent legally-recognized unions but also (and more often) relationships that one forms with those equally committed to dual-and communal witnessing.

Chapter 4

1. The plot of *Beloved* is based on the true story of Margaret Garner, an escaped slave who killed her two-year-old daughter rather than permit her child to be enslaved (Rody 93).

2. Jean Wyatt, for example, argues that the "peculiarities" of Morrison's narrative style—"its gaps, discontinuities, and surprises"—invite readers, through filling in structured blanks, to participate in the novel's meaning-making, that is, to dual-witness (2).

3. Beloved's identity is enigmatic. At various points, the novel suggests she may be an ordinary woman traumatized by years of captivity (119); the ghost of Sethe's African mother (Horvitz "Nameless Ghosts"); or, as Sethe and Denver come to believe, the embodied ghost of Sethe's murdered daughter (239). Symbolically, Beloved represents the specter of American slavery (Scheel 154).

4. Morrison's novels all depict psychosocial violence, which, Bouson recognizes, risks "alienating, or even unsettling or hurting, some of her readers" (*Quiet* 3). Still, her writing commands an engaged response. "My writing expects, demands participatory reading," Morrison writes. "The reader supplies the emotions . . . He or she can feel something visceral, see something striking. Then we [you, the reader, and I, the author] come together to make this

book, to feel this experience" (qtd. in Bouson *Quiet* 19). Alienating her readers through vivid depictions of trauma is a risk Morrison takes every time she writes and publishes a novel. In fact, because of the trauma depicted in *Beloved,* Morrison believed the novel would be the "least read" of her works (qtd. in Bouson *Quiet* 131). She wrote and published it anyway. In doing so, she reminds readers that her subject matter, howsoever difficult, must be witnessed primarily and secondarily.

5. Sethe is an unusual trauma victim in that a principal source of her trauma is the murder she has inflicted on her daughter. Paul D's horror at Sethe's Misery is thus understandable: she is not only a victim; she is also a victimizer. What makes Paul D's response problematic is not that he is appalled by what Sethe has done (readers share his revulsion) but that he refuses, first, to acknowledge Sethe's act and, second, to witness secondarily how and why she made the choice she did. Dual-witnessing does not dictate that secondary witnesses condone or understand everything a primary witness has experienced. The process asks reader-listeners instead to engage another's life narrative. Paul D promises to perform this service but refuses to follow through when he learns the scope of Sethe's traumatic history.

6. The symbol of the tree also evokes one's family tree, the biblical trees of life and the knowledge of good and evil, the trope of the bleeding tree (Ferber 219–20), the cross on which Jesus was crucified, and the trees on which lynched African Americans have been hanged. When Sethe's scars form a tree on her back and a forest rises up between Sethe and Paul D, these other trees likewise become emblazoned on Sethe's person and in her psyche as well as in the distance that separates Sethe from Paul D. To surmount the forest and dual-witness, Paul D must confront not only Sethe's and his own traumas but those of his family tree (including in its broadest scope all other slaves, African Americans, and Americans in general); the tribulations of life, the knowledge of good and evil; the woundedness of the bleeding tree and Christ's cross; and the trees used to hang men like Sixo and all those lynched persons who did not survive slavery and beyond. This forest offers Paul D a vast traumatic landscape to navigate, and he pales at the task. Nevertheless, this is the path that *Beloved* presents to Paul D and readers alike, for if we do not face the past, we cannot prevail over it.

7. Paul D's transformation may come down to a matter of choice. He chooses to witness Sethe now, whereas earlier he did not. In writing *Beloved,* Morrison may hope to encourage readers, alongside Amy and a reformed Paul D, to choose not to a-witness America's dark history or to accept institutionalized slavery and systemic racism casually but to decide to witness such historical traumas secondarily and communally.

8. Here, Paul D literally and figuratively embraces Jesus's commandment in John 13:14–15 to "wash one another's feet," that is, to love and serve one other, as Christ loved and served his disciples.

9. This loss may account for why Baby Suggs is eager to celebrate the return if not of her son, Halle, then of her daughter-in-law, Sethe, and granddaughter, Denver.

10. Although men like Paul D and Stamp Paid witness Sethe secondarily, the group that witnesses her communally is comprised of women. This nonpatriarchal chorus underscores the power of marginalized persons to surmount trauma through the strength of combined voices.

11. Perhaps for this reason, after Beloved disappears, characters continue to encounter traces of her footprints that "come and go," the sound of her skirts rustling, and the sensation of her "knuckles brushing [against their] cheek[s]" (324). One townswoman, Ella, "is not so sure" that Beloved has "passed on" at all, that she is not "waiting for another chance" (310) to reenter the narrative and their lives. The haunting of Beloved, even after she has

been witnessed and exorcised, illustrates that Morrison's characters can only do so much to witness with and for one another. The rest is up to those who will not "pass on" *Beloved's* story but will carry it forward: (ideally) the novel's readership.

12. Some critics suggest that the character Wild in Morrison's *Jazz* (1992) may in fact be the "resurfaced, pregnant Beloved who disappears at the end of *Beloved*" (Vickroy *Contemporary* 110). If this intertextual reading is correct, Beloved may resurrect as Wild in *Jazz* in an attempt to witness what she could not in Morrison's earlier work.

13. While the understanding of trauma as "beyond experience" typically refers to an individual's shattered psyche, it can also extend to members of a community who experience a shared cultural trauma, such as Hurricane Katrina (Eyerman *America* 40).

14. "Didn't my Lord deliver Daniel / Deliver Daniel, deliver Daniel / Didn't my Lord deliver Daniel / An' why not-a every man?" (17).

15. "Say, therefore, to the children of Israel, 'I am the LORD, and I will bring you out from under the burdens of the Egyptians, and I will deliver you from their bondage. I will also redeem you with an outstretched arm and with great judgments'" (Exodus 6:6). The flood also recalls God's destruction of the earth by water in Genesis 6–9.

16. Pantaleo placed Garner in a chokehold for selling individual cigarettes. The coroner ruled his death a homicide (Calabresi).

17. Jojo's mother is African American; his father is white.

18. Pop, like *Beloved's* Sethe, is an atypical primary witness in that the trauma he needs to work through is the violence he inflicted on another. He also evokes both schoolteacher and Sethe in this scene. Like schoolteacher, he tracks a fugitive slave. Like Sethe, he kills a fugitive slave (Richie/Beloved) rather than return him to slavery.

19. "Black eyes" is also a homophone for African American "I's" or selves, which Jojo, in engaging the ghosts, also witnesses secondarily.

20. In *Tears We Cannot Stop,* Michael Eric Dyson attributes this fable to Fannie Lou Hamer. However, in Hamer's version, the wise person is male, and the race of the children or the elder is not specified.

Conclusion

1. Kunta Kinte was born in the Mandinka village of Juffure in the Republic of Gambia (*Roots*).

2. LeVar Burton plays Kunta Kinte in parts 1 through 4 of *Roots*.

3. The miniseries *Roots* is based on Alex Haley's 1976 novel, *Roots: The Saga of an American Family.* Although Haley acknowledged that his novel was primarily fiction (he described the work as "faction," a blend of fact and fiction [*Roots* 899]), he also maintained that Kunta Kinte was an actual person, stolen from the African village of Juffure in what is now Gambia and forced into American slavery. Haley also claimed that Kinte was his great-great-great-great grandfather (*Roots* 899).

4. The student's misnaming of Kunta Kinte as "Toby" also bothered me, since the importance of the protagonist's Mandinka name is central to the episode.

5. While I initially focused on questions of reading trauma and race, I added considerations of gender to my research, inspired in part by Schweickart's feminist theories of reading, my discomfort expressing emotion in the classroom as a woman, my future experiences teaching gender studies, and the recognition that race is not an essential, contained category

but a socially constructed classification that intersects with other forms of difference including (but not limited to) gender.

6. My experience watching *Roots* also suggests that, even when one initially anti-witnesses (as I did empathically and ignorantly), one also has the opportunity to reposition oneself and strive to dual-witness again. Read in this light, the witnessing process must not end when a text or discussion does but can continue beyond a given experience, provided readers continue to engage the trauma they encounter.

Bibliography

Adichie, Chiminanda. *Americanah*. Alfred A. Knopf, 2013.

Ahrens, Courtney "Being Silenced: The Impact of Negative Social Reactions on the Disclosure of Rape." *American Journal of Community Psychology*, vol. 38, no. 3–4, December 2006, pp. 263–74.

Alexander, Michelle. *The New Jim Crow: Incarceration in the Age of Colorblindness*. New Press, 2010.

Amadeo, Kimberly. "Hurricane Katrina Facts, Damage, and Costs: What Made Katrina So Devastating." *The Balance: GDP and Growth*, July 4, 2018, www.thebalance.com /hurricane-katrina-facts-damage-and-economic-effects-3306023.

Anderson, Carol. *White Rage: The Unspoken Truth of Our Racial Divide*. Bloomsbury, 2016.

Andrews, Karen. "The Shaping of Joanna Burden in 'Light in August.'" *Pacific Coast Philology*, 26, no. 1/2, July 1991, pp. 3–12.

Andrews, Molly. "Beyond Narrative: The Shape of Traumatic Testimony." *We Shall Bear Witness: Life Narratives and Human Rights*, edited by Meg Jensen and Margaretta Jolly, University of Wisconsin Press, 2014, pp. 32–47.

Andrews, William. *To Tell a Free Story: The First Century of Afro-American Autobiography, 1760–1865*. University of Illinois, 1986.

Angelou, Maya. *I Know Why the Caged Bird Sings*. 1969. Ballantine Books, 2009.

Anzaldúa, Gloria. *Borderlands La Frontera: The New Mestiza*, 3rd ed., Aunt Lute, 2007.

Ashe, Bertram. *From within the Frame: Storytelling in African-American Studies*. Routledge, 2002.

Baker, Houston. "The Point of Entanglement: Modernism, Diaspora, and Toni Morrison's *Love*." *Contemporary African American Literature: The Living Canon*, edited by Lovalerie King and Shirley Moody-Turner, Indiana University Press, 2013, pp. 17–40.

———. *Workings of the Spirit: The Poetics of Afro-American Women's Writing*. University of Chicago, 1991.

Baker, Houston, and Patricia Redmond, editors. *Afro-American Literary Study in the 1990s*. University of Chicago, 1989.

Baldwin, James. "Down at the Cross." 1963. *Baldwin: Collected Essays*, edited by Toni Morrison, Library Classics of the United States, Inc. 1998.

Bambara, Toni Cade. "Foreword to the First Edition, 1981." *This Bridge Called My Back: Writings by Radical Women of Color*, edited by Cherríe Moraga and Gloria Anzaldúa, 4th ed., State University of New York Press, 2015, pp. xxiv-xxxii.

Barker, Deanna. "Indentured Servitude in Colonial America." *Frontier Resources*, 2004, mertsahinoglu.com/research/indentured-servitude-colonial-america/.

Barnett, Pamela. "Figurations of Rape and the Supernatural in Beloved." *PMLA*, vol. 112, no. 3, May, 1997, pp. 418–427.

Behar, Ruth. *The Vulnerable Observer: Anthropology That Breaks Your Heart*. Beacon, 1996.

"Behind the Eric Garner Video of a Deadly Confrontation with Police." YouTube, July 31, 2014, www.youtube.com/watch?v=N__5p_dNW3U.

Behind the Seams; by a Nigger Woman Who Took in Work from Mrs. Lincoln and Mrs. Davis and signed with an "X," the mark of "Betsey Kickley (nigger). National News Company, 1868.

Bennett, Ken. "The Language of the Blues in Faulkner's 'That Evening Sun.'" *Mississippi Quarterly: The Journal of Southern Culture*, vol. 38, no. 3 (Summer 1985), pp. 339–42.

Blanchfield, Patrick. "The Psychology of an Ethnic Fraud: Behind Rachel Dolezal's Invented Persecution." *The Daily Beast*, June 12, 2015, www.thedailybeast.com/articles/2015/06/13/the-psychology-of-an-ethnic-fraud-behind-rachel-dolezal-s-invented-persecution.html.

Bland, Sterling, Jr. "Bearing Witness: The Fugitive Slave Narrative and Its Traditions." *African American Slave Narratives: An Anthology*, edited by Sterling Bland, Jr., vol. 1, Greenwood, 2001, pp. ix-xxxi.

Block, Melissa. "Writing Mississippi: Jesmyn Ward Salvages the Stories of the Silenced." *NPR: All Things Considered*, August 31, 2017, www.npr.org/2017/08/31/547271081/writing-mississippi-jesmyn-ward-salvages-stories-of-the-silenced.

Bloom, Howard. *How to Read and Why*. Scribner, 2001.

Bloom, Howard, editor. *Zora Neale Hurston's Their Eyes Were Watching God: Bloom's Modern Critical Interpretations*. Blooms Literary Criticism, 2008.

Blow, Charles. *Fire Shut Up in My Bones*. Mariner Books, 2014.

Bollinger, Laura. "Narrating Racial Identity and Transgression in Faulkner's 'That Evening Sun.'" College Literature, vol. 39, no. 2 (Spring 2012), pp. 73–72.

Booth, Wayne. *The Company We Keep: An Ethics of Fiction*. University of California Press, 1988.

Borstein, Leon, Chinua Achebe, and Toni Morrison. "Things Fall Together." *Transition*, vol. 89, 2001, pp. 150–65.

Bouie, Jamelle. "Is Rachel Dolezal Black Just Because She Says She Is?" *Slate*, June 12, 2015, www.slate.com/articles/news_and_politics/politics/2015/06/rachel_dolezal_claims_to_be_black_the_naacp_official_was_part_of_the_african.html.

Bouson, J. Brooks. "Approaches to Morrison's Work: Psychoanalytic." *The Toni Morrison Encyclopedia*, edited by Elizabeth Ann Beaulieu. Greenwood Press, 2003, pp. 34–39.

———. *Quiet as It's kept: Shame, Trauma, and Race in the Novels of Toni Morrison*. State University of New York Press, 2000.

Boyd, Valerie. *Wrapped in Rainbows: The Life of Zora Neale Hurston*. Scribner, 2004.

Bracher, Mark. *Radical Pedagogy: Identity, Generativity, and Social Transformation.* Palgrave Macmillan, 2006.

Braxton, Joanne. *Black Women Writing Autobiography.* Temple University Press, 1989.

Brison, Susan. *Aftermath: Violence and the Remaking of a Self.* Princeton University Press, 2003.

Brown, Jeffrey. "Jesmyn Ward Answers Your Questions about 'Sing, Unburied, Sing.'" *PBS News Hour,* January 31, 2018, www.pbs.org/newshour/show/jesmyn-ward-answers-your -questions-about-sing-unburied-sing#transcript.

Brown, Sterling. "Review of *Their Eyes Were Watching God.*" *Zora Neale Hurston: Critical Perspectives Past and Present,* edited by A. K. Appiah and Henry Louis Gates Jr., Amistad, 1993, pp. 20–21.

Brownmiller, Susan. *Against Our Will: Men, Women, and Rape.* 1975. Ballentine, 1993.

Bruce, Dickson, Jr. *The Origins of African American Literature, 1680–1865.* University Press of Virginia, 2001.

Bush, Laura. "A Very American Power Struggle: The Color of Rape in *Light in August.*" *Mississippi Quarterly,* vol. 51, no. 3, Summer 1998, pp. 483–501.

Butler, Judith. *Frames of War: When Is Life Grievable?* Verso, 2010.

———. *Precarious Life: The Powers of Mourning and Violence.* Verso, 2004.

———. "Violence, Mourning, Politics." Emotions: A Cultural Studies Reader, edited by Jennifer Harding and E. Deidre Pribram, Routledge, 2009, pp. 387–402.

Byerman, Keith. *Remembering the Past in Contemporary African American Fiction.* University of North Carolina University Press, 2008.

Calabresi, Massimo. "Why a Medical Examiner Called Eric Garner's Death a Homicide." *Time,* December 4, 2014, time.com/3618279/ eric-garner-chokehold-crime-staten-island-daniel-pantaleo/.

Cannon, Katie Geneva. "Resources for a Constructive Ethic in the Life and Work of Zora Neale Hurston." *Journal of Feminist Studies in Religion,* vol. 1, no. 1, Spring 1985, pp. 37–51.

Carby, Hazel. *Reconstructing Womanhood: The Emergence of the Afro-American Woman Novelist.* Oxford University Press, 1999.

Carden, Mary Paniccia. "Models of Memory and Romance: The Dual Endings of Toni Morrison's *Beloved.*" *Twentieth Century Literature,* vol. 45, no. 4, Winter 1999, pp. 401–27.

Carmichael, Jacqueline. *Trumpeting a Fairy Sound: History and Folklore in Margaret Walker's Jubilee.* University of Georgia Press, 1998.

Caruth, Cathy. *Listening to Trauma: Conversations with Leaders in the Theory & Treatment of Catastrophic Experience.* Johns Hopkins University Press, 2014.

———. "Trauma and Experience." *Trauma: Explorations in Memory,* edited by Cathy Caruth, Johns Hopkins University Press, 1995, pp. 3–12.

———. *Unclaimed Experience: Trauma, Narrative and History.* Johns Hopkins University Press, 1996.

Castle, Terry. *The Apparitional Lesbian: Female Homosexuality and Modern Culture.* Columbia University Press, 1995.

Chawla, Sarika. "Black Women Are 3.5 Times More Likely to Die from Being Pregnant Than White Women." *Tonic,* September 13, 2017, tonic.vice.com/en_us/article/mb7j4p/black -women-are-3-times-more-likely-to-die-from-being-pregnant.

Chiaverini, Jennifer. *Mrs. Lincoln's Dressmaker: A Novel.* Plume, 2013.

Christian, Barbara. *Black Women Novelists: The Development of a Tradition, 1892–1976.* Greenwood. 1980.

Christiansë, Yvette. *Toni Morrison: An Ethical Poetics.* Fordham University Press, 2013.

Clarke, Deborah. *Robbing the Mother: Women in Faulkner.* 1994. University Press of Mississippi, 2006.

Coates, Ta-Nehisi. "Foreword." *The Origin of Others,* by Toni Morrison, Harvard University Press, 2017, pp. vii–xvii.

Colbert, Soyica Diggs. "Introduction: Do You Want to Be Well?" *The Psychic Hold of Slavery: Legacies in American Expressive Culture,* edited by Soyica Diggs Colbert, Robert Patterson, Aida Levy-Hussen, Rutgers University Press, 2016, pp. 1–16.

Collins, Patricia Hill. *Black Feminist Thought.* Routledge, 2000.

Collins, Patricia Hill, and Sirma Bilge. *Intersectionality.* Polity, 2016.

Condé, Mary. "Some African-American Fictional Responses to *Gone with the Wind.*" *Strategies of Reading: Dickens and After.* Special Number of *The Yearbook of English Studies,* vol. 26, 1996, pp. 208–217.

Cooley, John. "Faulkner, Race, Fidelity." *Connotations,* vol. 4, no. 3, 1994–95, pp. 300–12.

Coonradt, Nicole. "To Be Loved: Amy Denver and Human Need—Bridges to Understanding in Toni Morrison's *Beloved.*" *College Literature,* vol. 22, September 2005, pp. 168–87.

Crawford, Margo Natalie. "The Inside-Turned-Out Architecture of the Post-Neo-Slave Narrative." *The Psychic Hold of Slavery: Legacies in American Expressive Culture,* edited by Soyica Diggs Colbert, Robert Patterson, Aida Levy-Hussen, Rutgers University Press, 2016, pp. 69–85.

Cullick, Jonathan. "'I Had a Design': Sutpen as Narrator in 'Absalom, Absalom!'" *The Southern Literary Journal,* vol. 28, no. 2, Spring 1996, pp. 48–58.

Davis, Angela. "Foreword." *When They Call You a Terrorist: A Black Lives Matter Memoir* by Patrisse Khan-Cullors and Asha Bandele. St. Martin's, 2017, pp. xi–xiv.

———. *Freedom Is a Constant Struggle: Ferguson, Palestine, and the Foundations of a Movement.* Haymarket Books, 2016.

Davis, Bonnie. "Women." *William Faulkner Encyclopedia,* edited by Robert Hamblin and Charles Peek, Greenwood, pp. 439–42.

Davis, Charles, and Henry Louis Gates Jr., editors. *The Slave's Narrative.* Oxford University Press, 1985.

Davis, Doris. "'De Talkin' Game': The Creation of Psychic Space in Selected Short Fiction of Zora Neale Hurston." *Tulsa Studies in Women's Literature,* vol. 26, no. 2, Fall 2007, pp. 269–86.

Dawes, James. "Human Rights, Literature, and Empathy." *The Routledge Companion to Literature and Human Rights,* edited by Sophia McClennen and Alexandra Schultheis Moore, Routledge, 2016, pp. 427–32.

Decety, Jean. *Empathy: From Bench to Bedside.* MIT Press, 2014.

DeGruy, Joy. *Post Traumatic Slave Syndrome: America's Legacy of Enduring Injury and Healing.* Joy DeGruy, 2005.

Denard, Carolyn. "Introduction." *What Moves at the Margin: Selected Nonfiction. Toni Morrison.* University Press of Mississippi, 2008, pp. xi–xxvi.

Denton, Ren. "Telling the White Man: Decoding the Gendered Blues and Domestic Violence in Hurston's 'Sweat' and Faulkner's 'That Evening Sun.'" *Faulkner & Hurston,* edited by Christopher Rieger and Andrew Leiter. Southeast Missouri State University Press, 2017, pp. 91–109.

"Didn't My Lord Deliver Daniel?" *The Norton Anthology of African American Literature*, edited by Henry Louis Gates Jr. and Valerie A. Smith, vol. 1, W. W. Norton, 2014, pp. 17–18.

Dolezal, Rachel, with Storms Reback. *In Full Color: Finding My Place in a Black and White World*. BenBella Books, 2017.

Dubek, Laura. "'[J]us' listenin' tuh you': Zora Neale Hurston's *Their Eyes Were Watching God* and the Gospel Impulse." *The Southern Literary Journal*, vol. 41, no. 1, Fall 2008, pp. 109–30.

Du Bois, W. E. B. "Criteria of Negro Art." *African American Literary Theory: A Reader*, edited by Winston Napier, New York University Press, 2000, 17–23.

———. *The Souls of Black Folk*. 1903. Tribeca Books, 2013.

Duke, Annie. *Thinking in Bets: Making Smarter Decisions When You Don't Have All the Facts*. Penguin, 2018.

Dyson, Michael Eric. *Tears We Cannot Stop: A Sermon to White America*. St. Martin's, 2017.

———. *What Truth Sounds Like*. St. Martin's, 2018.

Ellerby, Janet. *Intimate Reading: The Contemporary Women's Memoir*. Syracuse University Press, 2001.

Ellison, Ralph. *Invisible Man*. 1947. Vintage, 1995.

Epstein, Randi. "When Doctors Don't Listen to Women." *The New York Times Book Review*, March 19, 2018, www.nytimes.com/2018/03/19/books/review/abby-norman-ask-me -about-my-uterus.html.

Eyerman, Ron. *Cultural Trauma: Slavery and the Formation of African American Identity*. Cambridge University Press, 2001.

———. *Is This America? Katrina as Cultural Trauma*. University of Texas Press, 2015.

Farrell, Kirby. *Post-Traumatic Culture: Injury and Interpretation in the Nineties*. Johns Hopkins University Press, 1998.

Faulkner, William. *Absalom, Absalom!* 1936. Vintage Books, 1991.

———. "Appendix/Compson, 1699–1945." *The Sound and the Fury, A Norton Critical Edition*, edited by David Minter, 2nd edition, W. W. Norton, 1993, pp. 203–15.

———. "April 15, 1957 Session Ten Visitors from Virginia Colleges." *The Sound and the Fury: A Norton Critical Edition*, edited by David Minter, 2nd edition, W. W. Norton, 1993, pp. 237.

———. *As I Lay Dying*. 1930. Vintage Books, 1991.

———. "Interview with Jean Stein vanden Heuvel." 1956. *The Sound and the Fury: A Norton Critical Edition* edited by David Minter, 2nd edition, W. W. Norton, 1993, pp. 232–34.

———. "An Introduction for *The Sound and the Fury*." *The Sound and the Fury: A Norton Critical Edition*, edited by David Minter, 2nd edition, W. W. Norton, 1993, pp. 225–28.

———. "A Letter to the Leaders of the Negro Race, 1956." *Essays, Speeches, & Public Letters*. 1956, edited by James Meriwether, the Modern Library, 2004, pp. 107–12.

———. *Light in August*. 1932. Vintage Books, 1991.

———. *Requiem for a Nun*. 1950. Vintage Books, 1975.

———. *Sanctuary. 1931*. Vintage Books, 1993.

———. *The Sound and the Fury*. 1929. Vintage Books, 1991.

———. "That Evening Sun." *1931. Collected Stories of William Faulkner*. Vintage Books, 1995, pp. 289–309.

———. "Upon Receiving the Nobel Prize for Literature, 1950." *Essays, Speeches, & Public Letters*. 1965, edited by James Meriwether, the Modern Library, 2004, pp. 119–21.

Felman, Shoshana. *The Juridical Unconscious: Trials and Traumas in the Twentieth Century.* Harvard University Press, 2002.

Felman, Shoshana, and Dori Laub. *Testimony: Crises of Witnessing in Literature, Psychoanalysis and History.* Routledge, 1991.

Fetterley, Judith. *The Resisting Reader: A Feminist Approach to American Fiction.* Indiana University Press, 1977.

Fish, Stanley. *Is There a Text in This Class? The Authority of Interpretive Communities.* Harvard University Press, 1980.

———. "Literature in the Reader: Affective Stylistics." *New Literary History,* vol. 2, no. 1, 1970, pp. 123–62.

Foster, Frances Smith. *Witnessing Slavery: The Development of Ante-Bellum Slave Narratives.* University of Wisconsin, 1994.

———. *Written by Herself: Literary Production by African American Women, 1746–1892.* Indian University Press, 1993.

Foster, Michèle. "Using Call-and-Response to Facilitate Language Mastery and Literacy Acquisition Among African American Students." *ERIC Digest.* Center for Applied Linguistics, 2002. eric.ed.gov/?id=ED468194

Fowler, Doreen. *Drawing the Line: The Father Reimagined in Faulkner, Wright, O'Connor, and Morrison.* University of Virginia Press, 2013.

———. "Introduction." *Faulkner and Race (Faulkner and Yoknapatawpha),* edited by Doreen Fowler and Anne J. Abadie, University Press of Mississippi, 2007, pp. vii–x.

French, Agatha. "MacArthur winner Jesmyn Ward writes socially conscious works set in the South." *Los Angeles Times,* October 10, 2017, www.latimes.com/books/la-et-jc-macarthur -fellow-ward-20171010-story.html#.

Friedman, Susan Stanford. "Both/And: Critique and Discovery in the Humanities." *PMLA,* vol. 132, no. 2, 2017, pp. 344–350.

Gates, Henry Louis Jr. "Introduction." *Talk That Talk: An Anthology of African-American Storytelling,* edited by Linda Goss and Marian Barnes, Touchstone, 1989, pp. 15–20.

———. *The Signifying Monkey: A Theory of African-American Literary Criticism.* Oxford University Press, 1989.

Gay, Roxane. *Hunger: A Memoir of (My) Body.* HarperCollins, 2017.

Gilmore, Leigh. *The Limits of Autobiography: Trauma and Testimony.* Cornell University Press, 2001.

———. *Tainted Witness: Why We Doubt What Women Say about Their Lives.* Columbia University Press, 2017.

Goldstein, Philip, and James Machor. "Introduction: Reception Study: Achievements and New Directions." *New Directions in American Reception Study,* edited by Philip Goldstein and James Machor, Oxford University Press, 2008, pp. xi–xxviii.

Goellner, Ellen. "By Word of Mouth: Narrative Dynamics of Gossip in Faulkner's *Light in August.*" *Narrative,* vol. 1, no. 2, May 1993, pp. 105–23.

Graham, Maryemma. "Black Is Gold: African American Literature, Critical Literacy, and Twenty-First-Century Pedagogies." *Contemporary African American Literature: The Living Canon,* edited by Lovalerie King and Shirley Moody-Turner, Indiana University Press, 2013, pp. 55–90.

———. "The Fusion of Ideas: An Interview with Margaret Walker Alexander." *Black South.* Spec. Issue of *African American Review,* vol. 27, no. 2, Summer 1993, pp. 279–86.

———. "Introduction." *Cambridge Companion to the African American Novel,* edited by Maryemma Graham, Cambridge University Press, 2004, pp. 1–13.

———. "Introduction." *How I Wrote Jubilee,* edited by Margaret Walker, Feminist Press at CUNY, 1993, pp. xiii–xxii.

———. "Introduction." *This Is My Century,* edited by Margaret Walker, University of Georgia Press, 1989, pp. xvii–xxxvi.

———. "'I Want to Write, I Want to Write the Songs of My People': The Emergence of Margaret Walker." *Fields Watered with Blood.* University of Georgia Press, 2001, pp. 11–27.

———. "Preface." *How I Wrote Jubilee,* edited by Margaret Walker, Feminist Press at CUNY, 1990, pp. vii–xii.

Graham, Maryemma, and Deborah Elizabeth Whaley. "Introduction." *Fields Watered with Blood.* University of Georgia Press, 2001, pp. 1–10.

Graham, Maryemme, and Jerry Ward, Jr. *The Cambridge History of African American Literature.* Cambridge University Press, 2011.

Gray, Richard. *The Life of William Faulkner: A Critical Biography.* Blackwell, 1994.

Guy-Sheftall, Beverly, editor. *Words of Fire: An Anthology of African American Feminist Thought.* New Press, 1995.

Hall, Stuart. *Representation: Cultural Representations and Signifying Practices.* SAGE, 1997.

Hardison, Ayesha. *Writing through Jane Crow: Race and Gender Politics in African American Literature.* University of Virginia Press, 2014.

Harris, Trudier. "African American Protest Poetry." *Freedom's Story, TeacherServe.* National Humanities Center. nationalhumanitiescenter.org/tserve/freedom/1917beyond/essays/aaprotestpoetry.htm.

Hartman, Geoffrey. "Trauma within the Limits of Literature." *European Journal of English Studies,* vol. 7, no. 3, December 2003, pp. 257–74.

Headlee, Celeste. *We Need to Talk: How to Have Conversations That Matter.* HarperCollins, 2017.

Henke, Suzette. *Shattered Subjects.* Palgrave Macmillan, 2000.

Herman, Judith. *Trauma and Recovery.* Basic Books, 1992.

Hill, Anita. *Speaking Truth to Power.* Anchor, 1998.

hooks, bell. *Sisters of the Yam: Black Women and Self-Recovery.* South End, 2005.

———. *Teaching to Transgress: Education as the Practice of Freedom.* Routledge, 1994.

———. *Yearning: Race, Gender, and Cultural Politics.* South End, 1999.

Hoover, Elizabeth. "Jesmyn Ward on Salvage the Bones." *The Paris Review,* August 30, 2011, www.theparisreview.org/blog/2011/08/30/jesmyn-ward-on-salvage-the-bones/.

Horvitz, Deborah. *Literary Trauma: Sadism, Memory, and Sexual Violence in American Women's Fiction.* State University of New York Press, 2000.

Humez, Jean. "Reading 'The Narrative of Sojourner Truth' as a Collaborative Text." *Frontiers: A Journal of Women Studies,* vol. 16, no. 1, 1996, pp. 29–52.

Hurston, Zora Neale. "Characteristics of Negro Expression." *Negro: An Anthology,* edited by Nancy Cunard, Continuum, 1970, pp. 24–46.

———. *Seraph on the Suwanee.* 1948. Harper Perennial, 1991.

———. *Their Eyes Were Watching God.* 1937. Harper Perennial Modern Classics, 2006.

Hutchins, Zachary. "Sojourner Truth: The Libyan Sibyl." *Documenting the American South.* University of North Carolina Library, 2004. docsouth.unc.edu/highlights/sojourner truth.html.

Iser, Wolfgang. *The Act of Reading: A Theory of Aesthetic Response.* Johns Hopkins University Press, 1987.

Jacobs, Harriet. *Incidents in the Life of a Slave Girl.* 1861. *I Was Born a Slave: An Anthology of Classic Slave Narratives,* edited by Yuval Taylor and Charles Johnson, vol. 2, Lawrence Hill Books, 1999, pp. 533–682.

Jaggar, Alison. "Love and Knowledge: Emotion in Feminist Epistemology." *Emotions: A Cultural Studies Reader,* edited by Jennifer Harding and E. Deidre Pribram, Routledge, 2009, pp. 50–68.

Jamison, Leslie. *The Empathy Exams: Essays.* Graywolf, 2014.

Janoff-Bulman, Ronnie. *Shattered Assumptions: Toward a New Psychology of Trauma.* New York Free Press. 1992.

Jauss, Hans Robert. *Toward an Aesthetic of Reception,* translated by Timothy Bahti, University of Minnesota Press, 1982.

Jerkins, Morgan. *This Will Be My Undoing: Living at the Intersection of Black, Female, and Feminist in (White) America.* Harper, 2018.

Johnson, Charles. "Introduction." *I Was Born a Slave: An Anthology of Classic Slave Narratives,* edited by Yuval Taylor and Charles Johnson, vol. 1, Lawrence Hill Books, 1999, pp. xv–xxxviii.

Johnson, James Weldon. *The Autobiography of an Ex-Colored Man.* 1912. Filiquarian, 2007.

Johnson, Mat. "Foreword." *Contemporary African American Literature: The Living Canon,* edited by Lovalerie King and Shirley Moody-Turner, Indiana University Press, 2013, pp. ix–xii.

Johnston, Kenneth. "The Year of Jubilee: Faulkner's 'That Evening Sun.'" *American Literature,* vol. 46, no. 1 (March 1974), pp. 93–100.

Jordan, June. "On Richard Wright and Zora Neale Hurston." *Black World,* vol. 23, August 1974, pp. 4–8.

Kaplan, Carla. "The Erotics of Talk: 'That Oldest Human Longing' in *Their Eyes Were Watching God. American Literature,* vol. 67, no. 1, March 1995, pp. 115–42.

Kearney, Richard. "Narrating Pain: The Power of Catharsis." *Paragraph: A Journal of Modern Critical Theory,* vol. 30, no. 1, March 2007, 51–66.

Keckley, Elizabeth. *Behind the Scenes or, Thirty Years a Slave and Four Years in the White House* 1868. Create Space, 2011.

Khan-Cullors, Patrisse, and Asha Bandele. *When They Call You a Terrorist: A Black Lives Matter Memoir.* St. Martin's, 2017.

King, Debra Walker. *African Americans and the Culture of Pain (Cultural Frames, Framing Cultures).* University of Virginia, 2008.

———. "Multiple Jeopardy, Multiple Consciousness: The Context of a Black Feminist Ideology." *Signs,* vol. 14, no. 1, Autumn 1988, pp. 42–72.

King, Lovalerie, and Shirley Moody-Turner. "Introduction." *Contemporary African American Literature: The Living Canon,* edited by Lovalerie King and Shirley Moody-Turner, Indiana University Press, 2013, pp. 1–13.

Kirschner, Luz Angelica. "Human Rights and Minority Rights: Argentine and German Perspectives." *The Routledge Companion to Literature and Human Rights,* edited by Sophia McClennen and Alexandra Schultheis Moore, Routledge, 2016, pp. 361–72.

Krumholz, Linda. "The Ghosts of Slavery: Historical Recovery in Toni Morrison's *Beloved.*" *African American Review,* vol. 26, no. 3, Fiction Issue, Autumn, 1992, pp. 395–408.

Kuyk, Dirk Jr., Betty Kuyk, and James Miller. "Black Culture in William Faulkner's 'That Evening Sun.'" *Journal of American Studies,* vol. 20, no. 1, April 1986, pp. 33–50.

LaCapra, Dominick. *Writing History, Writing Trauma.* Johns Hopkins University Press, 2000.

Ladd, Barbara. "The Direction of the Howling: Nationalism and the Color Line in *Absalom, Absalom!*" *American Literature,* vol. 66, no. 3, September 1994, pp. 525–51.

Late Night with Seth Meyers. "Jesmyn Ward Breaks Down How the South's History of Racism Affects the Present." *Youtube.com,* commentary by Seth Meyers and Jesymn Ward, September 29, 2017, www.youtube.com/watch?v=oLezj-UYr1c.

Lawson, Kimberly. "What Serena Williams's Birth Story Says about Racism in Healthcare." *Broadly,* January 12, 2018, broadly.vice.com/en_us/article/j5vak8/what-serena-williams -birth-story-says-about-racism-in-health-care.

Lee, Harper. *To Kill a Mockingbird.* 1959. Harper, 2010.

Lee, Jim. "The Problem of Nancy in Faulkner's 'That Evening Sun.'" *The South Central Bulletin,* vol. 21, no. 4, Studies by Members of S-CMLA, Winter, 1961, pp. 49–50.

Levinas, Emmanuel. *Entre-Nous: Thinking of the Other,* translated by Michael Smith and Barbara Harshav, Columbia University Press, 1998.

Levy-Hussen, Aida. *How to Read African American Literature: Post-Civil Rights Fiction and the Task of Interpretation.* New York University Press, 2016.

———. "Trauma and the Historical Turn in Black Literary Discourse." *The Psychic Hold of Slavery: Legacies in American Expressive Culture,* edited by Soyica Diggs Colbert, Robert Patterson, Aida Levy-Hussen, Rutgers University Press, 2016, pp. 195–211.

Lincoln. Directed by Steven Spielberg, performances by Daniel Day-Lewis and Sally Field, 2012.

Litwack, Leon F. "Hellhounds." *Without Sanctuary: Lynching Photography in America,* edited by James Allen, Twin Palms, 2000, pp. 8–37.

Locke, Alain. "Review of *Their Eyes Were Watching God.*" *Opportunity,* June 1, 1938, *Zora Neale Hurston: Critical Perspectives Past and Present,* edited by Appiah and Gates, Amistad, 1993, p. 18.

Lorde, Audre. "Age, Race, Class, and Sex: Women Redefining Difference." *Words of Fire: An Anthology of African-American Feminist Thought,* edited by Beverly Guy-Sheftall, W. W. Norton, 1995, pp. 284–92.

———. "The Master's Tools Will Never Dismantle the Master's House." *Sister Outsider: Essays and Speeches by Audre Lorde.* Crossing, pp. 110–13.

Marcus, Lilit. "Why I Only Read Books by Women In 2013." *Flavorwire,* December 12, 2013. flavorwire.com/429473/why-i-only-read-books-by-women-in-2013.

Martin, Reginald. "Faulkner's Southern Reflections: The Black on the Back of the Mirror in 'Ad Astra.'" *African American Review,* vol. 2, no. 1, Black South Issue Part 1 of 2, Spring, 1993, pp. 53–57.

Masur, Kate. "In Spielberg's 'Lincoln,' Passive Black Characters." The Opinion Pages. *The New York Times,* November 12, 2012, www.nytimes.com/2012/11/13/opinion/in-spielbergs -lincoln-passive-black-characters.html

McBride, Dwight. *Impossible Witness: Truth, Abolitionism, and Slave Testimony.* New York University Press, 2001.

McClennen, Sophia, and Alexandra Schultheis. "Aporia and Affirmative Critique: Mapping the Landscape of Literary Approaches to Human Rights Research." *The Routledge Companion to Literature and Human Rights,* edited by Sophia McClennen and Alexandra Schultheis Moore, Routledge, 2016, pp. 1–20.

———. "Impacts." *The Routledge Companion to Literature and Human Rights,* edited by Sophia McClennen and Alexandra Schultheis Moore, Routledge, 2016, pp. 399–404.

McDowell, Deborah. "Negotiating between the Tenses: Witnessing Slavery after Freedom—Dessa Rose." *Slavery and the Literary Imagination,* edited by Deborah McDowell and Arnold Rampersad, Johns Hopkins University Press, 1989, pp. 144–63.

——. "The Self and the Other: Reading Toni Morrison's *Sula* and the Black Female Text." *Critical Essays on Toni Morrison,* edited by Nellie McKay. G. K. Hall, 1988, pp. 77–88.

McIntosh, Peggy. "White Privilege: Unpacking the Invisible Knapsack." *Peace and Freedom,* July/August, 1989, pp. 9–10.

McKay, Nellie. "Introduction." *Morrison's Beloved: A Casebook,* edited by William Andrews and Nellie McKay, Oxford University Pres, 1999, pp. 3–20.

McKenzie, Mia. *Black Girl Dangerous: On Race, Queerness, Class, And Gender,* BGD, 2014.

Miles, Diana. *Women, Violence, and Testimony in the Works of Zora Neale Hurston.* P. Lang, 2003.

Miller, Nancy, and Jason Tougaw. *Extremities: Trauma, Testimony, and Community.* University of Illinois Press, 2002.

Miller, Shawn. "'Some Other Way to Try': From Defiance to Creative Submission in *Their Eyes Were Watching God.*" *The Southern Literary Journal,* vol. 37, no. 1, Fall, 2004, pp. 74–95.

Mills, Charles. "White Ignorance." *Race and the Epistemologies of Ignorance,* edited by Shannon Sullivan and Nancy Tuana, State University of New York Press, 2007, pp. 11–38.

Minter, David. *Faulkner's Questioning Narratives: Fiction of His Major Phase.* University of Illinois Urbana Champaign, 2004.

Mitchell, Angelyn, and Danielle K. Taylor, editors. *The Cambridge Companion to African American Women's Literature.* Cambridge University Press, 2009.

Mitchell, Margaret. *Gone with the Wind.* 1939. Scribner, 2011.

Mobley, Marilyn Sanders. "A Different Remembering: Memory, History, and Meaning in *Beloved.*" *Toni Morrison: Critical Perspectives Past and Present,* edited by Henry Louis Gates Jr. and Kwame Anthony Appiah, Amistad, 1993, pp. 356–68.

Moraga, Cherríe. "Catching Fire: Preface to the Fourth Edition." *Writings by Radical Women of Color,* edited by Cherríe Moraga and Gloria Anzaldúa, 4th edition, State University of New York Press, 2015, pp. xv–xxvi.

——. "La Güera." *This Bridge Called My Back: Writings by Radical Women of Color,* edited by Cherríe Moraga and Gloria Anzaldúa, 4th edition, State University of New York Press, 2015, pp. 22–29.

Moraga, Cherríe, and Gloria Anzaldúa. "Introduction, 1981." *This Bridge Called My Back: Writings by Radical Women of Color,* edited by Cherríe Moraga and Gloria Anzaldúa, 4th edition, State University of New York Press, 2015, pp. xliii–xlvii.

Musiol, Hanna. "Sites of Human Rights Theory." *The Routledge Companion to Literature and Human Rights,* edited by Sophia McClennen and Alexandra Schultheis Moore, Routledge, 2016, pp. 389–98.

Morrison, Toni. *Beloved.* 1987. Vintage Books, 2004.

——. *The Bluest Eye.* 1970. Vintage Books, 2007.

——. *God Help the Child.* Vintage Books, 2015.

——. "The Nobel Lecture in Literature." *What Moves at the Margin: Selected Nonfiction.* University Press of Mississippi, 2008, pp. 198–203.

——. *Playing in the Dark: Whiteness and the Literary Imagination.* Vintage Books, 1992.

——. "Rootedness: The Ancestor as Foundation." In *What Moves at the Margin: Selected Nonfiction.* University of Mississippi, 2008, pp. 56–64.

———. "The Site of Memory." *What Moves at the Margin: Selected Nonfiction.* University Press of Mississippi, 2008, pp. 65–82.

———. "Unspeakable Things Unspoken: The Afro-American Presence in American Literature." *The Tanner Lectures on Human Values,* October 7 1988. tannerlectures.utah .edu/_documents/a-to-z/m/morrison90.pdf

Nance, Kimberly. *Can Literature Promote Justice?: Trauma Narrative and Social Action in Latin American Testimonio.* Vanderbilt University Press, 2006.

Naylor, Gloria. *The Women of Brewster Place.* Penguin, 1983.

Newton, Adam Zachary. "Humanism with a (Post) Social Face: A Reply to Daniel R. Schwarz." *Narrative,* vol. 5, 1997, pp. 207–21.

Nudelman, Franny. "Harriet Jacobs and the Sentimental Politics of Female Suffering Author(s)." *ELH,* vol. 59, no. 4, Winter, 1992, pp. 939–64.

Oluo, Ijeoma. *So You Want to Talk about Race.* Seal, 2018.

O'Neill, Ann. "Identifying victims a grueling task." *CNN,* September 9, 2005, www.cnn. com/2005/US/09/09/katrina.morgue/index.html.

Orton, Richard. "Learning to Listen: One Man's Work in the Anti-Rape Movement." *Transforming a Rape Culture,* edited by Emilie Buchwald, Pamela Fletcher, and Martha Roth, Milkweed, 2005, pp. 235–48.

Painter, Nell Irvin. "Introduction." *Narrative of Sojourner Truth.* Penguin Classics, 1998, vii–xx.

Pandit, Eesha. "Making Movement Mistakes: What to Do When You F@*ck Up." *The Crunk Feminist Collection,* edited by Brittney Cooper, Susanna Morris, Robin Boylorn, Feminist, 2017, pp. 164–65.

Pérez-Peña, Richard. "Black or White? Woman's Story Stirs Up a Furor." *The New York Times,* June 12, 2015, www.nytimes.com/2015/06/13/us/rachel-dolezal-naacp-president -accused-of-lying-about-her-race.html?_r=0.

Petry, Ann. *The Street.* 1946. Mariner, 1998.

Phelan, James. "Toward a Rhetorical Reader-Response Criticism: The Difficult, the Stubborn, and the Ending of *Beloved.*" *Toni Morrison: Critical and Theoretical Approaches,* edited by Nancy Peterson, Johns Hopkins University Press, 1997, pp. 225–44.

Pickens, Therí. "Political Flesh XII: The Dynamics of Disclosure." *A Scholar's Thoughts.* December 15, 2013, www.tpickens.org/2013/12/15/political-flesh-xii-the-dynamics-of-disclosure/.

Plant, Deborah. *Every Tub Must Sit on Its Own Bottom: The Philosophy and Politics of Zora Neale Hurston.* University of Illinois Press, 1995.

Pogrebin, Letty Cottin. *How to Be A Friend to a Friend Who's Sick.* PublicAffairs, 2014.

Raine, Nancy. *After Silence: Rape and My Journey Back.* Three Rivers, 1998.

Rankine, Claudia. "The Condition of Black Life Is One of Mourning." *The Fire This Time: A New Generation Speaks about Race,* edited by Jesmyn Ward, Scribner, 2016, pp. 145–55.

Ratcliffe, Krista. *Rhetorical Listening: Identification, Gender, Whiteness (Studies in Rhetorics and Feminisms).* Southern Illinois University Press, 2006.

Rich, Adrienne. "When We Dead Awaken: Writing as Re-Vision." *College English,* vol. 34, no. 1, 1972, pp. 18–30.

Rieger, Christopher. "As I Lay Trying: How to Read William Faulkner." *MPR News,* April 26, 2016, www.mprnews.org/story/2016/04/26/books-advice-for-reading-william-faulkner.

Roberts, Diane. *Faulkner and Southern Womanhood.* University of Georgia, 1995.

Rody, Caroline. "Toni Morrison's *Beloved*: History, 'Rememory,' and a 'Clamor for a Kiss.'" *American Literary History,* vol. 7, no. 1, Spring 1995, pp. 92–119.

Rosenblatt, Louise. *The Reader, the Text, the Poem: The Transactional Theory of the Literary Work*. Southern Illinois University Press, 1978.

Roswell, Charles. "Poetry, History, and Humanism: An Interview with Margaret Walker." *Conversations with Margaret Walker*. University Press of Mississippi, 2002, pp. 19–31.

Rothberg, Michael. "Preface: Beyond Tancred and Clorinda—Trauma Studies for Implicated Subjects." *The Future of Trauma Theory: Contemporary Literary and Cultural Criticism*, edited by Gert Puelens, Sam Durrant, and Roger Eaglestone, Routledge, 2014, pp. xi–xviii.

Russell-Brown, Katheryn. "While Visions of Deviance Danced in Their Heads." *After the Storm: Black Intellectuals Explore the Meaning of Hurricane Katrina*, edited by David Dante Troutt, New Press, 2006, pp. 111–26.

Ryan, Barbara. "Kitchen Testimony: Ex-Slaves' Narratives in New Company." *Callaloo*, vol. 22, no. 1, Winter, 1999, pp. 141–56.

Ryan, Judylyn. "Language and Narrative Technique in Toni Morrison's Novels." *The Cambridge Companion to Toni Morrison*, edited by Justine Tally, Cambridge University Press, 2007, pp. 151–61.

Sandberg, Sheryl, and Adam Grant. *Option B: Facing Adversity, Building Resilience, and Finding Joy*. Alfred A. Knopf, 2017.

——. "Sheloshim." *Facebook*. June 3, 2015, www.facebook.com/sheryl/posts/10155617891025177:0.

Santamarina, Xiomara. "Behind the Scenes of Black Labor: Elizabeth Keckley and the Scandal of Publicity." *Feminist Studies*, vol. 28, no. 3, Autumn, 2002, pp. 514–37.

Scarry, Elaine. *The Body in Pain: The Making and Unmaking of the World*. Oxford University Press, 1985.

Scheel, Charles. "Toni Morrison's *Beloved*: A Traumatic Book on the Trauma of Slavery?" *Syllabus Review: Human & Social Science Series*, vol. 1, 2009, pp. 153–69.

Schreiber, Evelyn Jaffe. *Race, Trauma, and Home in the Novels of Toni Morrison*. Louisiana State University Press, 2010.

——. *Subversive Voices: Eroticizing the Other in William Faulkner and Toni Morrison*. University of Tennessee Press, 2001.

Schweickart, Patrocinio. "Reading Ourselves: Toward a Feminist Theory of Reading." *Readers and Reading*, edited by Andrew Bennett, Routledge Press, 2013, 66–93.

——. "Understanding an Other: Reading as a Receptive Form of Communicative Action." *New Directions in American Reception Study*, edited by Philip Goldstein and James Machor, Oxford University Press, 2008, pp. 3–22.

Sedgwick, Eve. *Epistemology of the Closet*, 2nd edition, University of California Press, 2008.

Silverman, Kaja. *The Threshold of the Visible World*. Routledge, 1996.

Simmons, Ryan. "'The Hierarchy Itself': Hurston's *Their Eyes Were Watching God* and the Sacrifice of Narrative Authority. *African American Review*, vol. 36, no. 2, Summer 2002, pp. 181–93.

Slater, Lauren. *Lying*. Penguin, 2000.

Smith, Valerie. *Not Just Race, Not Just Gender: Black Feminist Readings*. Routledge, 1998.

Smitherman, Geneva. *Talkin and Testifyin: The Language of Black America*. Houghton Mifflin, 1977.

Solnit, Rebecca. *Call Them by Their True Names: American Crises (and Essays)*. Haymarket Books, 2018.

——. *Hope in the Dark: Untold Histories, Wild Possibilities*. Haymarket Books, 2016.

———. *Men Explain Things to Me.* Haymarket Books, 2014.

———. *The Mother of All Questions.* Haymarket Books, 2017.

Spataro, Joanne. "Doctors Don't Always Believe You When You're a Black Woman." *Vice,* February 2, 2018, tonic.vice.com/en_us/article/qvedxd/doctors-dont-always-believe-you -when-youre-a-black-woman.

Spencer, Stephen. "The Value of Lived Experience: Zora Neale Hurston and the Complexity of Race." *Studies in American Culture.* Spec. issue of *Studies in Popular Culture,* vol. 27, no. 2, Studies in American Culture, Oct. 2004, pp. 17–33.

Stepto, Robert. *From behind the Veil: A Study of Afro-American Narrative.* University of Illinois, 1979.

Stern, Jessica. *Denial.* Ecco, 2010.

Stockett, Kathryn. *The Help.* Putnam, 2008.

Strozier, Charles. *Until the Fires Stopped Burning: 9/11 and New York City in the Words and Experiences of Survivors and Witnesses.* Columbia University Press, 2011.

Sullivan, John Jeremiah. "How William Faulkner Tackled Race—and Freed the South from Itself." *New York Times Magazine,* June 28, 2012, www.nytimes.com/2012/07/01/magazine /how-william-faulkner-tackled-race-and-freed-the-south-from-itself.html.

Tal, Kali. *Worlds of Hurt: Reading the Literatures of Trauma.* Cambridge University Press, 1995.

Tate, Claudia. "Black Woman Writers at Work: An Interview with Margaret Walker." *Fields Watered with Blood.* Athens: University of Georgia Press, 2001. 44–54.

Taylor, Sonya Renee. *The Body Is Not an Apology.* Berrett-Koehler, 2018.

Thorbecke, Catherine. "Serena Williams opens up about harrowing medical ordeal she faced after giving birth to her daughter." *ABCNews,* January 10, 2018, abcnews.go.com/ Entertainment/serena-williams-opens-harrowing-medical-ordeal-faced-giving/story ?id=52248260.

Thorpe, Vanessa. "Jesmyn Ward: 'So much of life is pain and sorrow and willful ignorance.'" *The Guardian,* November 12, 2017, www.theguardian.com/books/2017/nov/12/jesmyn -ward-sing-unburied-sing-interview-meet-author.

Thrasher, Steven. "Rachel Dolezal Exposes Our Delusional Constructions and Perceptions of Race." *The Guardian,* June 12, 2015, www.theguardian.com/commentisfree/2015/jun/12 /rachel-dolezal-delusional-construction-perception-of-race.

"Trauma." *APA.org.* American Psychological Association, 2014, www.apa.org/topics/trauma/

Trezise, Thomas. "Between History and Psychoanalysis: A Case Study in the Reception of Holocaust Survivor Testimony." *History and Memory,* vol. 20, no. 1, 2008, pp. 7–47.

Troutt, David Dante. "Many Thousands Gone, Again." *After the Storm: Black Intellectuals Explore the Meaning of Hurricane Katrina,* edited by David Dante Troutt, New Press, 2006, pp. 3–28.

Truth, Sojourner, and Nell Irvin Painter. *Narrative of Sojourner Truth.* 1850. Penguin Classics, 1998.

Turner, Justin, and Linda Lovitt Turner. *Mary Todd Lincoln: Her Life and Letters.* Knopf, 1972.

Urgo, Joseph, and Noel Polk. *Reading Faulkner: Absalom, Absalom!* University Press of Mississippi, 2010.

U.S. Constitution. Amend. XIII, Sec. 1.

Uwarjaren, Jarune, and Jamie Utt. "Why Our Feminism Must Be Intersectional." *Everyday Feminism,* January 11, 2015, everydayfeminism.com/2015/01/why-our-feminism-must -be-intersectional/.

Van der Kolk, Bessel. *The Body Keeps the Score: Brain, Mind, and Body in the Healing of Trauma*. Penguin Books, 2014.

Vickroy, Laurie. *Reading Trauma Narratives: The Contemporary Novel & the Psychology of Oppression*. University of Virginia Press, 2015.

——. *Trauma and Survival in Contemporary Fiction*. University of Virginia, 2002.

Vint, Sherryl. "'Only by Experience': Embodiment and the Limitations of Realism in Neo-Slave Narratives." *Science Fiction Studies*, vol. 34, no. 2, Afrofuturism, July 2007, pp. 241–61.

Wadlington, Warwick. "Conclusion: The Stakes of Reading Faulkner—Discerning Reading." *The Cambridge Companion to William Faulkner*, edited by Philip Weinstein. Cambridge University Press, 1995, pp. 197–220.

Walker, Alice. *The Color Purple*. 1982. Mariner, 2003.

Walker, Margaret. "How I Wrote Jubilee." *How I Wrote Jubilee: And Other Essays on Life and Literature*. Feminist Press at CUNY, 1993, pp. 50–68.

——. "The Humanistic Tradition of Afro-American Literature." *How I Wrote Jubilee: And Other Essays on Life and Literature*. Feminist Press at CUNY, 1993, pp. 121–33.

——. *Jubilee*. 1966. Mariner, 1999, pp. vii–xii.

——. "Phillis Wheatley and Black Women Writers." *On Being Female, Black, and Free: Essays by Margaret Walker: 1932–1992*. University Press of Tennessee, 1997, pp. 35–40.

——. "Reflections on Black Women Writers." 1983. *On Being Female, Black, and Free: Essays by Margaret Walker: 1932–1992*. University Press of Tennessee, 1997, pp. 41–56.

——. "Willing to Pay the Price." *How I Wrote Jubilee*. Feminist Press at CUNY, 1993, pp. 15–25.

Wall, Cheryl. "*Their Eyes Were Watching God*." *The Oxford Companion to African American Literature*, edited by William Andrews, Frances Smith Foster, and Trudier Harris, Oxford University Press, 1997, p. 724.

Walters, Wendy. "Lonely in America." *The Fire This Time: A New Generation Speaks about Race*, edited by Jesmyn Ward, Scribner, 2016, pp. 33–58.

Ward, Jesmyn. "Introduction." *The Fire This Time: A New Generation Speaks about Race*, edited by Jesmyn War, Scribner, 2016, pp. 3–11.

——. "Racism Is 'Built into the Very Bones' of Mississippi." *The Atlantic*, March 1, 2018, www.theatlantic.com/magazine/archive/2018/02/jesmyn-ward-mississippi/552500/.

——. *Salvage the Bones: A Novel*. Bloomsbury, 2011.

——. *Sing, Unburied, Sing: A Novel*. Scribner, 2017.

Warren, Kenneth. *What Was African American Literature?* Harvard University Press, 2012.

Warren, Robert Penn. "'William Faulkner: The South, the Negro, and Time,' *Southern Review*, 1, Summer 1965." *William Faulkner: Critical Assessments*, edited by Henry Claridge, vol. IV, Helm Information, 1999, pp. 325–246.

Washington, Booker T. 1901. *Up from Slavery*. W. W. Norton, 1995.

Watkins, Ralph. "'It Was like I Was the Woman and She Was the Man': Boundaries, Portals, and Pollution in 'Light in August.'" *The Southern Literary Journal*, vol. 26, no. 2, Spring 1994, pp. 11–24.

Weinstein, Arnold. *Recovering Your Story: Proust, Joyce, Woolf, Faulkner, Morrison: Understanding the Self through Reading Five Great Modern Writers*. Random House, 2006.

Weinstein, Philip. "Marginalia: Faulkner's Black Lives." *Faulkner and Race (Faulkner and Yoknapatawpha)*, edited by Doreen Fowler and Anne Abadie, University Press of Mississippi, 2007, pp. 170–91.

——. *What Else but Love? The Ordeal of Race in Faulkner and Morrison*. Columbia University Press, 1996.

White, Deborah Gray. *Ar'n't I a Woman? Female Slaves in the Plantation South.* W. W. Norton, 1999.

White, John Valery. "The Persistence of Race Politics and the Restraint of Recovery in Katrina's Wake." *After the Storm,* edited by David Dante Troutt, New Press, 2006, pp. 29–40.

Whitehead, Anne. *Trauma Fiction.* Edinburgh University Press, 2004.

Whitehead, Colson. *The Underground Railroad.* Random House, 2016.

Whitlock, Gillian. "Sorry Business." *The Routledge Companion to Literature and Human Rights,* edited by Sophia McClennen and Alexandra Schultheis Moore, Routledge, 2016, pp. 206–14.

"Witness." *Oxford English Dictionary Online.* 2010. oed.com/witness.

Wittenberg, Judith Bryan. "Race in *Light in August*: Wordsymbols and Obverse Reflections." *The Cambridge Companion to William Faulkner,* edited by Philip Weinstein, Cambridge University Press, 1995, pp. 146–67.

Wood, Amy Louise. *Lynching and Spectacle: Witnessing Racial Violence in America: 1890–1940.* University of North Carolina Press, 2009.

Woolf, Virginia. *A Room of One's Own.* 1929. Penguin, 2012.

Woolfork, Lisa. *Embodying American Slavery in Contemporary Culture.* University of Illinois Press, 2009.

Wright, Richard. "Between Laughter and Tears." *New Masses,* October 5, 1937, pp. 22–23.

———. *Native Son.* 1940. Harper Perennial Modern Classics, 2005.

Wyatt, Jean. *Love and Narrative Form in Toni Morrison's Later Novels.* University of Georgia Press, 2017.

Yellin, Jean Fagan. "Harriet Jacobs." *The Oxford Companion to African American Literature,* edited by William Andrews, Frances Smith Foster, and Trudier Harris, Oxford University Press, 1997, p. 394.

———. *Harriet Jacobs: A Life.* Basic Civitas Books, 2005.

———. "Texts and Contexts of Harriet Jacobs' *Incidents in the Life of a Slave Girl: Written by Herself.*" *The Slave's Narrative,* edited by Charles Davis and Henry Louis Gates, Jr, Oxford University Press, 1985, pp. 262–82.

Index

Page numbers in italics refer to figures.

Absalom, Absalom!, 100–114; anti- and a-witnessing in, 103, 104; Bon, 103; double marginalization in, 104; dual-witnessing in, 108; learned racism and classism, 100–101; of marginalized race, 106; readers witness secondarily, 107; trauma, 112; Venn liminality in, 100

Afra-Americans: as doubly marginalized, 18, 38, 104; emancipatory testimonials, 39; as enslaved persons, 48, 54; in *Their Eyes Were Watching God*, 120–21. *See also* marginalized

African American literature: as collection of testimonial works, 37; defining, 33–38; emancipatory narratives, 28; intersecting with trauma theory, 33; as political speech, 36; protest fiction, 116; provoking readers to "face the truth," 36–37; on slavery as trauma, 32. *See also* African American testimonial literature; American slavery and literature; trauma fiction

African American testimonial literature, 31, 35; African American literature as collection of, 37; author's traumatic

consciousness in, 62; interplay of race and gender in, 38; need for empathic reader-listener, 5; role of reader-respondent and, 7; *Their Eyes Were Watching God* as, 116. *See also* American slavery and literature; autobiography

African American Vernacular English (AAVE), 125; as dual-witnessing in *Their Eyes Were Watching God*, 117–18

"Age, Race, Class, and Sex" (Lorde), positions of marginalization, 154

aggressive anti-witnessing, 11–15; Sethe's killing of daughter as, 147–48; violence of, 150; in *The Women of Brewster Place*, 13–15. *See also* anti-witnessing

Ahad, Sadia Sahar, 33

Alcoholics Anonymous, 10

Allende, Isabel, 14

American postbellum literature, 30–32. *See also* African American literature; African American testimonial literature

American slavery, 32–38; and African American literature and trauma theory, 33; as a-witnessing enslaved personhood, 151; *Beloved* as

221

witnessing aftermath of, 39, 145–63; as contaminating all, 133, 138; effects of Margaret Walker, 129, 132; Jesmyn Ward, 163; *Jubilee*, 128–29; as open wound in culture, 146; as national trauma, 4; and postbellum literature, 31; sexual assault in, 63–64; Toni Morrison, 163; traumatic aftermath of, 145; witnessing, 32–33. *See also* African American literature; African American testimonial literature; *Behind the Scenes*; *Incidents in the Life of a Slave Girl*; life writing

Amy Denver: recognition of Sethe's blackness, 155; as secondary witness, 152–54. *See also* interracial female dual-witnessing; Sethe

Andrews, Karen, on *Light in August*, 83–85

Andrews, Molly, 20; on appropriating primary witness, 17

Andrews, Penelope, 185

Andrews, William, 48; emancipatory narratives, 42; *To Tell a Free Story*, 44

Angelou, Maya, *Incidents in the Life of a Slave Girl*, 43

anti-witnessing, 11–20, 22–25; in *Absalom, Absalom!*, 103; in *Behind the Seams*, 72; danger of in *Beloved*, 146, 159–60; in dual-witnessing and Venn Liminality, 189; fictive, 28–30; in *Incidents in the Life of a Slave Girl*, 51; in *Lincoln*, 72; propensity toward, 24–25; by readers in *Behind the Scenes*, 66–70; Sethe, 145; in *The Sound and the Fury*, 80; in *Their Eyes Were Watching God*, 122–23, 127; voyeuristic, 11. *See also* aggressive anti-witnessing; a-witnessing; Faulkner, William

Ashe, Bertram: on gender roles in *Their Eyes Were Watching God*, 121; Janie as embodied dual-witness, 124

autobiography. *See* life writing

Autobiography of an Ex-Colored Man (Johnson), 5

a-witnessing, 15–17; in *Absalom, Absalom!*, 103; in *Beloved*, 150–51; damage of,

21–22; Hazel Carby, 52; in *Incidents in the Life of a Slave Girl*, 50; as "innocent bystander," 11; of personhood of enslaved, 151; risk emphasizing progress and success, 66; *vs.* discomfort of dual-witnessing, 26. *See also* anti-witnessing

Awkward, Michael, 33

Baby Suggs, 159

Baker, Houston, 70–71

Bambara, Toni Cade, 186

Barker, Deanne, 154

Barnett, Pamela, on *Beloved*, 150

Behar, Ruth, on *The Vulnerable Observer*, 14

Behind the Scenes Or, Thirty Years a Slave and Four Years in the White House (Keckley), 42, 62–76, 120; readers' anti-witnessing of, 66–72; secondary by proxy witnessing of sexual assault in, 63–64

Behind the Seams; by a Nigger Woman Who Took in Work from Mrs. Lincoln and Mrs. Davis, 71–72

Bell, Bernard, 78

Beloved: as co-optive anti-witness, 149; as depleting Sethe, 149–51; exorcism of, 161–62; murder of, 156. *See also* ghosts; Sethe

Beloved (Morrison), 35, 120; Amy Denver 152–55; appropriative and co-optive anti-witnessing, 148–49; Baby Suggs, 147; as bearing witness to slavery trauma, 146; Beloved as co-optive anti-witness, 149; communal witnessing, 158; disremembering slavery, 162; exorcising of Beloved *vs.* Kayla's witnessing, 179; intergendered dual witnessing, 155; interracial female dual-witnessing, 152–54; Mr. and Miss Bodwin, 148–49; Mr. Garner, 148; neighborhood women communally witnessing, 16; Paul D, 147; readers' response to, 163; Sethe's aggressive anti-witnessing, 147–48; Sethe's Misery, 155, 159–60; slavery as a-witnessing, 151; Sweet Home, 147–48,

151; ; tree as metaphor, 156–57; witnessing in aftermath of slavery, 145–63. *See also* American slavery

Bennett, Ken, 96–97

Black Lives Matter: communal witnessing, 10; *Tears We Cannot Stop*, 16

Blackness, 34–35, 82–84, 86, 88–89; in *Absalom, Absalom!*, 100; in *Beloved*, 149; witnessing in *Their Eyes Were Watching God*, 116; and womanhood, 79

Bland, Sterling, 50; androcentric emancipatory narratives, 42

Bloom, Harold, 184

Blow, Charles, *Fire Shut Up in My Bones*, 5, 7–8

Blue, 174–77

Bluest Eye, The (Morrison), 10

Body in Pain, The (Scarry), 3

Body Is Not an Apology, The (Taylor), 26

Booth, Wayne, 30

Bouson, J. Brooks, 146; *Beloved*, 157–58; *Quiet as It's Kept*, 36

Boyd, Valerie, on *Their Eyes Were Watching God*, 121

Bracher, Mark, 184

Braxton, Joanne, 38, 48, 75; *Narrative of the Life of Frederick Douglass* as emancipatory narrative, 42

Brent, Linda. *See* Jacobs, Harriet

Brison, Susan, 22; conflict between "will to deny" and "to proclaim" catastrophe, 6

Brown, Sterling, 116; *Their Eyes Were Watching God*, 42

Brownmiller, Susan, *Against Our Will*, 85

Bruce, Dickson, 34

Bush, Laura, 84

Butler, Judith, 185; *Frames of War*, 22; speaker-survivor and reader-listener as "undone," 21

Byerman, Keith: African American literature as provoking, 36–37; African American literature and trauma theory, 33

"By Word of Mouth" (Goellner), 87

Caddy Compson: in *The Sound and the Fury*, 78; "That Evening Sun," 98

Can Literature Promote Justice? (Nance), 184

Cannon, Katie Geneva, on *Their Eyes Were Watching God*, 116

Carby, Hazel, 52

Carden, Maria Paniccia, 155

Carter, Hodding, on *The Sound and the Fury*, 79

Caruth, Cathy, 4–5, 7, 9, 21, 30–32; *Trauma*, 33; trauma theory from literary criticism, 30; *Unclaimed Experience*, 3

Celan, Paul, 9

Celie, 9

"Characteristics of Negro Expression" (Hurston), 117

Charles Bon, 78, 103. *See also* blackness

Chiaverini, Jennifer, *Mrs. Lincoln's Dressmaker*, 72–75

Child, Lydia Marie, 51

Christian, Barbara, 38

Christiansë, Yvette, 146

Chun, Wendy, *Extremities*, 20

Clark, Lee, 164

Claudia MacTeer, 10

Clytie, 106

Coates, Ta-Nehisi, *The Origin of Others*, 13

Color Purple, The (Walker), 8–9

communal witnessing: audience called to, 142, 159; in *Beloved*, 160; call and response as, 158; challenges of, 21; in *Jubilee*, 128; on social media, 10; in *The Women of Brewster Place*, 10–11

Compson family, 79

Condé, Mary, on *Jubilee*, 130

constriction: Judith Herman, 5; as response to trauma, 4; secondary by proxy witnessing sexual assault in slavery, 63–64

Coonradt, Nicole, 152–53

co-optive anti-witnessing, 17–19; aligning with speaker-survivor, 11; master-slave bond, 148; violence of, 150

Davis, Angela, 16

Davis, Charles, 185

Davis, Doris, 117, 120

Davis, Thadious, on *The Sound and the Fury*, 79

Dawes, James, 184–85
Decety, Jean, 21
DeGruy, Joy, *Post Traumatic Slave Syndrome*, 15
Denton, Ren, 99–100; Nancy as double victim, 95; "That Evening Sun," 92
Denver, 148–50, 155
Dilsey Gibson: "Dilsey's chapter," 79; as stereotypical "mammy," 78–80. *See also* Faulkner, William
Dolezal, Rachel, 17–18
Douglass, Frederick, 11, 42
Dozier, Elvira Ware, 129
dual-witnessing, 7, *189*; *Absalom, Absalom!*, 108–9; across race and gender, 100; African American literature as promoting, 36; in *Beloved*, 152; challenges of, 21; in *The Color Purple*, 9; group therapy as, 10; heightened consciousness *vs.* self-congratulation, 24; interracial female model of, 39; learning, 19–28; non-verbal, 170–71; in *Their Eyes Were Watching God*, 117–18; transformative power of, 121; in *The Women of Brewster Place*, 10–11
Duke, Annie, *Thinking in Bets*, 28
Dyson, Michael Eric: interview with Kamala Harris, 32; *Tears We Cannot Stop*, 16; *What Truth Sounds Like*, 36; white Americans a-witnessing antiblack violence, 16

Ebony, "If I Were a Negro" article, 81
81st Blow, The (Guri), 22
Eliot, T. S., *The Waste Land*, 157–58
Ellerby, Janet, 7, 22
Ellison, Ralph, *Invisible Man*, 16–17
emancipatory narratives: nineteenth-century American, 9, 28, 30–31, 41–75. *See also* African American testimonial literature
Epistemology of the Closet, The (Sedgwick), 55
Eric Garner, 169
Esch, 170; Hurricane Katrina, 166–68
Eulalia Bond, 106
Extremities (Chun), 20

Eyerman, Ron, 5; on Hurricane Katrina, 164–65

Farrell, Kirby, 3
Faulkner, William, 77; African American characters as stereotypes, 77–78; anti-witnessing African American women, 90–91, 106–7; awareness of Dilsey's character as failure, 81–82; intertextual dual-witnessing, 100–101; marginalized characters, 78–81, 84; Nobel Prize acceptance speech, 81; as privileging reader, 113–14. *See also* anti-witnessing; co-optive anti-witnessing; gender; race
  Characters: Caddy Compson, 78; Compson family, 79; Dilsey Gibson, 79–81; Henry Sutpen, 103; Jesus, 94; Joanna Burden, 83; Joe Christmas, 78; Mrs. McEachern, 78; Nancy, 92–100; Quentin Compson, 92–100, 100–114; Rosa Coldfield, 10; Shreve, 100, 106, 108, 110–13; Temple Drake Stevens, 5; Thomas Sutpen, 100
  Works: *Absalom, Absalom!*, 78, 100–114, 105–6; appendix to *The Portable Faulkner*, 80–81; "If I Were a Negro," 81; *Light in August*, 78, 82–91; *Requiem for a Nun*, 5; *Sanctuary*, 4; *The Sound and the Fury*, 79–81; "That Evening Sun," 92–100
Felman, Shoshana, 3, 5; impossibility of witnessing on another's behalf, 9; trauma theory from literary criticism, 30
Fetterley, Judith, 184
Fire Shut Up in My Bones (Blow), 5, 7–8
Fire This Time, The (Ward), 10
Foster, Frances Smith, 47–48, 50; a-witnessing *Narrative of Sojourner Truth*, 52; *Witnessing Slavery*, 44
Foster, Michèle, 159
Frames of War (Butler), 22

Garners, 150–51
Gates, Henry Louis, Jr., 185; *The Signifying Monkey*, 117–18; *Talk That Talk*, 37

Gay, Roxanne, *Hunger*, 6, 121
gender: intersection with race and class, 134; in *Their Eyes Were Watching God*, 121; witnessing, 38–39. *See also* anti-witnessing; Faulkner, William; race
genocide, 3
ghosts: Jojo's ability to witness with, 174–77; Jesmyn Ward, 163; Kayla witnessing with, 178–79; as witnessing beyond death, 172. *See also* Beloved
Gilbert, Olive, 52; co-optive anti-witnessing by, 59–61. See also *Narrative of Sojourner Truth*
Gilmore, Leigh, *Tainted Witness*, 13
Given, 172
Goellner, Ellen, "By Word of Mouth," 87
Gone with the Wind (Mitchell), 130
Graham, Maryemma: *Jubilee* as nation's memoir, 139; Vyry Brown as "black everywoman," 132; Walker's use of fiction to witness, 130
Guri, Chaium, *The 81st Blow*, 22

Halle, 149–51
Hardison, Ayesha, 94
Harris, Kamala, 32
Harris, Trudier, 116
Hartman, Geoffrey, 30
Headlee, Celeste, *We Need to Talk*, 23–24
Heilbrun, Carolyn, 185
Henderson, May Gwendolyn, 35
Henke, Suzette, 5; "scriptotherapy," 41
Henry Sutpen, 103
Herman, Judith, 5, 7, 126; blocking off victim's witnessing, 15; difficulties facing traumatized life writers, 48; hyperarousal and trauma, 97; impulse to align with perpetrator, 12–13; on psychological trauma, 6; trauma as "affliction of the powerless," 4
hooks, bell, 5, 38
Horvitz, Deborah, 3
How to Be a Friend to a Friend Who's Sick (Pogrebin), 25
Hunger (Gay), 6
Hunt, Lynn, 185

Hurricane Katrina: a-witnessing African American survivors of, 165; and continuum of injustice, 167; John Valery White, 164–65; as national trauma, 4, 163–65; in *Salvage the Bones*, 164–66
Hurston, Zora Neale: "Characteristics of Negro Expression," 118; *Their Eyes Were Watching God*, 115–28
Hutchins, Zachary, on *Narrative of Sojourner Truth*, 61–62
Hyperarousal, 4, 7

"If I Were a Negro" (Faulkner), 81
Incidents in the Life of a Slave Girl (Jacobs), 35, 42; anti-witnessing, 51; intended audience as Northern white women, 44–45; interracial female dual-witnessing, 45–48; witnessing and a-witnessing sexual trauma, 43–52. *See also* American slavery; life writing
Innis Brown, 140–42
intergendered dual witnessing: Sethe and Paul D, 155; Tea Cake and Janie, 123–25
interracial female dual-witnessing: in *Incidents in the Life of a Slave Girl*, 45–48; Sethe and Amy, 152–54
intrusion: Judith Herman, 5; of response to trauma, 4
Invisible Man (Ellison), 116; white people's a-witnessing of protagonist, 16–17
I Was Born a Slave: An Anthology of Classic Slave Narratives (Johnson), 32

Jacobs, Harriet ("Linda Brent"), 42; *Incidents in the Life of a Slave Girl*, 35, 43–52
Jamison, Leslie, 18–20
Janie Crawford, 115–28; husbands of, 120
Janoff-Bulman, Ronnie, 15; anti-witnessing, 13
Jauss, Hans Robert, 7
Jerkins, Moran, *This Will Be My Undoing*, 17–18
Jesus, 94
Joanna Burden, 83
Jody Starks: as anti-witnessing, 122–23; difficulty of defining race, 120

Joe Christmas, 78, 82–84, 89. *See also* blackness
John Dutton, 135, 139–42
Johnson, Charles, *I Was Born a Slave*, 32
Johnson, James Weldon, *Autobiography of an Ex-Colored Man*, 5
Johnson, Mat, 37–38; race as socially constructed illusion, 34
Jojo, 168; ability to dual-witness, 170–72; secondarily witnessing Richie's ghost, 173. *See also* ghosts; Kayla
Jordan, June, 117
Jubilee (Walker): antebellum South, 128; cruelty of American slavery, 130–31; difficulty of primary witnessing, 140; importance of dual witnessing, 128; John Dutton, 135, 139–42; primarily and communally witnessing, 128; race and gender constructs with class, 134; secondary witnessing, 115, 128–43; Sis Hetta, 135; Vyry witnessing from many perspectives, 130. *See also* American slavery; *Their Eyes Were Watching God*

Kaplan, Carla, 125–27
Katrina, Hurricane. *See* Hurricane Katrina
Kayla, 171; Jojo dual-witnessing with, 170–71; witnessing with the dead, 178–79
Kearney, Richard, "Narrating Pain," 17
Keckley, Elizabeth: *Behind the Scenes*, 42, 62–76, 120; *Lincoln* as anti-witnessing, 72. *See also* African American testimonial literature; American slavery
King, Lovalarie, 37–38
Kinney, Arthur, 113
Kirschner, Luz Angelica, 186
Krumholz, Linda: Beloved as personifying slavery, 150; individual and collective recovery in *Beloved*, 146

LaCapra, Dominick, 4, 8, 12, 19
Ladd, Barbara, on *Absalom, Absalom!*, 103
"La Güera" (Moraga), 20, 180
Laub, Dori, 24, 48; impossibility of witnessing on another's behalf, 9; *Testimony*, 22; trauma survivor's need to tell their story, 5

Leafy, 120
Lee, Harper, *To Kill a Mockingbird*, 19
Leonie, 169
Levy-Hussen, Aida: African American literature as political speech, 36; on African American literature and trauma theory, 33
life writing: as allowing primary witnesses control, 5; memoir *vs.* trauma fiction, 29; as ways of witnessing through, 41; as witnessing, 8–9. *See also* African American testimonial literature
Light in August (Faulkner): African American characters as stereotypes, 78; anti-witnessing in, 86–91; co-optive anti-witnessing, 87–89; engagement with race and gender, 85; Faulkner's difficulty witnessing blackness and womanhood, 82–91; racial essentialism, 82; rape, 84–85; witnessing in, 105
Lincoln, Mary Todd, *Behind the Scenes*, 62, 65–79
literary criticism, 3
literature, African American. *See* African American literature; African American testimonial literature
Locke, Alain, on *Their Eyes Were Watching God*, 116
Logan Killicks, 120
Lorde, Audre, 85; positions of marginalization, 154
Luckhurst, Roger, 4
Lucy, 131–32
Lying (Slater), 4
Lynching and Spectacle (Wood), 8

maafa, 32
Marcus, Lilit, 186
marginalized: doubly, 38, 104; enslaved Afra-Americans as, 54; *Jubilee*, 134; perspective of, 168; race and gender, 42; status of, 4; *Their Eyes Were Watching God*, 116–17, 121; triply, 54. *See also* American slavery; Faulkner, William; Ward, Jesmyn
Martin, Trayvon, 10
Masur, Kate, on *Lincoln*, 72

Matthias, Robert, 58–59
McBride, Dwight, on *Incidents in the Life of a Slave Girl*, 44
McClennen, Sophia, 184
McIntosh, Peggy, on "White Privilege," 81
McKay, Nellie, 146
McKenzie, Mia: heightened consciousness vs. self-congratulation, 24; witnessing trauma as compelling action, 185
memoir. *See* life writing
Miles, Diana, *Women, Violence, and Testimony*, 36
Miller, Nancy, 4, 8, 12, 32; on cultural addiction to trauma narratives, 14
Miller, Shawn, on *Their Eyes Were Watching God*, 124
Mills, Charles, 95
Minter, David, 107
Misery, 155, 159–60
Miss Bodwin, 148–49
Mitchell, Margaret, *Gone with the Wind*, 130
Mobley, Mamie Till, 9–10
Moody-Turner, Shirley, 37–38
Moraga, Cherríe, *"La Güera,"* 20
Morrison, Toni: difficulty defining African American literature, 34; Nobel Prize acceptance speech, 180; Pecola Breedlove, 22; trauma fiction as witnessing, 29–30; Venn space as already encoded, 31
  Characters: Amy Denver, 152–55; Baby Suggs, 147, 159; Beloved, 149–51, 156, 161–62; Mr. and Miss Bodwin, 148–49, 160–61; Mr. Garner, 148; Halle, 149–51; Paul D, 147, 150, 155–58; schoolteacher, 147, 150, 156; Sethe, 35, 145, 147–56, 159–60; Stamp Paid, 155–56, 162–63
  Works: *Beloved*, 145–63; *The Bluest Eye*, 10; *The Origin of Others*, 13; "Rootedness," 37; "Unspeakable Things Unspoken," 36–37
Mr. Bodwin: and communal witnessing, 160–61; Sethe's attack on, 160–61
Mrs. Lincoln's Dressmaker (Chiaverini), 72–75
Mrs. Turner, 125

multiethnic and multigendered witnessing, 145. *See also* intergendered dual-witnessing; interracial female dual-witnessing

Nance, Kimberly, *Can Literature Promote Justice?*, 184
Nancy, 92–100, 174–77
Nanny, 119
"Narrating Pain" (Kearney), 17
Narrative of Sojourner Truth (Truth), 42; co-optive anti-witnessing of, 59–62; omission from a-witnessing, 52; religion as dual-witnessing with God, 57–59; secondary witness by proxy, 52–55; textual gaps in, 55–56. *See also* African American testimonial literature; Gilbert, Olive; life writing
Narrative of the Life of Frederick Douglass (Douglass), 42
narrative: emancipatory, 31; "first-person appropriative," 81; as witness to psychosocial injury, 3
natural disaster, 3
Naylor, Gloria, *The Women of Brewster Place*, 10–11, 14–16
Newton, Adam Zachary, 30
Nussbaum, Martha, 185

Oluo, Ijeoma, 185; dual-witnessing, 26–28; *So You Want to Talk about Race*, 10
Option B: Facing Adversity, Building Resilience, and Finding Joy (Sandberg), 7
Origin of Others, The (Morrison), 13
Orton, Richard, 21

Painter, Nell Irvin: on *Behind the Scenes*, 62; difficulty finding facts of Sojourner Truth's life, 56–57; race as idea vs. fact, 34
Pandit, Eesha, 27–28
Parchman Prison, 168. See also *Sing, Unburied, Sing*; Ward, Jesmyn
Paris Review, 81–82
patriarchal stereotypes, 78
Paul D, 147, 150; and Sethe's scar, 156; as witness, 155, 157–58
Pecola Breedlove, 22

Pennebaker, Jamie, 7
Petry, Ann, *The Street*, 21–22
Phelan, James, 7–8
Pheoby Watson, 115–18, 121, 127; as model
    secondary witness, 125–26
Pickens, Theri, 74. *See also* autobiography
Plant, Deborah, 125
Pogrebin, Letty Cottin, *How to Be a Friend
    to a Friend Who's Sick*, 25–26
Pop/River, 168–78
Portable Faulkner, The (Faulkner), 80–81
Post Traumatic Slave Syndrome (DeGruy), 15
primary witnessing, 8–11, 27–28; as speaking
    the unspeakable, 108. *See also* African
    American testimonial literature;
    anti-witnessing; a-witnessing; dual-
    witnessing; life writing; secondary
    witnessing
psychosocial effects and injury: and sec-
    ondary witnessing, 184; and trauma
    narratives, 3

Quentin Compson, 92–114
*Quiet as It's Kept: Shame, Trauma, and
    Race in the Novels of Toni Morrison*
    (Bouson), 36

race: in African American testimonial
    literature, 38; as cultural construct,
    34; difficulty of defining, 34; as forms
    of oppression, 63; and gender, 84,
    91; as idea *vs.* fact, 34; interracial
    female dual-witnessing, 152–54; in
    Light in August, 83; need to testify to
    difference, 38; as social categoriza-
    tion, 34–35; as social construct, 121;
    stereotypes of, 79; in *Their Eyes Were
    Watching God*, 119–21; witnessing,
    38–39. *See also* blackness; Faulkner,
    William; marginalized; racism
racial oppression, 119–21
racism: continuing to pollute America, 163;
    systemic, 5; witnessing, 119–21. *See also*
    anti-witnessing; Faulkner, William;
    race; Ward, Jesmyn
"Racism Is 'Built into the Very Bones' of
    Mississippi" (Ward), 163–64

Randall Ware, 139–40
rape: of Afra-American slaves, 31, 48–49; of
    black women, 135–36; challenges of
    witnessing, 48; depictions of, 3
reader: as listener, 8, 15, 21, 78, 184, *189*;
    respondent role of, 7
reception theory, 8; and trauma, 37
Requiem for a Nun (Faulkner), 97; Temple
    Drake Stevens, 5
Rich, Adrienne, 21, 24
Richie, 172; and anti-black violence, 164;
    dual-witnessing with Pop/River,
    174–77; and link to Eric Garner, 169
River. *See* Pop/River
Roberts, Diane, on *The Sound and the Fury*,
    79–80
"Rootedness" (Morrison): African American
    literature inspiring reader participa-
    tion, 37
"Roots," 181
Rorty, Richard, 185
Rosa Coldfield, 10; female characters as
    patriarchal stereotypes, 78
Rothberg, Michael, 4
Russell-Brown, Katheryn, 165
Ryan, Judylyn, 179

Salvage the Bones (Ward), 163–80; Hurricane
    Katrina, 164–66; witnessing aftermath
    of American slavery, 163–80. See also
    Sing, Unburied, Sing; Ward, Jesmyn
Sanctuary (Faulkner), 4; Temple Drake
    Stevens, 5
Sandberg, Sheryl, 19–20, 25; *Option B*, 7
Santamarina, Xiomara: on *Behind the
    Seams*, 70; Elizabeth Keckley and
    Mary Todd Lincoln, 71
Scarry, Elaine, 12, 16; traumatized narrator, 9;
    Unclaimed Experience, 3, 30
schoolteacher, 147, 150, 156
Schweickart, Patrocinio: on readers' respon-
    sibility, 30; "Reading Ourselves," 182;
    traumatic text, 8
secondary witnessing, 8, 115–28, 152–54;
    in *Absalom, Absalom!*, 103, 106–10;
    American slavery and its aftermath,
    32–33; carrying primary witness

through trauma, 172–73; as compre-
hending the incomprehensible, 108;
"heteropathic identification," 20;
from multiple viewpoints, 136–37;
needing empathic attention, 108–10;
promise of in *Beloved*, 146; Quentin
Compson attempting, 98–99; in *Their
Eyes Were Watching God*, 125–28;
trauma narratives as, 3; trauma of, 20;
Venn liminality, 20, 24; with animals
and ghosts, 171–72. See also *Jubilee*;
primary witnessing; secondary witnessing by proxy
secondary witnessing by proxy: not witnessing on behalf of another, 9; testifying
on behalf of primary witnesses, 9;
Their Eyes Were Watching God, 52–55
Sedgwick, Eve, on *The Epistemology of the
Closet*, 55
Sethe, 145, 147–48, 155; depleted by Beloved,
149–51; and interracial female dual-
witnessing, 152–54; *Misery*, 159–60;
murder of Beloved, 147–48, 156; scar
as effects of trauma, 147. *See also* Amy
Denver; Beloved
sexual abuse: of Afra-American slaves,
48–49; of black women, 135–36; challenges of witnessing, 48
Shreiber, Evelyn Jaffe, 7
Shreve, as co-optive anti-witness and
a-witness, 111–12; as secondary wit-
ness, 100
Signifying Monkey, The (Gates), 117–18
Silverman, Kaja, 20
Simmons, Ryan, 128
Sing, Unburied, Sing (Ward), 37, 52; collective witnessing, 177–79; mass African
American incarceration as slavery, 168;
witnessing aftermath of American slav-
ery, 163–80. *See also* American slavery
Sis Hetta, 135
Skeetah, 167–68, 170
Slater, Lauren, *Lying*, 4
slavery. *See* American slavery
Smith, Valerie, 38; on Harriet Jacobs's
escape, 45
Smitherman, Geneva, 158

sociocultural positioning, 4
Sojourner Truth. *See* Truth, Sojourner
Sound and the Fury, The (Faulkner), 78–80;
fall of South, 79; as Faulkner's "most
splendid failure," 81–82; first-person
narratives by white characters in,
79. *See under* Faulkner, William:
Characters
So You Want to Talk about Race (Oluo), 10
Spencer, Stephen, 117
Spielberg, Steven, *Lincoln*, 72. See also
Behind the Scenes
"Stakes of Reading Faulkner, The" (Wadling-
ton), 113
Stamp Paid, 162–63; and Sethe's scar, 155–56
Standardized American English (SAE), 118
Stein, Jean, 81–82
Stepto, Robert, 126; on androcentric emanci-
patory narratives, 42; *Their Eyes Were
Watching God*, 118–19
Stern, Jessica, 16
Stewart, Jeffrey, on *Narrative of Sojourner
Truth*, 60
Stowe, Harriet Beecher, 56
Street, The (Petry), 21–22

Tainted Witness (Gilmore), 13
Talk That Talk (Gates), 37
Taylor, Sonya Renee, *The Body Is Not an
Apology*, 26
Tea Cake, 120; and communal witnessing,
123–24; and intergendered dual–witnessing, 123–25; killing of, 121, 125
*Tears We Cannot Stop: A Sermon to White
America* (Dyson), 16
Temple Drake Stevens, 5–6
testimonial literature. *See* African American
testimonial literature
Testimony (Laub), 22
"That Evening Sun" (Faulkner), 92–100
Their Eyes Were Watching God, 117–18,
189; black male critics, 116; as black
protest fiction, 116, 119–21; communal
witnessing, 123–24; intergendered dual
witnessing, 123–25; James Baldwin, 116;
linguistic witnessing, 118–19; secondary witnessing, 115–27, 128–43; use of

African American Vernacular English in, 117; witnessing black women's trauma, 120; witnessing of racial oppression, 119–21. See also *Jubilee*

Thinking in Bets: Making Smarter Decisions When You Don't Have All the Facts (Duke), 28

This Bridge Called My Back (Moraga). *See* Moraga, Cherríe

This Will Be My Undoing: Living at the Intersections of Black, Female, and Feminist in (White) America (Jerkins), 17–18

Thomas Sutpen, 100

Till, Emmett, 9–10

Till, Mamie. *See* Mobley, Mamie Till

Titus, Frances, 61–62

To Kill a Mockingbird (Lee), 19

torture, 3

To Tell a Free Story (Andrews): emancipatory narratives, 42; skeptical audience on self-writers, 44

trauma: as "affliction of the powerless," 4; and African American literature, 33; and constriction, 63–64; in conversation with literature, 30; as creating communal witnessing, 29; difficulty of staying responsive to another's, 22; Dominick LaCapra, 4, 8, 12, 19; intersection of with African American literature 33; narratives, 12; narratives and psychosocial injury, 3; obstacles to witnessing, 7; as psychosocially productive, 146; and reception theory, 37; secondary effects of, 112; and secondary witnessing, 20; as secondary witnessing by proxy, 77; slavery as national, 4, 132, 163; surmounting through communal witnessing, 161; survivor's need to tell their story, 7; and Venn consciousness, 12; witnessing responses to, 15–16; witnessing sexual assault in slavery, 63–64. *See also* Weinstein, Arnold

Trauma: Explorations in Memory (Caruth), 33

traumatic narratives: entry into another's testimony, 12; in fiction, 29; Philip Weinstein, 29

trauma theory. *See* trauma

Truth, Sojourner, *Narrative of Sojourner Truth*, 42, 52–62

Unclaimed Experience: Trauma, Narrative and History (Scarry), 3, 30

Underground Railroad, The (Whitehead), 30

"Unspeakable Things Unspoken" (Morrison), 36–37

Up from Slavery (Washington), 66

Utt, Jamie, 28

Uwarjaren, Jarune, 28

Van der Kolk, Bessel: primary witnessing and secondary witness, 8; trauma and everyday life, 20

Venn: consciousness, 12, 128; diagram of secondary witnessing, 12, 146, *189*; readings, 39

Venn liminality, 5, 7, 24; *Absalom! Absalom!*, 100; as encoded in language and literature, 31; "heteropathic identification," 20; reader as secondary witness, 12; working through personal and cultural traumas, 146

Vickroy, Laurie, 3, 5; postbellum American fiction and effects of trauma, 30; reader's "double position," 19; trauma as phenomenon, 4; trauma fiction, 29

Vint, Sherryl, 146

Vulnerable Observer, The (Behar), 14

Vyry Brown, 128, 130; as fictional version of Walker's great-grandmother, 129; as prototype of Afra-American agency, 133

Wadlington, Warwick, 113

Walker, Alice, *The Color Purple*, 8–9

Walker, Margaret: "How I Wrote Jubilee," 129, 138; *Jubilee*, 36–37, 128–45; *This Is My Century*, 130; "Willing to Pay the Price," 132

Ward, Jesmyn: importance of dual-witnessing, 163; mass incarceration of African Americans as form of slavery, 163; novels from perspective of poor black children, 168–69; Parchman Prison as slave plantation, 168; secondary witnessing, 168; Twitter as forum to witness, 10; and voices of marginalized, 168–70

Works: *The Fire This Time*, 10; "Racism Is 'Built into the Very Bones' of Mississippi," 52; *Salvage the Bones*, 163–80; *Sing, Unburied, Sing*, 37, 163–80

warfare, 3

Warren, Robert Penn, 92

Washington, Booker T., on *Up from Slavery*, 66

Waste Land, The (Eliot), 157–58

Watkins, Ralph, 83

Weinstein, Arnold: Faulkner's African American characters, 77; trauma fiction and reality, 29

Weinstein, Philip: Clytie as "sparely represented," 106; Dilsey as mothering Compson family, 79–80; *Light in August*, 90; traumatic fiction, 29

We Need to Talk: How to Have Conversations That Matter (Headlee), 23–24

What Truth Sounds Like (Dyson), 36

White, Deborah, 38; slaves responsible for their sexual victimization, 48

White, John Valery, 164–65

Whitehead, Ann: responsibility of secondary witnesses, 19; trauma as "seismic" event, 4; witnessing as collaborative, 8

Whitehead, Colson, 29–30; *The Underground Railroad*, 30

"White Privilege," 81

Whitlock, Gillian, 185

"Willing to Pay the Price" (M. Walker), 132

Winks, Robin, 50

witnessing: challenge of, 48; as dual and active, 8; as empowering, 7; in fiction *vs.* nonfiction, 28–29; in postbellum American literature, 30–32; race and gender, 38–39; and sexual abuse, 48; temporary suspension of, 27

Witnessing Slavery: The Development of Ante-Bellum Slave Narratives (Foster), 44. *See also* anti-witnessing; a-witnessing; communal witnessing; dual-witnessing; secondary by proxy witnessing; secondary witnessing

Wittenberg, Judith Bryant, on *Light in August*, 90

womanhood and blackness, 79

Women, Violence, and Testimony (Miles), 36

Women of Brewster Place, The (Naylor): communal and dual-witnessing in, 10–11; dangers of aggressive anti-witnessing, 14–15

Wood, Amy Louise, *Lynching and Spectacle*, 8

Woolfork, Lisa, 33

Wright, Richard, on *Their Eyes Were Watching God*, 116

Yellin, Jean, 52

About the Author

Credit: Laura Novak at Little Nest Studios

Dr. Eden Wales Freedman is an associate professor of English, the director of diversity studies, and the department chair of communication, literature, and arts at Mount Mercy University, where she also serves as Dr. Thomas R. Feld Chair for Teaching Excellence and deputy Title IX coordinator. She lives in Cedar Rapids, Iowa.

CPSIA information can be obtained
at www.ICGtesting.com
Printed in the USA
BVHW032105201120
593834BV00021B/219